That Godless Court?

RONALD B. FLOWERS

That Godless Court?

Supreme Court Decisions on Church–State Relationships

Westminster John Knox Press
Louisville, Kentucky

Scripture quotations from the Revised Standard Version of the Bible are copyright 1946, 1952, © 1971, 1973 by the Division of Christian Education of the National Council of the Churches of Christ in the U.S.A. and are used by permission.

Book design by Drew Stevens
Cover design by Peyton Tabb Talbott, III

First edition

Published by Westminster John Knox Press
Louisville, Kentucky

This book is printed on acid-free paper that meets the American National Standards Institute Z39.48 standard. ∞

PRINTED IN THE UNITED STATES OF AMERICA

94 95 96 97 98 99 00 01 02 03 — 10 9 8 7 6 5 4 3 2 1

Library of Congress Cataloging-in-Publication Data

Flowers, Ronald B. (Ronald Bruce), date.
    That godless court? : Supreme Court decisions
on church-state relationships / Ronald B. Flowers. — 1st ed.
        p.   cm.
    Includes bibliographical references.
    ISBN 0-664-25562-0 (acid-free paper)
    1. Church and state—United States.   2. Freedom of religion—
United States.   I. Title.
KF4865.F57   1994
342.73′0852—dc20
[347.302852]   94-11019

To Ambrose Edens
former teacher and longtime dear friend
who, although not single-handedly,
inspired me to become a teacher

and

Sidney E. Mead
teacher extraordinary
who made me read my first Supreme Court case

Contents

Introduction

In 1962 and 1963, as a reaction to its decisions banning school-sponsored prayer in the public schools, the Supreme Court was frequently called "godless" by those who opposed those decisions. Is that a fair representation of the Court? Or is it more accurate to say that the Court was then and is now simply trying to maintain neutrality between church and state? My purpose in this book is to throw some light on such questions.

Why a book of this sort? First, the relationship between religion and civil authority in this country is a legal, ultimately a *constitutional*, concept. The Supreme Court is the final arbiter of constitutional issues. Second, there is frequently much confusion about what the Supreme Court has ruled, often because the primary information people get comes from the media. Unfortunately, most media reports are usually brief and superficial and do not include the scope or applicability of the Court's rulings. Furthermore, the nonlawyer is likely to be intimidated by the prospect of reading a Supreme Court decision, thinking that surely it will "read like an insurance policy," filled with "legalese." Actually, the language of these opinions is often very clear and expresses great principles of freedom. The goal of this book is to try to help people get beyond those perceived barriers to better understand the Court and its church–state opinions.

I am both a professor and a church person, and I am writing for clergy and laypeople within religious communities. In these times when church–state issues are so much in the public consciousness, I can imagine that clergy are frequently asked questions by parishioners about issues such as prayer in public schools, tax exemptions for religious institutions, or the possibility of political action by religious institutions. Most clergy are not prepared by their training in theological seminaries to give answers to such questions much beyond what they have read in the media. Although there is considerable discussion of church–state issues in scholarly (particularly legal) journals and in scholarly books, clergy are not likely to look at those sources, because of time constraints or lack of training. This book is designed to help clergy and laypeople to understand church–state issues and the Supreme Court's role in defining what is permissible and what is not. I hope that it may help clergy to find resources for preaching and for other forums in which they deal with the laypeople of their congregations. I would hope, for example, that study groups or social action committees of religious institutions might find the book useful as an introduction to church–state questions.

The reader should know that I am a rather strict separationist in my view of church–state relationships. I am convinced that the Constitution demands substantial separation between religion and civil authority and, at the same time, mandates that religious freedom should be unfettered, limited only by the necessity of maintaining peace and order in society. Such a relationship is of benefit both to the state and to religion. Strict separation is not hostile to religion, as many have claimed, but will provide the best conditions for religion to flourish. Indeed, by keeping government out of religion, separation is best seen as a way to maximize the free exercise of religion.

It is important to realize that when church–state relationships are discussed, "church" and "state" are oversimplified, shorthand terms. On reflection, the reason for this is obvious. There is no single "church" in America; there is a multiplicity of religious bodies. Of course, there are groups that do not even use the word "church" when they speak of their corporate bodies, but may speak, rather, of "synagogue," "mosque," "Kingdom Hall," or "spiritual assembly." The pluralism of American religion makes the term "church" only an approximation. Likewise, there is not a single "state." The term encompasses the federal government, the various state governments, county and city governments, and governmental agencies such as boards of education, zoning commissions, regulatory agencies, and, frequently in time of war, draft boards. All or any of these can interact with and impact religious people or groups. The better phrase for the subject at hand is "relationships between religion and civil authority." But here, for the sake of convenience and because of the familiarity of the phrase, I shall write of "church and state." Please remember that the phrase masks a much more complicated reality, on both sides of the conjunction.

Some readers may want to read one or more of the cases referred to in the book. Citations are given in endnotes. These references are not as intimidating or as opaque as those unfamiliar with them might think. Supreme Court opinions are printed by the government in *United States Reports*, which is designated by the "U.S." in the middle of the reference. If the reference says "S.Ct.," it means that the case has not yet been printed in *United States Reports* and can be found in *The Supreme Court Reporter*, published by West Publishing Company. The left-hand number refers to the volume number and the right-hand number designates the first page of the case. So, *Everson v. Board of Education* 330 U.S. 1 begins on page 1 of volume 330 of *United States Reports*. (Where a reference reads "1 at 5," the reference is to page 5 of a case that begins on page 1.) The books can be found in any law library and in many public or university libraries. For those who do not have access to law books, or who would like to have the cases for a personal or church library, or for the use of a study group, the texts of most of the major church–state cases can be found in *Toward Benevolent Neutrality: Church, State, and the Supreme Court*, by Robert T. Miller and Ronald B. Flowers, 4th ed. (Waco, Tex.: Baylor University Press, 1992). Beginning in the summer of 1993, an annual cumulative supplement was published for this book, to bring it up to date on the decisions of the Court. To facilitate reading the cases for those who use that source, the notes here will give page references to "Miller and Flowers" or "Miller and Flowers Supplement" as well as the regular legal citation.

As does living itself, the scholarly enterprise requires the help of others. To get a sense of the utility of this book for clergy and the church, I asked the following people to read the manuscript: Clark Ford, minister of Memorial Christian Church, Midland, Texas; Rudy Pulido, minister of Southwest Baptist Church, St. Louis, Missouri; Rick Spleth, minister of Creekwood Christian Church, Flower Mound, Texas; Dr. Bryan Feille, Harold Glen Brown Lecturer in Pastoral Ministry, Brite Divinity School of Texas Christian University; and Pamela G. Holt, a student at Brite and a minister at South Hills Christian Church, Fort Worth, Texas. Two practitioners of church–state law also read the manuscript: Steven K. Green, legal counsel, Americans United for Separation of Church and State, and Mitchell A. Tyner, associate general counsel, General Conference of Seventh-day Adventists. These critics have saved me from errors of both style and fact. Their help is gratefully acknowledged. Whatever errors remain result from my stubbornness in not following their suggestions. Thanks are due also to Walter Sutton of Westminster John Knox Press, whose suggestion to write this book stimulated me to go ahead and do what I had been thinking about for quite some time.

Finally, but far from least, a huge expression of gratitude goes to my wife, Leah, who endured more missed family time and blank stares during conversations than was proper or fair. And to Jennifer, Philip, and Paul, who, although now gone from home, still wonder how and why their father can get so excited about writing stuff. But, in spite of the puzzlement and missed togetherness, they all have been enormously supportive. I hope my appreciation has been evident.

1

The Court and Its Procedures

As Americans think of the three branches of their government, it is likely that the Supreme Court is more mysterious to most people than either the Presidency or Congress. This is because the Court is less public in its operations than either of the other two. Our first task, then, is to look at the inner workings of the Court.

SELECTING CASES: THE FIRST STEP

The Court makes its pronouncements on various issues, including church and state, by handing down opinions, which express decisions about cases. A case is a controversy between two parties (individuals or institutions, including the government), each of which has an interest in and will be affected by the outcome of the decision. The Court will not give opinions on abstract or merely philosophical questions. Only real controversies come before the Court: somebody *versus* somebody. A person may not challenge a law through a lawsuit unless his or her rights are somehow directly affected. This adversarial system of jurisprudence means that the Court does not set its own agenda, in the sense of going out and looking for controversies to resolve; it deals only with what is brought to it. However, as will be seen, the Court does set its own agenda by choosing from among the cases that come before it. The adversarial system also means that the questions before the Court will be formed more sharply and argued more vigorously than merely philosophical questions might be. Furthermore, a question of vital interest to two parties may be of importance to many others in the country. Of course, we know this is true from the public outcry Supreme Court decisions sometimes elicit.

Cases get to the Court through either the federal court system or the court system of a state. In the federal system, cases normally begin at the district court, or "trial court" level. There are currently ninety-four district courts. Here the controversy is fully aired by counsel for both sides, including the questioning of witnesses. Normally a constitutional question such as those involving religion will be heard by one federal judge. However, when the constitutionality of a state action is involved, the case will sometimes be

1

heard before a three-judge panel. A written opinion is virtually always handed down by the judge or judges. The losing party may appeal that opinion to a federal court of appeals, one of twelve that would hear religion cases. (Appeals of three-judge panel cases go directly to the Supreme Court.) Here the judges do not rehear the witnesses, but rather examine the record of the trial in the lower court, including its opinion, read written statements by opposing counsel, and listen to arguments. On the basis of this evidence a decision is reached, again virtually always expressed in a written opinion. The decisions at this level may uphold the decision of the lower court or overturn it. The loser may want to appeal to the Supreme Court, but, as you will see, the trip there is neither automatic nor easily traversed.

The courts of the fifty states hear the majority of cases in this country. Judicial systems vary from state to state, but it is possible to generalize about them. As in the federal system, there are trial courts and courts of appeal. In populous states there are often four layers of courts, rather than three. Losers may appeal their cases upward. Of course, state courts hear cases involving state law. But state laws, either by their nature or by their enforcement, may have federal constitutional dimensions. So state courts may hear cases involving federal issues. If a case gets to a state supreme court, and *if it involves a federal question* (as a church–state question would), it is a candidate for being heard at the U.S. Supreme Court.

In both the federal and state systems, appeal of a case from a trial court to a court of appeals is generally a matter of right to the loser in a case. That is, the appeals court must accept the appeal from the lower court. In the vast majority of cases, the decision of the appeals court is where the case stops because appeal beyond one level is not a matter of right. The U.S. Supreme Court will be our example, since it is the focus of this book. There is a small category of cases, mostly having to do with conflicts between state laws and the federal Constitution, in which there is the right of appeal, that is, the Court must deal with those cases. Cases that come to the Court on appeal are often decided summarily without full argument, either affirming or reversing the decision of the court below. These affirmations or reversals are usually on the basis of precedents already decided by the Court. These are "decisions" of the Court, even though there is no written opinion. But the Court may simply dismiss an appeal because it lacks jurisdiction over the question presented or because the case fails to pose a substantial federal question. Again, only a small percentage of the cases on appeal are scheduled for oral argument before the Court. Those cases are deemed important enough for oral argument and full opinions and are put on the Court's docket for that purpose.

The vast majority of cases do not come on appeal, and the Court has "discretionary power" over those cases; in short, it can refuse to hear them. This is the Court's way of managing its workload and focusing only on those cases which will clarify the law and/or have national significance. In the last decade the Court's workload has become almost unbearable. In the 1989–90 term 5,746 cases came before it for consideration, 6,316 cases in the 1990–91 term, 6,770 cases in the 1991–92 term, and 7,245 cases in the 1992–93 term.[1] Of course, it would be impossible to give full consideration to all these cases. The procedure to winnow out the less-important cases is called the "writ of certiorari." "Certiorari" literally means "to be made more certain." The writ is a command "from a higher court requiring the record of a case in the court below to be sent up to itself for re-determination."[2] When a case comes to the Court, it is accompanied by all the materials that have been generated in the lower courts. The record of each case is examined and a preliminary judgment is made on the merit of the case. If a determination is made that a case is not worthy of discussion by the full Court, that case goes on a "nondiscussion list." If all the nine justices have made that judgment, the case is dismissed without any discussion. If any one of the nine believes that a case is worthy of discussion, it is put on a list for conference. When the justices come together in conference, a vote is taken on each case on the "discuss list." If four of the justices vote for a case, it is carried over for oral arguments, "cert. granted." Even at the stage of conference, most cases are denied certiorari and thus are not ever decided by the full Court. There are many reasons why the Court refuses to hear a case. For example, the case may not represent a real controversy, it may not present a federal question, or it may not be of national importance. But the Court does not have to give reasons for refusing to hear a case and usually does not.

What does it mean when the Court refuses to hear a case, when the response is "cert. denied"? It means only that. It should not be construed as meaning that the refusal to hear a case is an endorsement of the decision of the lower court. Certainly the decision of the lower court stands and becomes effective, since the Supreme Court has chosen not to review it. But in denying certiorari, the Court is not taking a position on the merits of the case or on the decision of the court below. It means, as much as anything, that no matter how important the issue is to the parties in the case, the Court, with a huge workload, simply cannot take all cases and chose not to take this one. Perhaps this was best summarized by Chief Justice William Howard Taft:

> No litigant is entitled to more than two chances, namely, to the original trial and to a review, and the intermediate courts of review are provided for that purpose. When a case goes beyond that, it is not primarily to preserve the rights of the litigants. The Supreme Court's function is for the purpose of expounding and stabilizing principles of law for the benefit of the people of the country, passing upon constitutional questions and other important questions of law for the public benefit. It is to preserve uniformity of decision among the intermediate courts of appeal.[3]

One of the main reasons the Court will accept a case for review is mentioned in the last sentence of Chief Justice Taft's comment. Sometimes similar cases will come up through two or more courts of appeal and these courts will reach contradictory conclusions. Put simply, one court has decided "yes" and another court has decided "no" on the same issue. The Supreme Court will hear one of those cases (or combine two or more cases into one), in order to eliminate confusion and bring stability and consistency to the federal law on that subject. Examples of this procedure are the conscientious objector cases of 1965, discussed in chapter 5, and the public school prayer decisions of 1963, discussed in chapter 7.

This description of the procedure of winnowing out cases, particularly the fact that the Court must decide between conflicting opinions from lower courts, brings up the fact that the Court gets hard cases. Usually the Court accepts for oral argument those cases which are most complicated and which will have the most impact on the conduct of life in American society. They are cases in which both parties seem to have persuasive arguments firmly based in law. In short, they are very difficult cases to decide. One Supreme Court justice is reported to have said: "I can think of a thousand hypothetical cases that we could dispose of simply by reference to the words of the Constitution. But, doggone it, our Court never seems to get a case like that to decide."[4] Church–state cases are frequently of this most difficult type.

DECIDING CASES AND CLARIFYING THE LAW

As noted, the justices have already received the materials about each case from lower courts. When a case has been accepted for oral argument, the lawyers for each litigant submit additional briefs, arguing their viewpoint and marshaling all the legal rationale they can to persuade the justices to decide in their favor. Of course, because cases that come before the Court are often of great importance, parties or groups other than the litigants are frequently vitally interested in the outcome of a case. Such groups will often file *amicus curiae*, or "friend of the court," briefs. These may support either side in the suit and will sometimes ask the Court to look at other angles of the case than those articulated by the litigants.[5] Consequently, the justices may have a mountain of paper to read through in informing themselves about the case and ultimately reaching a decision.

In oral arguments, the counsel for each side makes a presentation to the Court, summarizing the legal issues for the justices and telling them why they should decide for his or her client. They are expected not to read from a prepared text. Each side is allowed only thirty minutes to present its argument. Furthermore, the justices may—and do—break into the argument at any moment to ask questions. (The justices have already read much of the paperwork about the case and often come to the bench with a written summary of the case; they come prepared to ask questions.) It is a pressure-packed situation for the lawyers.

When oral arguments are over, the justices meet in conference to discuss the case. Only the nine justices attend these secret conferences. Given the caseload of the modern Court, the discussion of the case is not intense or meticulous. Its primary purpose is to see where the various justices stand in their view of how the case should be decided: is there consensus, or is the Court divided? It is here that the chief justice, whose vote is no more weighty than that of any other justice, may exercise the primary authority of the office, assigning opinions, although that authority is not absolute. If in the majority, the chief justice will assign one justice to write the opinion for the Court. If the chief is not in the majority, the assignment will be made by the most senior associate justice who is in the majority.

The person assigned will write an opinion expressing the views of the majority, and this will become the decision in the case at hand. But, as suggested already, there may be justices who do not see the case that way. They are free to write dissenting opinions. No one assigns these opinions; any justice who is not with the majority may write a dissent. All these opinions are circulated to all the justices, who read them and react. Sometimes dissenters are won over to the majority and dissenting opinions are withdrawn. Sometimes some may break from the majority and join with the dissenters. (Occasionally a dissenting opinion becomes the majority opinion.) The process is a debate on paper. Each justice who writes an opinion tries to be as persuasive to colleagues as possible, to win them to his or her position. Although they talk about the case in conference on more than one occasion, it is essentially through the opinion-writing process that the alignments of the justices are produced and the decision reached.

Sometimes justices agree with the conclusions or result of the majority, but do not agree with the reasoning or the legal principles by which they arrived at the result. These justices will frequently write concurring opinions. In extreme cases, a majority is not reached. For example, three justices may join "the opinion of the Court," and two others may "concur in the judgment," to produce a "plurality opinion" of 5–4. Such opinions tell who won and who lost, but not why. They therefore do not fulfill a major responsibility of the Court: clarifying the meaning of the law. When all the justices have decided where they want to be positioned in the result of a case, the decision is then made public. That is the "decision of the Court." That final decision may be of a unanimous Court, although that is rare,[6] or it may be made up of several concurring and dissenting opinions. The existence of these, particularly dissents, shows that it was impossible for the majority writer to persuade all colleagues to reach a consensus about the case. Dissent is important, however, because it compels the author of the majority opinion to be more precise and to try to answer the objections of the dissenters.

When there are dissents, particularly when the vote is 5–4, there is a tendency to think that one person decided the case. People are often concerned about this "law by one person" concept, particularly if they do not like the decision in the case. But although if one justice had voted differently the decision would have been different, it is important to remember that in those close, split-vote decisions it was *five* or *six* justices who voted a particular way, not just one or two. It simply is not realistic to expect that all cases will be unanimous or voted preponderantly one way, especially given the complex world in which we live and the perplexing cases brought before the Court.

Law Clerks

How can the justices handle the enormous amount of paperwork by themselves? They cannot. Each of the justices may have up to four clerks, except for the chief justice, who may have up to five. The clerks are of immense help to the justices. They are young lawyers, recent graduates from some of the best law schools in the country, who may have had experience clerking in a lower federal court. Clerks are chosen by each justice to work in his or her office for a year or two.

In the certiorari process described earlier, the clerks summarize each case and make a recommendation to the justice as to whether that case should be on the list for discussion. When a case is accepted for oral argument, the clerk will read the paperwork on it and prepare a summary for the justice to take to the bench on the day that case is argued. When a justice is assigned to write an opinion, or chooses to write a concurring or dissenting opinion, a clerk is responsible for doing the necessary research on the case. Some justices even ask their clerks to write first drafts of opinions for them to consider. Of course, the way clerks are used varies from justice to justice, but all the justices use their clerks to help bear the burden of a crushing workload.

The question is frequently raised as to whether this situation means that the business of administering justice for the nation has, in reality, passed from the hands of the justices to the law clerks. There is no doubt that the justices now give less attention to each case than they were able to in earlier times. (The first clerk was hired in 1882: prior to that time the workload was such that justices could do it all themselves. As recently as 1970, each justice had only two clerks.) But, even today, even with those justices who have clerks write first drafts of opinions, each justice looks carefully at the clerks' work, often edits it heavily or even rewrites it, and makes sure that the opinion says what the justice wants to say before he or she signs it. It is, in reality, the justice's decision. So, the situation seems to be not "justice by clerks" but "justice with the important help of clerks."[7]

Stare Decisis and Obiter Dicta

It is important to look at two legal concepts at this point. One is *stare decisis*, "let the decision stand." This is the principle of precedent, which is so important to the law. It is the principle of "not reinventing the wheel." This means that courts will routinely follow their previous decisions. So lower courts are bound to follow the precedents set by the Supreme Court and the Supreme Court itself will ordinarily follow the precedents set by its previous decisions. This principle of precedent allows the Court more latitude in refusing to hear cases that raise questions well-settled by previous decisions. It is the concept that enables lawyers to advise clients of their rights and their prospects of winning any proposed litigation. Precedent provides continuity to the law, in that it provides the justices benchmarks and concepts that aid them in deciding on the litigation before them. A decided case and the rationale for the decision carry great weight in analogous cases before the Court.

The other principle of importance is *obiter dictum* (pl. *dicta*), "remark in passing." In writing opinions, the justices articulate legal principles that are central to the decision of the case. Often, however, they do not confine themselves to the technicalities of the case at hand, but comment more widely about history, philosophy, patriotism, and other topics that embellish the decision and enlighten its readers. Such comments are *dicta* and do not have the same binding or precedential effect on future cases that the actual decision on the case has.

Sometimes people say about a statement in a decision, "Oh, that is just *dictum*," as if to minimize its importance. That is too bad, for often the *dictum* is quite wonderful, both in the sense of being good literature and in the sense of being instructive on matters of American history—even religious history, in the instance of church–state cases.

Dicta can influence later cases. For example, a dissenting opinion is clearly *dictum*, since it does nothing to decide the case and define the legal principles of the decision. But sometimes a dissent can be so persuasive that it can become the majority opinion in a later case on the same or similar issue. A good example is the Jehovah's Witnesses flag salute cases, discussed in chapter 3. In *Minersville School District* v. *Gobitis*,[8] the Court ruled that school districts could compel Jehovah's Witness students to salute the American flag, even though it was contrary to their religious beliefs to do so. Justice Harlan Stone wrote a strong dissent. Three years later the Court reexamined the issue in *West Virginia Board of Education* v. *Barnette*.[9] The Court reversed itself, that is, it overruled the *Gobitis* case and said the Jehovah's Witness children had the constitutional right, based on their religious belief and the Free Exercise Clause of the First Amendment, to refuse to salute the flag in the public school context. The majority opinion in *Barnette* was based largely on Justice Stone's dissent in *Gobitis*.

Occasionally, as in this example, the Court will reverse itself. The principle of *stare decisis* is not absolute. And *dicta* often carry great force, even though they may not focus precisely on the case at hand. We shall have occasion to look at some stirring *dicta* in the chapters that follow. Indeed, I shall include many direct quotes, because most who read this book have probably never before read any Supreme Court opinions. I think it is important for you to get a sense of how these opinions read. But, much more important, frequently statements of the Court eloquently, even powerfully, articulate principles of freedom and church–state separation. I hope you will be instructed by reading the Court's own words. But first it is necessary to look at the background of the religion clauses of the Constitution, which are critical to church–state relations in this country.

2

Background of
Constitutional Principles

Christianity became the official religion of the Roman Empire in the fourth century. In the language of church–state relations, it became the "established" religion. Here and throughout this book "establishment" means an official, formal, symbiotic relationship between religion and the civil authority. This relationship was assumed to be good for both the state and the church in those early days. It was beneficial for the state in that the moral precepts taught by the church provided an ideology and moral basis for government. It was good for the church, in that it provided the church with political status and influence, protection from competition, and, in some eras, financial assistance from tax monies collected by the state for the benefit of the church.

The arrangement persisted for centuries in the Western world; the Catholic Church was the established church. One might think that when the Protestant Reformers broke with the Roman church, they would also have abandoned its concept of establishment. But that was not the case. Because everyone was so immersed in the idea that it was necessary to have an establishment in order to have a stable political order, the new Protestant movements continued the practice. Even though, with the proliferation of religious movements, church–state alignments became enormously more complicated, the principle and practice of establishment persisted in Western Europe. The most prominent early examples were the Lutheran state churches in Germany and, later, Scandinavia, Henry VIII's Church of England (Anglican), and the established Reformed churches in Huldreich Zwingli's Zurich and John Calvin's Geneva. There is one exception to this generalization: the Anabaptists believed that the civil authority should have nothing to do with matters of religion. But this idea was regarded as heretical by the majority and was a major reason the Anabaptists were persecuted as they were.

Because everything was complicated by the multiplicity of religious groups, in 1555 a treaty was signed, the Peace of Augsburg, which set forth, for Germany, the principle of *cujus regio, ejus religio*, "whose the rule, his or hers the religion." The actual phrase was not used until 1648, in the treaty called the Peace of Westphalia, which expanded the principle to apply to all of Europe. Under this principle, the ruler of a territory had the right to determine the religion of that territory.

The relevance of this for the American situation is that this proestablishment philosophy and this operating principle, "whose the rule, his or hers the religion," were transported to the New World with its earliest permanent settlers.

THE SEVENTEENTH CENTURY:
A VARIETY OF CHURCH–STATE RELATIONSHIPS

It is frequently said that the founders of the first American colonies came to the New World for religious freedom. That is not entirely accurate. The earliest of the permanent settlers were those who created the colony of Virginia. They were members of the Anglican Church, which was the established church in England at the time. As such, in England they were not persecuted or otherwise disadvantaged because of their religion. They came to the New World at least as much for its adventure and economic potential as out of missionary zeal. When they created a government for the Virginia colony, they established the Anglican Church; it was to be the only church in the colony. In the traditional style of an establishment, clergy were provided public support in the forms of money or, more often, land and tobacco. "Dale's laws" (1610), named after one of the first governors of the colony, required attendance at Anglican worship by all the citizens of the colony, and persistent violation of the law carried the death penalty. There were also laws against blasphemy and criticism of the Anglican Church or any of its particular doctrines. Again, depending on the seriousness of the profanity, penalties could range from mutilation of one's tongue to death. There is no clear evidence that the laws were rigorously enforced or that the ultimate penalties were ever inflicted. But it is clear that there was no religious freedom in early Virginia.[1] Anglicanism was also at least nominally established in North and South Carolina, Georgia, and, in the eighteenth century, Maryland and New York.

There were in England, however, some people who did not conform to the Church of England. Although they disagreed among themselves about the extent to which they should separate from the national church, they agreed that it should be purified of what they considered to be the residue of Roman Catholicism within it—thus the name "Puritans." When it became clear that the Anglican Church would not follow their admonitions on the purification of the church and that they might lose their wealth or even their lives if they persisted in their criticism, they left for the New World.

Some of the Puritans landed at what is now Plymouth, Massachusetts, in 1620 and a larger group at Massachusetts Bay in 1628. Here they attempted to create the ideal church and state, a commonwealth based on the Bible, "a due form of Government both civil and ecclesiastical,"[2] an establishment. Because of the form of church government they followed, their church was called "Congregationalist." Puritan laws compelled the observance of Congregationalist faith and practice by all the citizens of the colony. They wanted to keep their religion pure. As one early leader, Nathaniel Ward, said, after naming a list of unacceptable religions, they "shall have free Liberty to keep away from us, and such as will come to be gone as fast as they can, the sooner the better."[3] Did the Puritans mean that? Yes; dissenters were often tried and physically punished, sometimes banished from the colony.[4] Between 1659 and 1661 four Quakers were executed by hanging, including Mary Dyer, the first woman martyr for religious liberty in the New World.[5] In short, these Puritans came to America for religious liberty, but when they got here they created an establishment just as repressive as that from which they had escaped.

> It is important to understand that they never intended to launch a colony which would be open to all persons of all religious persuasions—or none. The Puritans and Pilgrims came to create a pure church, conduct a holy experiment in a wilderness where none would interfere, none would oppose or even distract. They were not hypocrites who came to America for freedom of religion, then would allow a similar freedom to no one else. That was never the plan, never the errand. They came to prove that one could form a society so faithful, a church so cleansed, that even old England would be transformed by witnessing what determined believers had managed to achieve many thousands of miles away.[6]

The Congregationalist church was also established in Connecticut and New Hampshire.

Exceptions and Precursors

There were exceptions to the pattern of establishment. The most notable were Rhode Island and Pennsylvania. The former was founded by Roger Williams, the most vigorous advocate for religious freedom in the colonial period. He was concerned for the purity of the church and the spiritual welfare of those within it. To preserve that purity, he believed, the church should be separated from the corrupting influences of the state and the "natural man." Consequently, he founded Rhode Island in 1636 on the principle of religious liberty, and the colony became a haven of freedom for those who were persecuted for their religion in other colonies.

Pennsylvania was founded in 1682 by William Penn, a Quaker. The Quakers believed in the concept of the "inner light," something of God in each person, which both sanctified human life and potentially revealed God to the individual. Because one's experience with God could be direct and immediate and persons could understand the inner light differently, the Quakers believed that religion should be free of state-imposed uniformity in thought or practice. However, even in Pennsylvania, political office was available to Christians only. In spite of that restriction, Penn's "Holy Experiment" granted the broadest religious freedom in colonial America.

"Whose the rule, his or hers the religion." That principle was dominant in the early seventeenth century. Most governments chose to try to enforce religious uniformity and exclusivism, although the denominations differed from colony to colony. But others were willing to accommodate religious diversity. In any case, the shape of religion in a colony was dependent on the beliefs of those in power. However, as time progressed, a number of factors emerged to change this situation.

THE EIGHTEENTH CENTURY:
THE PROCESS OF DISESTABLISHMENT

Pluralism

Pluralism is one of the principal features of American religion. "Pluralism" means that in this country we have a multiplicity of religions, each of which thinks of itself as being different enough from others to merit separate existence. It has been that way from the country's beginning. Consequently, it may be artificial to introduce the concept of pluralism under the heading of the eighteenth century, for, as the seventeenth progressed, Dutch Reformed, Lutherans, Roman Catholics, Jews, Baptists, and many nonbelievers journeyed to America. In the eighteenth century, pluralism increased as groups such as the Presbyterians, Mennonites, German Reformed, and Moravians began to arrive in numbers.

My point is that with the increasing diversity of the population it became more difficult for any government to maintain religious homogeneity within its borders. Thus one of the traditional arguments for an establishment, a stable political order based on an official theology and set of moral ideas, became progressively irrelevant. In addition, Rhode Island and Pennsylvania, which were flourishing, demonstrated that it was possible to have orderly government and a stable society even without religious uniformity. They were successful "laboratory schools" of religious pluralism.

Furthermore, from the perspective of the various religious groups, there was a very practical implication of this pluralism. None of them was large enough or powerful enough to become the dominant, much less the sole, religious group in an area. Each decided that if it could not have that kind of power for itself, it did not want any other group to have it either. Stated differently, groups perceived that if any one group was given political power, all others would be disadvantaged. Better that all religious groups be equal before the law. So pluralism was one of several factors in the eighteenth century that contributed to the eventual separation of church and state in America.

Religious Revivalism

Beginning in the 1720s with regional outbursts and reaching its peak from 1740 to 1742, the Great Awakening contributed significantly to the process of disestablishment. The Great Awakening was a revival movement that swept the eastern seaboard, spread primarily by the enormously talented preacher George Whitefield. The revival sought to enliven the churches, which many religious leaders saw as spiritually dead or at least in the doldrums, by preaching a message of spiritual renewal and discipline. It was not enough to be a lukewarm Christian; one should know that he or she was a sinful creature, estranged from God, before receiving God's forgiveness. But, by God's grace, salvation and spiritual revitalization were available. Much of this preaching was done not in churches, but in open-air meetings, thus reaching large crowds. Many people had conversion experiences. It is difficult to know how many conversions there were; eighteenth-century preachers were not much better at accurately reporting such numbers than modern ones. But historians are convinced that the churches of various denominations were revitalized and enlarged by the Great Awakening.

Historically it had been argued that it was necessary to have an establishment to get people into the churches; the police power of the state would be used to compel people to attend worship. (Remember "Dale's laws.") But those who responded to the revival preachers did so voluntarily, because they were attracted to the gospel. There was no coercion, yet people came to listen to preachers, worship, and join churches. Some began to wonder why, if it was possible to attract people to religion and churches through persuasion, it was necessary to continue the establishment pattern? Such thinking later contributed to the formulation of the concept of separation of church and state.

Pietism

In addition to the persuasive power of orthodox Christian preaching, many people at the time drew antiestablishment conclusions from the theology itself: Human beings are sinful; their stiff-necked pride causes them to rebel against God, thus distorting, if not destroying, the relationship between humans and God that God originally intended. This sin manifests itself in all sorts of ways, from minor peccadilloes to deeds of abject evil.

Human beings cannot restore this relationship with God themselves. God, in an act of ultimate mercy, sent Jesus Christ to be the savior of humankind.

Those who heard this good news and in whom God ignited faith (Calvinist) or who responded to the message (Arminian) were brought into a restored relationship with God; they were Christian. But this was an individual experience. Without discounting the church as the place where the gospel was rightly preached and the sacraments rightly administered, as the community of the faithful gathered for mutual support and spiritual nurture, nonetheless the experience of salvation was ultimately an individual experience.

In the American environment, some began to make a connection between the personal experience of salvation and political religious freedom. The experience of becoming Christian was dependent on the work of the Holy Spirit within one, not the theological dictates of a state-controlled church. The liberating experience of salvation meant freedom from the "principalities and powers," not only from sin, but the political powers as well. Furthermore, there was no guarantee that all should respond to the call of God in the same way. "Hence the pietist did not have the heart . . . longer to justify coerced uniformity under Establishment."[7]

Rationalism

Another contributor to eventual separation was the opposite of pietism: rationalism. In this age of the Enlightenment, many became convinced of the virtual invincibility of human reason. Reason could perceive and understand all that was worth knowing; it could formulate ethical principles; it could devise systems of government. There was great emphasis on the worth and abilities of human beings. Rationalists were not unanimous in their views of religion. Some said that reason took the place of God: by relying on reason, humans no longer had need for God; religion was only antiquated superstition. Others took the position that reason could demonstrate the existence of God; for example, the complexity and precision of the universe implied the existence of a Designer. This theistic form of rationalism was known as Deism and was the position of many of those great men who were responsible for writing the Constitution. Their Deism greatly influenced their views of church–state relationships. They were convinced that any institution that hindered reason, interfered with free, creative thought, shackled the minds of men and women, was bad. They knew history well enough to know that the established church had had just such an impact. Theological orthodoxy imposed by law, the medieval Inquisitions, and the heresy trials and executions of the American colonies taught them that an established church was inimical to political and intellectual freedom. Consequently, they were not willing to make establishment a characteristic of the new nation they were creating.

The Virginia Experience

In sum, a variety of factors, practical, theological, and philosophical, contributed to constitutional disestablishment. A final factor was the almost laboratory experience of Virginia. By 1779 Virginia had become as religiously pluralistic as the other colonies and many of its inhabitants were rethinking church–state relationships. The Anglican establishment was considerably weakened.

In 1784 a taxation bill was introduced in the Virginia legislature that was intended for the support of the Christian religion rather than any particular sect. The tax was to be collected by the civil authorities, but the taxpayer could designate which Christian group would receive the money. If one chose no Christian organization to receive the tax, it would go to education. The principal sponsor of the bill was Patrick Henry, who argued that governmental support of religion was necessary in order to have a moral society. The principal opponent of the bill was James Madison, who expressed his opposition in a document entitled "Memorial and Remonstrance against Religious Assessments" (see Appendix A). Madison marshaled rationalistic and philosophical arguments against any tax bill whatsoever, in the process making the case for religious freedom in a variety of forceful ways. No document has argued for religious freedom more eloquently: it is an American classic.

Madison's purpose in writing the piece was to sway public opinion against the taxation bill. In that he was extraordinarily successful. In 1785 the legislature defeated the taxation bill. Madison took advantage of this moment to reintroduce to the legislature Thomas Jefferson's "Bill for Establishing Religious Freedom" (Appendix B). Jefferson had first introduced this bill in 1779, and it had been tabled by the legislature every year since. But now, in the climate created by the "Memorial and Remonstrance," the bill was enacted into law in January 1786. The importance of these events is not only that Virginia became a trailblazer in the American movement toward the separation of church and state, but also that it gave Madison the opportunity to crystallize and articulate his thoughts on the question of religious liberty before he went to Philadelphia to work on the Constitution, to which we now turn.

THE CONSTITUTION

When the statesmen who founded this country wrote the Constitution, they mentioned religion in only one place, Article VI. What they wrote is a prohibition. In Article VI, as a part of the requirement that state and federal officeholders take an oath or make an affirmation to support the Constitution, the founders wrote: "but no religious Test shall ever be required as a Qualification to any Office or public Trust under the United States." There is no reference to God or to any religious tradition in the Constitution. Apparently this was not an oversight.

Does that mean that the founders were hostile to religion or even to Christianity? No, it means that they recognized, given the multiplicity of religions in the new nation and the distressing history of governmental oppression in the name of religion, that it would be better for them to leave the question alone. To avoid getting involved in a quagmire of competing religious loyalties, the government should remain neutral. Furthermore, it was a way of asserting the limited nature of government. The state had no powers that were not enumerated in the Constitution. By not mentioning religion, the founders were not expressing animosity toward religion, but rather keeping the sacred matter of religion from the reach of government. In the words of Madison, the Constitution was not to grant "a shadow of right in the general government to intermeddle with religion."[8] However, since the government obviously needed to set the requirements for public office, the authors addressed themselves to this question. Public office would be independent of religious belief or the lack thereof.

This provision of Article VI did not create the separation of church and state. But it went a long way to minimize in the new nation the possibility of the religious strife and oppression that had been known in the history of the Western world. Apparently the majority of Americans were satisfied with the Constitution's virtual silence on the question of religion, for it was ratified in 1789. But many were not satisfied by the silence of the Constitution on the larger question of the freedoms of citizens, including the freedom of religion. Consequently, the founders drew up a list guaranteeing particular freedoms: the Bill of Rights.

The Establishment Clause

The historical record on the process of writing the religion clauses of the First Amendment is not completely clear. The record of the debate in the House of Representatives is brief, perhaps more a paraphrase or summary than a verbatim report. The Senate debate was conducted in secret, although there is a record of the votes on various proposals. The information available indicates that the religion provisions of the Bill of Rights went through several modifications before the final wording was decided on.

What is of importance to contemporary debate on the meaning of the clauses, especially the Establishment Clause, is that there were several proposals that, while clearly prohibiting the government from establishing one particular religious group, would have allowed it to aid all religions on a nondiscriminatory, nonpreferential basis. For example, there were two proposals in the Senate: "Congress shall make no law establishing one religious sect or society in preference to others," and "Congress shall not make any law infringing the rights of conscience, or establishing any religious sect or society." Some of the proposals in the House were similar. But the First Congress rejected that language. When members of the House and Senate came together in conference committee, they produced the language that became the religion clauses of the First Amendment: "Congress shall make no law respecting an establishment of religion, or prohibiting the free exercise thereof."

By the end of the eighteenth century, the colonial establishments described earlier had changed. None of them was any longer the establishment of a single religious group. No longer was the Anglican Church, the Congregational Church, or any other religious group exclusively established anywhere. As a result of many of the factors described earlier, especially pluralism, all the establishments had become "multiple establishments." By the time the Bill of Rights was ratified in 1791, only six states had any sort of establishment. Of those, three gave government support to Protestantism and three to Christianity—none to a specific denomination.

I mentioned earlier the bill proposed in the Virginia legislature that would have levied a tax "for the Christian religion," in which each taxpayer could designate which group would receive the tax payment, so long as the group was Christian. The result would have been a "multiple establishment," and if Virginia had passed that bill it would have brought to seven the number of states to have such an arrangement. The only variation among these states was that three excluded Catholicism by favoring only Protestant groups. Thus multiple establishment was the pattern at the time the First Congress was debating the language of the religion provisions of the Bill of Rights.

Some of the proposals presupposed this multiple-establishment arrangement and wanted to preserve it by prohibiting the government from giving its favor and support to only one denomination. This is known as the "nonpreferential" view of establishment: establishment is permitted so long as it is nondiscriminatory, showing no preference between religions. This view is also known as the "accommodationist" approach: the proper relationship between church and state is for the state to accommodate the church.

But the final language of the First Amendment went beyond this view; it took the "separationist," or "no aid," approach. The founders were familiar with the no-preference approach, but they wrote that there was to be "no law respecting an establishment of religion." The government was not to establish one religion, neither was it to establish multiple religions. This was one more way the founders articulated their view that government was to be limited.

Every bit of evidence goes to prove that the First Amendment, like the others, was intended to restrict Congress to its enumerated powers. Since the Constitutional Convention gave Congress no power to legislate on matters concerning religion, Congress had no such power even in the absence of the First Amendment. It is, therefore, unreasonable to believe that an express prohibition of power—"Congress shall make no law respecting an establishment of religion"—creates the power, previously nonexistent, of supporting religion by aid to one or all religious groups. The Bill of Rights, as Madison said, was not framed "to imply powers not meant to be included in the enumeration."[9]

The meaning of the Establishment Clause on this issue is currently a topic of intense debate. The debate is over what the founders originally intended by the First Amendment, especially the Establishment Clause. Although the evidence is strong, as just described, that the founders were "separationist" in their understanding of what they were doing, some argue that they were "nonpreferentialists." This "original intent" controversy is covered in detail in chapter 9.

Application of Constitutional Principles
by the States

When the Bill of Rights was ratified, it was understood by everyone that it applied only to the federal government, not to the states. On the subject of religion, the founders believed that each state should handle the issue at the state level. The effect of this is easily illustrated. Most of the states wrote provisions into their constitutions that also provided for separation of church and state and guaranteed religious freedom. Sometimes the language was more detailed and stringent than the First Amendment. But three states—New Hampshire, Connecticut, and Massachusetts—continued their multiple establishments until long after the First Amendment became law. Massachusetts, in 1833, was the last to abolish its establishment. So, religious freedom was guaranteed against federal encroachment, but at the state level the concept still was basically "whose the rule, his or hers the religion."

After the Civil War, the Thirteenth, Fourteenth, and Fifteenth Amendments to the Constitution were ratified to eliminate slavery and to guarantee civil rights and the vote to freed slaves. The following clause, known as the Due Process Clause, is in the Fourteenth Amendment, section 1: "[N]or shall any State deprive any person of life, liberty, or property, without due process of law." This demands that the *states* be diligent in preserving the liberties of their citizens.

In the twentieth century, the Supreme Court began to decide some cases by applying the liberties of the First Amendment to the states through the Due Process Clause of the Fourteenth Amendment. Lawyers call this "incorporation," meaning that the liberties of the First Amendment are incorporated into the Fourteenth. Specifically, because of the Fourteenth Amendment, the liberties guaranteed by the Establishment and Free Exercise Clauses are among the liberties the various states may not deny to their citizens. So, in the current understanding of the principle, no governmental unit, from Congress to the local school board, may make a law establishing religion or prohibiting its free exercise.

When Americans think of the late eighteenth century, they think of the Revolutionary War, by which independence was gained from Britain. But no less revolutionary was the separation of church and state. This was the first time in human history that a nation had written into its legal charter the idea of separation and religious freedom. Never before had a nation been bold enough to guarantee to its citizens the right to be religious or nonreligious, and, if religious, to practice that religion according to the dictates of their conscience. Revolutionary! That constitutional guarantee is preeminent among the features that make America the great country it is. But, of course, it has been necessary for the Supreme Court to interpret the meanings and boundaries of the guarantee. In chapter 3 we begin an examination of that exposition.

3

Defining the Scope of
Religious Freedom: Prior to 1963

A survey of the decisions of the Supreme Court on church–state relations must begin with the Free Exercise Clause, because cases about that clause came to the Court long before Establishment Clause cases. The First Amendment demands that "Congress shall make no law . . . prohibiting the free exercise [of religion]." The obvious meaning is that government may not prohibit religious activity. The religion clauses mean, among other things, that a person can believe what she or he wants in the area of religion. However, it would be a hollow freedom if one were told, "You can believe whatever you want, so long as you do not do anything about it." Religious freedom goes much beyond that. The Free Exercise Clause guarantees the right to implement one's religious beliefs, to put them into action. But does that mean that "anything goes," that whatever one does in the name of religion is constitutionally protected?

MORMON CASES

The Supreme Court began to confront the issue of the scope of free exercise in the late nineteenth century, in cases brought by the Church of Jesus Christ of Latter-day Saints, the Mormons. The controversy was over polygamy. The founder of the church, Joseph Smith, Jr., had taught in the late 1830s and early 1840s that polygamy was divinely commanded and a religious obligation. That belief was a part of the theology of the church for the rest of the century. When the Mormons began to establish their communities in Utah and surrounding territories, the Congress responded with laws forbidding plural marriages. The laws applied to federal territories, which enabled the Supreme Court to judge cases that came from Utah and Idaho even before the incorporation of the First Amendment. The key case is *Reynolds* v. *United States*.[1] Reynolds, a Mormon who had two wives, was convicted for violating the law prohibiting polygamy. But he asserted that the Free Exercise Clause protected his behavior because it was based on religious belief.

The Supreme Court did not accept that argument. It held that one can believe whatever one wants, because the government may not interfere with religious belief, but one may not put those beliefs into action *if* those actions are somehow harmful to persons or even the moral structure of society. "Congress was deprived of all legislative power over mere opinion, but was left free to reach actions which were in violation of social duties or subversive of good order."[2] The Court held that the practice of polygamy tended to instill in people the attitude of despotism or authoritarianism (since a home with so many wives and children had to be "ruled with an iron hand"). Such an attitude was contrary to the needs of a democratic society. Furthermore, polygamy historically had been held to be immoral and unacceptable in the Western world, and that was the reason the laws prohibiting plural marriages had been passed by Congress. Because the law, and the Court, assumed polygamy to be harmful to the moral fiber of society, the law was constitutional and Reynolds was not protected by the fact that his practice of polygamy was religiously based.

In *Reynolds* the Court established a precedent that has persisted, in some form, to the present. Although religious freedom is a constitutionally guaranteed right, it is not absolute. It is subject to government interference if the government can show that a practice has harmful effects. In *Reynolds*, the Court held that government latitude is very wide in defining what is unacceptable to society. Although belief is protected, the government may prohibit any practice it determines has a negative impact on an individual, group, or society as a whole, even if it is religiously motivated. The Court did not give government officials any guidelines as to how to define what was negative and what was not. So this case gave the government extremely broad authority to interfere with religious behavior, and the government retained that judicially defined power for more than sixty years.[3]

JEHOVAH'S WITNESSES CASES

In the 1930s and 1940s the Supreme Court heard a large number of cases brought by the Jehovah's Witnesses. This prompts a short but important discussion. Often cases are brought to the Court by groups, or individuals representing groups, that are looked down on by the general population. In the 1940s the Jehovah's Witnesses were widely despised, just as the Mormons had been in the late nineteenth century. They found that the laws were written or enforced in such a way that their religious liberty was curtailed. Consequently, they initiated litigation to try to improve their situation. Of course, they had to invoke constitutional principles that applied to everybody (or were supposed to). The result was that in looking out for their own interests, these people elicited decisions from the Court that actually broadened the liberties of all Americans. So we all are in the debt of groups like the Mormons, Jehovah's Witnesses, Seventh-day Adventists, Native Americans, or individuals like Guy Ballard and Madalyn Murray O'Hair, who have braved the scorn of society to provide for clearer definitions and applications of the religion clauses of the First Amendment.[4]

Evangelizing on Public Property

Several of the Jehovah's Witnesses cases had to do with proselytizing or evangelizing on public property. The Witnesses believe that theirs is the only true religion and they are the only ones who understand God's activity in history, and thus it is their responsibility to tell as many people as possible about their faith. Furthermore, because they make no distinction between clergy and lay members, they believe that every baptized member of their organization is a minister with the obligation to engage in evangelization. In the 1930s and 1940s they were especially vigorous in this activity, often going into the streets and parks of communities in large groups to proclaim the word of God as they understood it. Not only did many residents of these towns regard the Witnesses as a nuisance to be gotten rid of, but they sometimes resented their message so much that they retaliated. The issue was not so much that the Witnesses were proclaiming the impending return of Jesus Christ to judge the earth, but their assertion that that judgment would be inflicted on all who were not among God's true people, the Witnesses. In those days the Witnesses preached in no uncertain terms that all organized religion was evil and the Roman Catholic Church was the worst of the lot. This message frequently led to hostile responses rather than conversions. Consequently, communities tried to keep the Witnesses out, and the Witnesses responded by going to court, claiming free-exercise rights.

One of the cases that grew out of these confrontations was *Cantwell* v. *Connecticut*.[5] It is such a significant case that it merits a detailed explanation.

Newton Cantwell and his two sons went to New Haven, Connecticut, to proclaim the Witnesses' message. A city statute required all outsiders to apply to a city official for a license to solicit funds or distribute material within the city limits. If the official determined that the cause was religious or a bona fide charity, the license would be given. If the cause was not, the license would be withheld. The Cantwells did not apply for a license because they believed that the city official would not certify the Witnesses as a religion. They simply proceeded to proclaim their religion on the streets and sidewalks. They spread their message by passing out literature to those who would take it and make a small contribution. They also played records on a small hand-held, spring-driven phonograph for those who would consent to listen. One of the records, entitled "Enemies," was a vigorous attack against the Roman Catholic Church. When some Catholics listened to the record, they threatened the Cantwells with violence if they did not leave. The Cantwells did leave, with no argument, but were later arrested for inciting a breach of the peace. They were also charged with not having obtained the required license.

Application to the States

The Supreme Court decided in favor of the Cantwells. In the process, it set forth some very important principles. *Cantwell* is the first case in which the Court incorporated the Free Exercise Clause into the Fourteenth Amendment. Never before had the clause been applied to state law; since then it always has been. No clearer explanation of the concept can be found than this statement from *Cantwell*, written by Justice Owen Roberts:

> We hold that the statute, as construed and applied to the appellants, deprives them of their liberty without due process of law in contravention of the Fourteenth Amendment. The fundamental concept of liberty embodied in that Amendment embraces the liberties guaranteed by the First Amendment. The First Amendment declares that Congress shall make no law respecting an establishment of religion or prohibiting the free exercise thereof. The Fourteenth Amendment has rendered the legislatures of the states as incompetent as Congress to enact such laws. The constitutional inhibition of legislation on the subject of religion has a double aspect. On the one hand, it forestalls compulsion by law of the acceptance of any creed or the practice of any form of worship. Freedom of conscience and freedom to adhere to such religious organization or form of worship as the individual may choose cannot be restricted by law. On the other hand, it safeguards the chosen form of religion. Thus the Amendment embraces two concepts,—freedom to believe and freedom to act. The first is absolute but, in the nature of things, the second cannot be. Conduct remains subject to regulation for the protection of society. . . . In every case the power to regulate must be so exercised as not, in attaining a permissible end, unduly to infringe the protected freedom.[6]

Impermissible Prior Restraint

The Court went on from this magnificent statement of what the freedom of religion is all about to say that New Haven, in attempting to attain a permissible end, had unduly infringed the Cantwells' religious freedom: the requirement to obtain a license to go into the streets to distribute literature and evangelize functioned as an impermissible prior restraint. A government official could not have the authority to decide what is a religion and what is not and accordingly issue or withhold an enabling license. Of course a city may maintain some control over what happens in its streets. "But to condition the solicitation of aid for the perpetuation of religious views or systems upon a license, the grant of which rests in the exercise of a determination by state authority as to what is a religious cause, is to lay a forbidden burden upon the exercise of liberty protected by the Constitution."[7] The effect of *Cantwell* was to broaden the liberty of all religious groups to be free from governmental prior restraint, that is, to be free from having to seek government approval to engage in religious activities, activities that may even determine its right to survive.

Clear and Present Danger

On the question of whether the Cantwells were guilty of incitement to breach of peace, the Court struck another blow for religious liberty. It ruled that before government may prohibit religious activity it must show that the activity presents a "clear and present danger" or an "immediate threat" to public safety, peace, or order. In other words, the Court considerably narrowed the latitude given the government in *Reynolds* v. *United States* to interfere with religious activity. No longer could the government inhibit religious activity on the basis that it presented *some* danger to society. Now the government had to show that the religious behavior presented a grave, significant, and current danger to society before it could be curtailed by government intervention. In short, since *Cantwell* religious freedom has been the rule, government interference the exception. It is a landmark case because it incorporated the Free Exercise Clause and applied it to the states and because it broadened the dimensions of religious liberty by both prohibiting prior restraints and articulating the clear and present danger test.

Taxing Evangelism Efforts

A variation on the effort to keep Jehovah's Witnesses, and anyone else who would attempt to evangelize in public places, from doing so was to levy a tax on the enterprise. Many cities in the late 1930s and early 1940s passed laws to require a permit and the payment of a tax for the permission to evangelize. The Court held such behavior also to be a form of prior restraint prohibited by the Free Exercise Clause (*Murdock* v. *Pennsylvania*).[8] But cities could maintain public order by placing time, place, and manner restrictions on the public evangelizing (*Cox* v. *New Hampshire*).[9] So government may not require the payment of a tax or the permission of a city official as a condition of evangelizing in public streets and parks,[10] but it may require the members of the evangelizing group to identify themselves and may have regulations on when, where, and how the evangelization is done. Thus cities are still in control of their streets and parks, in that they may insist that evangelization not be disruptive of a reasonably normal flow of traffic, not be harmful to citizens, or not overwhelm the police protection of the city.

Children as Evangelists

The Court also ruled that minor children may not be employed in preaching and literature distribution on public thoroughfares (*Prince* v. *Mas-*

sachusetts).[11] A Jehovah's Witness parent brought her minor children with her into a downtown area to preach on the streets. This preaching included the distribution, in return for a voluntary contribution, of literature, principally *The Watchtower* magazine. The child labor laws in the jurisdiction in which Sarah Prince lived prohibited the sale of literature and other goods on the public thoroughfares by boys under twelve and girls under eighteen years of age. When Prince was arrested for the violation of child labor laws, she protested that the children were ministers of the religion and their preaching was protected by the Free Exercise Clause. The Court ruled that whereas adults may practice their religion by preaching on the streets, children may not. Child labor laws, which are more restrictive of the kinds of employment children may engage in than they are with adults, show that the state has a strong interest in the health and safety of children.[12] Consequently, the Free Exercise Clause cannot protect the activity of using children to evangelize on the public streets. In this case, the Court made a rather expansive statement: "Parents are free to become martyrs themselves. But it does not follow that they are free, in identical circumstances, to make martyrs of their children before they have reached the age of full and legal discretion when they can make that choice for themselves."[13]

Blood Transfusions

Prince has a current application beyond evangelizing. Jehovah's Witnesses believe that ingesting blood into the body in any way, including transfusions, is contrary to the will of God.[14] Consequently, while they accept modern medicine, they are not willing to accept blood transfusions, even in the face of possible death absent the transfusion. But courts have ruled, based on *Prince*, that the children of Witnesses may be compelled to receive blood transfusions when adults may not.[15] Hospitals and physicians may obtain from judges legal authorization to administer blood to minors over the objection of their Jehovah's Witness parents. In short, the free-exercise rights of children are narrower than those of adults, if it can be shown that the religious behavior of any group or individual is harmful to the physical or mental welfare of the child.[16]

Saluting the Flag

The Jehovah's Witnesses also have religious objections to saluting the flag of any country. The basis of this is their belief that to salute a flag is to recognize the sovereignty of the country the flag represents. Jehovah's Witnesses believe there is only one sovereign worthy of the recognition of humans—God. Their reason for not saluting the flag is not contrariness or lack of appreciation for the country, but their adherence to the priorities they believe are taught by the Bible—loyalty to God should take precedence over loyalty to country. Furthermore, to salute a flag is to make a graven image and to engage in idolatry.[17] This practice became a legal matter when public school districts compelled Witness children to recite the pledge of allegiance and to salute the flag at the beginning of each school day.

On this issue, we see the Court's deliberative process at work. First, in 1940 the Supreme Court ruled that children could be forced to say the pledge of allegiance even though they claimed that the Free Exercise Clause protected their religious objections to the ceremony (*Minersville School District* v. *Gobitis*).[18] The Court's reasoning, as written by Justice Felix Frankfurter, was that the nation needs the loyalty and unity of the people and the flag salute is a primary way of achieving it; a national interest of the highest importance was at stake. "National unity is the basis of national security. . . . The ultimate foundation of a free society is the binding tie of cohesive sentiment. . . . 'We live by symbols.' The flag is the symbol of our national unity, transcending all internal differences, however large, within the framework of the Constitution."[19]

However, three years later the Court examined the issue again, for at least two reasons. First, three new justices had come on the Court. Second, after *Gobitis* school districts across the country had made even more stringent rules requiring the recitation of the pledge. When Witnesses continued to be faithful to their religious convictions and refused to salute the flag, shameful persecution was inflicted on them. This persecution included the burning of Witness meeting places, mob violence against Witnesses, at least one castration, and forcible removal from the communities where they lived. Sometimes they were made to drink castor oil and then paraded publicly through city streets.

In *West Virginia Board of Education* v. *Barnette*[20] the Court reversed *Gobitis*, Justice Robert Jackson writing for the majority. Arguing on both free speech and free exercise of religion grounds, the Court ruled that the state may not force one to say what one does not believe. Since the flag salute was a form of expression, Witness children could not be compelled to say the pledge of allegiance. Without denying that the flag is the symbol of national solidarity, on which national security rests, the Court held that freedom of religion and speech take precedent over even such important interests. Indeed, the very freedom that the flag symbolizes includes the freedom not to salute it. Mindful of the terror of Nazism, which was sweeping Europe at the time, the Court said:

> Those who begin coercive elimination of dissent soon find themselves exterminating dissenters. Compulsory unification of opinion achieves only the unanimity of the graveyard. It seems trite but necessary to say that the First Amendment to our Constitution was designed to avoid these ends by avoiding these beginnings.[21]

Robert Jackson, one of the best writers to serve on the Court, went on to make what has become a famous statement about the scope of liberties Americans enjoy.

> But freedom to differ is not limited to things that do not matter much. That would be a mere shadow of freedom. The test of its substance is the right to differ as to things that touch the heart of the existing order.
>
> If there is any fixed star in our constitutional constellation, it is that no official, high or petty, can prescribe what shall be orthodox in politics, nationalism, religion, or other matters of opinion or force citizens to confess by word or act their faith therein.[22]

This is *dictum* at its finest, by which all Americans should be instructed!

THEOLOGY: A FORBIDDEN AREA

A final free-exercise case prior to 1963 did not involve the Jehovah's Witnesses, but raised a very important issue of religious freedom. Guy Ballard was the leader of the "I Am Movement." He claimed to have had extraordinary spiritual experiences, including personal encounters with Saint-Germain and Jesus. As a result, he believed he knew the spiritual secret of good health and could heal people of even those diseases which doctors said were incurable. He and his family sent out mailings making these claims and encouraging people to send in money and partake of the healing the Ballards had available for them. The government claimed that the Ballards knew the representations they made were not true, and thus they were guilty of defrauding the public through the mail.

The question before the Court was whether the truth or falsity of the Ballards' theology could be presented to a jury. Stated differently, does a civil court or the government have the right to evaluate the religious beliefs of a person or a group? The Court answered that question with a resounding "No" in *United States* v. *Ballard.*[23] The fact that individuals or groups may believe what they want about religion means that the government is not permitted even to make a judgment about the validity of the beliefs. As Prof. Harry W. Jones put it, "Could we tolerate for a moment a principle that the free exercise of religion means only the free exercise of 'true' religion, and that judges and juries are empowered to decide whose religious faiths are true and whose are untrue?"[24] Both the Establishment Clause and the Free Exercise Clause point in that direction. To make that point, Justice William O. Douglas, writing for the Court, again clearly expressed the freedom that Americans enjoy.

> Freedom of thought, which includes freedom of religious belief, is basic to the society of free men. It embraces the right to maintain theories of life

and of death and of the hereafter which are rank heresy to followers of the
orthodox faiths. Heresy trials are foreign to our Constitution. Men may
believe what they cannot prove. They may not be put to the proof of their
religious doctrines or beliefs. Religious experiences which are as real as life
to some may be incomprehensible to others. Yet the fact that they may be
beyond the ken of mortals does not mean that they can be made suspect
before the law. . . . Man's relationship to his God was made no concern of
the state. He was granted the right to worship as he pleased and to answer
to no man for the verity of his religious views. The religious views es-
poused by [the Ballards] might seem incredible, if not preposterous, to
most people. But if those doctrines are subject to trial before a jury
charged with finding their truth or falsity, then the same can be done with
the religious beliefs of any sect. . . . The First Amendment does not select
any one group or any one type of religion for preferred treatment. It puts
them all in that position.[25]

Today when people seem to be so concerned about "cults" and even want
the government to take some action against them, these words are important
for us to remember. A similar idea was expressed in a dissenting opinion by
Justice Robert Jackson.

The chief wrong which false prophets do to their following is not financial.
The collections aggregate to a tempting total, but individual payments are
not ruinous. . . . But the real harm is on the mental and spiritual plane.
There are people who hunger and thirst after higher values which they feel
wanting in their humdrum lives. They live in mental confusion or moral
anarchy and seek vaguely for truth and beauty and moral support. When
they are deluded and then disillusioned, cynicism and confusion follow.
The wrong of these things, as I see it, is not in the money the victims part
with half so much as in the mental and spiritual poison they get. But that is
precisely the thing the Constitution put beyond the reach of the prosecu-
tor, for the price of freedom of religion or of speech or of the press is that
we must put up with, and even pay for, a good deal of rubbish.[26]

This concept, which prevents judicial or governmental evaluation of the
merits of theology, is to the benefit of all those who are religious, not just to
the "fringe" groups. *Ballard* does not mean that religions are immune from
prosecution for fraud. For example, they may not promise to do one thing
with money and then do another. Local churches or television evangelists
may not solicit money, promising to send it to foreign missions, and then use
it for local expenses without running afoul of law against fraud. But, in every
case, the government must proceed without making judgments about the
veracity of the theology of the group.

By 1963 the free exercise of religion had been defined by the Court very
broadly. Religious freedom was the rule, governmental interference in reli-

gious behavior was the exception. And in the area of religious belief, government intrusion was prohibited altogether. For the most part, these principles have remained unmodified. We Americans are the beneficiaries of a wonderful system of government in matters of religion.

4

The Uncertain Status of
Religious Freedom: 1963–1990

The year 1963 as the break between the chapters on free-exercise cases was not chosen arbitrarily. In that year the Court handed down a decision which "regularized" Free Exercise Clause jurisprudence for over a quarter of a century. Just as the "clear and present danger" test of *Cantwell* v. *Connecticut* prevailed from 1940 until 1963, the "*Sherbert* test" controlled free-exercise cases until 1990. This balancing test preserved the broad scope of religious freedom for Americans while continuing to hold that government may interfere in religious behavior if conditions merit it.

THE "*SHERBERT* TEST"

Unemployment Compensation

The key case in this development is *Sherbert* v. *Verner*.[1] Adell Sherbert, an employee in the textile mills of South Carolina, was a Seventh-day Adventist. Adventists believe that the seventh day of the week, Saturday, is the proper day of worship. Their belief is based on two biblical ideas. First is the concept that God rested on the seventh day from the labors of creating the earth. That God rested at the end of the creative process means that this pattern of work and rest is built into the nature of reality and thus should be observed by humans. Second, the Fourth Commandment teaches that humans are to "remember the sabbath day, to keep it holy," thus adding the dimension of worship to the seventh day.[2] This observance of Saturday as a day of worship and rest is considered to be a religious obligation by Seventh-day Adventists.

Ms. Sherbert's troubles began when her employer changed her work week to include Saturday. She refused Saturday work because of her sincerely held religious beliefs, and was fired. When it became clear that it was not possible to find employment that did not involve Saturday work, she applied to state authorities for unemployment compensation. She was denied compensation on the ground that the state supplied unemployment benefits for people for whom work was unavailable, not for people who were unavailable for work. Because Sherbert had essentially quit her job, albeit for religious reasons, she was not available for work and thus not entitled to compensation. At that point Sherbert sued, claiming that this situation was an imposition on her free exercise of religion. She argued that she had been forced to choose between employment and her religious practice. But when she had chosen the latter, she was denied state benefits and thus penalized for being faithful to her religion. The state supreme court ruled that her free exercise was not burdened. She could practice her religion as she chose, she just could not do that *and* receive unemployment payments. In an opinion by Justice William Brennan, the United States Supreme Court reversed that decision.

In the process of ruling on this case, the Court set forth a procedure for deciding free-exercise cases. The procedure has become known as the "*Sherbert* test." This test balances government interests against the religious behavior at issue. The best way to understand this procedure is to think of it as a series of questions to be asked about the parties involved in the controversy.

1. Has the government placed a burden on the religious actions of the plaintiff (the one bringing the suit alleging government infringement on religion)? That is, has the government somehow impaired, interfered with, or prevented the person's or group's exercise of religion? If the answer is no, the case is over—the government has won and the plaintiff lost. But if the answer is yes, then the inquiry must go to a second question.

2. Does the government have a compelling interest which justifies burdening the religious activity in question? It is assumed that the government has some legitimate end or goal for the public good that it is trying to accomplish. The question is whether the government has a compelling interest in reaching that goal? "Compelling" means here "very important," "of the highest magnitude." The Court expressed it this way: "It is basic that no showing merely of a rational relationship to some colorable state interest would suffice; in this highly sensitive constitutional area, '[o]nly the gravest abuses, endangering paramount interests, give occasion for permissible limitation.' "[3] If the answer to the question is negative, the government loses the case and the plaintiff wins. But if the answer is affirmative, the inquiry goes to a third question.

3. Even if the compelling interest exists, does the government have an alternative means to reach its legitimate goal without burdening religious action? Can the government do an "end run" around religious action and still accomplish its objective? If the answer is affirmative, the government is obligated to employ the alternative procedure to reach its goal and cease its oppression of religious action. If the answer is negative, the government has won the case and the plaintiff has lost.

In *Sherbert*, the inquiry stopped with the second question. The Court ruled that the state had burdened Sherbert's exercise of religion. "To condition the availability of benefits upon this appellant's unwillingness to violate a cardinal principle of her religious faith effectively penalizes the free exercise of her constitutional liberties."[4] To be sure, the state had an interest in preserving unemployment compensation funds and thwarting fraudulent claims. But these interests were not compelling enough to override the constitutionally guaranteed right of free exercise of religion. Sherbert won, South Carolina lost.

This case replaced the "clear and present danger" test (*Cantwell* v. *Connecticut*; see chapter 3) without nullifying its benefits for religious liberty. The importance of *Sherbert* is that it set forth a more sophisticated procedure to decide free-exercise controversies, which was designed to preserve the concept that freedom of religion is broad, the possibility of government interference is narrow. This is not to say that "anything goes" in the name of religion; the government still has the authority to prevent harmful religious behavior. But in balancing religious freedom and government intervention, religious freedom is clearly the weightier. The existence of the Free Exercise Clause in the Constitution demands that it be so!

Compulsory Education Laws

A frequently cited example of the effect of the "*Sherbert* test" is not an unemployment compensation case, but rather *Wisconsin* v. *Yoder*, which in 1972 decided the question of whether government is obligated to accommodate the religious belief of the Amish about the education of their children.[5] The Amish, descendants of the sixteenth-century Anabaptists, believe that the world is evil and that it is imperative that the follower of Christ maintain distance from the world, in order to prevent being corrupted by the contact. Consequently, the Amish maintain a lifestyle specifically designed to emphasize their difference from the world. One of the features of their lifestyle is to prevent their children from receiving any kind of formal education beyond the eighth grade. Any "book learning" beyond that time would present their children with too much of the evil world. So the Amish withdraw their children after the completion of the eighth grade and continue their education at home, emphasizing domestic and farming skills, those things which are most needed for living in the Amish community.

Wisconsin, like most states, has a compulsory education law that demands that children continue in formal education beyond the eighth grade. The state demanded that Amish parents obey the law. The Amish refused, in spite of fines and short jail sentences, stating that their views on education are firmly based in their religious belief and claiming Free Exercise Clause protection.

The issue reached the Supreme Court in *Wisconsin* v. *Yoder*. The Court weighed the state's interest in public education against the Amish religious beliefs. It was clear that the state's interest in an educated citizenry was very weighty, but the constitutionally protected religious practices of the Amish were weightier still. In making this determination, but writing about the importance of the free exercise of religion in general, Chief Justice Warren Burger said for the Court: "The essence of all that has been said and written on the subject is that only those interests of the highest order and those not otherwise served can overbalance legitimate claims to the free exercise of religion."[6] Government may intervene in religious practice, but the burden of proof is on the government that it has an overwhelmingly important reason to do so. Religious freedom is the rule, government interference is the exception.

Additional Unemployment Issues

The Court rendered decisions on several other unemployment compensation cases after *Sherbert*. Although the facts were somewhat different, the issues were essentially the same.

Issues of Theology

A Jehovah's Witness who was employed in a steel mill was transferred to a department manufacturing turrets for military tanks. This activity was contrary to his religious belief[7] and, because his employer had moved to all military-related work, he quit his job. He was denied unemployment compensation and went to court, claiming Free Exercise Clause protection. The Supreme Court found in his favor in *Thomas* v. *Review Board of Indiana*.[8]

Two issues are worthy of note in this case. First, the state argued that Thomas should not be awarded unemployment compensation because other Jehovah's Witnesses working in the factory had no objection to making armaments. The Court held that a civil court could not determine who, within a group of believers, is more accurately holding the beliefs of the group. Furthermore, one should not be penalized because one does not express one's faith well. Chief Justice Burger wrote:

> Courts should not undertake to dissect religious beliefs because the believer admits that he is "struggling" with his position or because his beliefs are not articulated with the clarity and precision that a more sophisticated person might employ. . . . Particularly in this sensitive area, it is not within the judicial function and judicial competence to inquire whether the petitioner or his fellow worker more correctly perceived the commands of their common faith. Courts are not arbiters of scriptural interpretation.[9]

This is a variation on and reaffirmation of the theme, articulated in *Ballard* (pp. 27–29, above), that the state, including its courts, may not get involved in theological/doctrinal issues. Freedom of religion demands the limitation of the state in this area.

Second, the *Thomas* case is important because the Court used it to reassert principles for interpreting the Free Exercise Clause, again taking the position that the state may not unduly burden the free exercise of religion, even indirectly.

> Where the state conditions receipt of an important benefit upon conduct proscribed by a religious faith, or where it denies such a benefit because of conduct mandated by a religious belief, thereby putting substantial pressure on an adherent to modify his behavior and to violate his beliefs, a burden upon religion exists. While the compulsion may be indirect, the infringement upon free exercise is nonetheless substantial.[10]

This is an elaboration of the "*Sherbert* test," giving it more specificity, and reasserting the broad scope of religious liberty.

Religious Converts

In *Hobbie* v. *Unemployment Appeals Commission of Florida*,[11] involving a Seventh-day Adventist who was denied unemployment compensation when she refused to work on Saturday, the Court again decided in favor of the worker. What makes this case unique is that the worker converted to the Adventist faith after she was employed, in contrast to both *Sherbert* and *Thomas*, in which a previously acceptable job became religiously unacceptable because of changes brought about by the employer. Florida claimed that the worker rather than the employer was the "agent of change" and consequently the state should not have to pay the unemployment compensation. It was the decision of the worker, by converting to a religion that had stipulations about when a believer should work, that created the condition in the workplace that made continued employment impossible. Of course, if this contention became law it would have a "chilling effect" on evangelism by churches. If employees thought they potentially were putting their jobs in jeopardy by converting to a religious belief, they would likely be much less receptive to evangelization. This would impose a subtle but real limitation on the religious freedom of individuals. The Court did not accept the "agent of change" argument; it would not give less favorable treatment to a convert. In another expression of the preeminence of religious freedom, Justice Brennan wrote: "The First Amendment protects the free exercise rights of employees who adopt religious beliefs or convert from one faith to another after they are hired."[12]

Personal Religious Belief

In *Frazee* v. *Illinois Department of Employment Security*,[13] a case in which a person refused to work on Sunday because of religious convictions, the state claimed that he was not entitled to unemployment compensation because he was not a member of a group that taught abstention from work on Sunday. In cases involving Seventh-day Adventists, for example, people who refused Saturday work did so because of the clear teaching of their church. But Frazee's refusal to work on Sunday was based only on his own personal theological convictions, not the doctrine of any organized group. The Supreme Court found in his favor anyway. Purely personal religious belief receives as much protection from the Free Exercise Clause as that tied to the theological propositions of an organized religious group.

Laws of General Applicability: Drug Use

In 1990, an Oregon unemployment compensation case came to the Court, this time involving not conscientious objection to workdays, but the use of drugs. Two counselors in a program for chemically dependent persons had agreed, as a condition of employment, not to use any addictive substances. But they were members of the Native American Church, an organization that has traditionally used peyote as part of its worship service.[14] Peyote is a mild hallucinogenic drug derived from the mescaline cactus. It was on Oregon's list of illegal drugs. When their employer found out that they used peyote they were dismissed from their jobs. When they applied for unemployment compensation it was denied because their firing was based on misconduct.

The issue came to the Supreme Court in *Employment Division of Oregon* v. *Smith*.[15] Justice Antonin Scalia was the author of the opinion. For the first time in an unemployment compensation case, the Court found against the believer and for the State. The reason is that Oregon's law proscribing certain drugs, peyote among them, was a "law of general applicability"; it applied to everybody, not just religious groups. The Court ruled that the Free Exercise Clause cannot be used as a defense against laws of general applicability. That is, one cannot claim that one's free exercise of religion should take precedence over a law that was not designed to burden religious behavior. A law specifically designed to inhibit religious activity would be unconstitutional, but a law of general applicability that has that effect is not.

This decision also specifically discontinued the use of the "*Sherbert* test" except in a very narrow set of circumstances. No longer is the burden of proof on the government to show that it has a very important reason, a "compelling interest," to interfere with religious freedom. All it has to show is that it has a need to regulate citizen behavior by means of a law of general applicability. If that law has the effect of inhibiting or prohibiting religious activity, so be it.

The effect of *Smith* was essentially to declare the Free Exercise Clause null and void and to restrict religious liberty in the United States, except in a very narrow set of circumstances. The decision eliminates the advances in interpreting the Free Exercise Clause described in this chapter and takes the status of the law back to 1879 and *Reynolds* v. *United States*, which had given civil authorities virtually unlimited right to interfere with religious freedom. Justice Sandra Day O'Connor wrote an opinion concurring in the result of this case but dissenting from the methodology of the Court. She declared that the Court had done violence to its long-standing policy in support of religious freedom and deplored the abandoning of the compelling state interest test. We shall have occasion to look at this disastrous decision again in chapter 9.

ANIMAL SACRIFICE

A case was decided in 1993 that many thought and hoped the Court would use as an opportunity to reverse the *Smith* decision, that is, to return to the use of the compelling state interest test and restore the Free Exercise Clause to its rightful place as a freestanding constitutional principle with some authority. The case was *Church of the Lukumi Babalu Aye* v. *City of Hialeah*.[16] The religion involved was Santeria and the issue was its practice of animal sacrifice.

Santeria had its origin in Cuba in the nineteenth century. Many of the Yoruba tribe of eastern Africa were captured and brought to Cuba as slaves. The principal cultural task that faced these newly enslaved people was how to preserve their traditional African religion in Roman Catholic Cuba. The Yoruba accomplished this by adopting Catholic saints' names and some of the practices associated with them and applying them to the deities and spirits of their traditional religion. It is likely that their captors thought that the Yoruba had converted to Catholicism, but the Yoruba knew that they were actually following their ancestral religion, only now under the guise of Catholicism. It was a defense mechanism by the Yoruba to prevent their traditional culture from being obliterated. Thus was born Santeria, "the way of the saints." It is a syncretism, a combining of two traditions into what is essentially a new religion. A central belief of Santeria is the existence of *orishas*, or spirits. These spiritual beings influence the lives of human beings. It is necessary for one to maintain a personal relationship with the *orishas*, and one of the principal forms of devotion is animal sacrifice. Furthermore, although the *orishas* are powerful, they are not immortal. They derive vitality from the devotion of their worshipers. Consequently, it is a cardinal belief of the Santeria that animal sacrifice is necessary for the survival of the *orishas*. For that reason, among the Santeria, sacrifices are performed at the birth of a child, at marriage ceremonies and funerals, for the cure of the sick, and for the initiation of new members and consecrating of priests, among other reasons. Santeria devotees sacrifice chickens, pigeons, doves, ducks, guinea pigs, goats, sheep, and turtles. In every case, the animals are killed by cutting the carotid arteries in the neck.

The Santeria religion was brought to the United States principally by exiles from the Cuban revolution. In Hialeah, Florida, it had usually been practiced in secret, in people's homes. But in the late 1980s the Church of the Lukumi Babalu Aye declared its intention to build a building for worship and to establish a cultural center and museum. In response to that announced intention, the city council of Hialeah, in 1987, passed a series of ordinances that prohibited the killing of animals in religious rituals. There were several laws that came at the issue from a variety of directions, but the prohibition of sacrifice was the intent of them all. The church responded by filing suit, claiming that its free exercise of religion was violated by the city council's actions.

As noted above, many church–state watchers hoped that the Court would use this case to revisit its recent gutting of the Free Exercise Clause by renouncing its *Smith* decision along the lines that Justice Sandra Day O'Connor had suggested in her opinion in that case. Their hopes were disappointed. The Court arrived at its decision by applying the *Smith* concept, that a neutral law of general applicability is not unconstitutional even though it has the effect of hindering or even prohibiting religious activity. But *Smith* had also said that if a law targeted religion specifically and hindered or prohibited that activity, then that law would be subjected to "strict scrutiny" (the compelling state interest test) by the Court. That was the case with Hialeah's laws. Justice Anthony Kennedy wrote the Court's opinion. He began with an admonition that applies not only to this case, but to religious freedom in general: "Although the practice of animal sacrifice may seem abhorrent to some, 'religious beliefs need not be acceptable, logical, consistent, or comprehensible to others in order to merit First Amendment protection.' "[17] When he turned to the issue at hand, it boiled down to this: Hialeah had passed laws that were aimed only at Santeria practice. This was clear because they prohibited practices involved in animal sacrifice that were allowed if they were done for secular purposes. Two of many examples will illustrate the point.

A principal justification Hialeah put forth for its laws was the prevention of cruelty to animals. Thus, it prohibited the killing of animals in religious ritual. But it did not prohibit the killing of animals by slaughterhouses, in Jewish kosher slaughter, or even by individual hunters and people who fish, who may bring their prey home to kill it in their own homes. The city had also expressed concern about the disposal of the sacrificed animals, and so passed laws prohibiting the disposal of the carcasses of sacrificed animals in open public places. But the laws did not prohibit hunters, fishers, or even the owners of small farms within the city limits from disposing of animals in public places. In short, the laws were discriminatory as opposed to being of general applicability. That is unconstitutional even under the *Smith* interpretation of the Free Exercise Clause.

> In sum, the neutrality inquiry leads to one conclusion: The ordinances had as their object the suppression of religion. The pattern we have recited discloses animosity to Santeria adherents and their religious practices; the ordinances by their own terms target this religious exercise; the texts of the ordinances were gerrymandered with care to proscribe religious killings of animals but to exclude almost all secular killings; and the ordinances suppress much more religious conduct than is necessary in order to achieve the legitimate ends asserted in their defense. These ordinances are not neutral, and the court below committed clear error in failing to reach this conclusion.[18]

As a result of this analysis, Justice Kennedy concluded his opinion with an admonition to government officials (and to all Americans) to be sensitive to that most precious of our liberties, freedom of religion. It is one of those "quotable" passages because it expresses so well an important and durable truth about the American system:

> The Free Exercise Clause commits government itself to religious tolerance, and upon even slight suspicion that proposals for state intervention stem from animosity to religion or distrust of its practices, all officials must pause to remember their own high duty to the Constitution and to the rights it secures. Those in office must be resolute in resisting importunate demands and must ensure that the sole reasons for imposing the burdens of law and regulation are secular. Legislators may not devise mechanisms, overt or disguised, designed to persecute or oppress a religion or its practices. The laws here in question were enacted contrary to these constitutional principles, and they are void.[19]

CLERGY AND PUBLIC OFFICE

Early in the history of this nation, it was widely held that clergy should not hold public office. There were laws to that effect in most of the states of the time. Seven of the original states and six more of the early additions to the Union had laws excluding clergy from holding public office. There were two primary reasons usually given for this. One was that the clergy had such a high calling and were engaged in such exalted activity, the proclamation of the Word of God and the care of souls, that they should not be involved in the mundane and often messy activity of politics and governing. The other was that the nation had just begun the experiment of separation of church and state. One way to guarantee the success of this disestablishment was to prevent clergy from holding office. The fear was that if they were in office, they might attempt to impose their religious views on the body politic.

However, even in these early days, there were also arguments against the exclusion of clergy. James Madison argued that such a law punished a religious profession with the denial of a civil right, which struck right at the heart of the concept of religious freedom. As time progressed, many were persuaded by that argument. Furthermore, many people believed that there were sufficient safeguards against establishment that the exclusion of clergy from public office was unnecessary. Consequently, clergy exclusion laws were gradually rescinded until, by 1977, Tennessee was the only state with such a law. The constitutionality of that was tested before the Supreme Court in *McDaniel v. Paty*.[20]

Tennessee had a law that said that nobody who was ineligible for service in the state legislature could be a delegate to a state constitutional convention. A Baptist minister named McDaniel ran to be a delegate and was elected. But in response to a suit by an opponent who claimed that his election was illegal, he was denied his place in the convention by the state supreme court. The U.S. Supreme Court reversed that decision. Although there was some disagreement among the justices about the rationale for the decision, the Court held that Tennessee's law denied McDaniel the free exercise of his religion. It had forced him to choose between his religious activity, which was also his profession, and a civil right. The Free Exercise Clause will not permit that. In Chief Justice Warren Burger's words:

> [T]he right to the free exercise of religion unquestionably encompasses the right to preach, proselyte, and perform other similar religious functions, or, in other words, to be a minister of the type McDaniel was found to be. . . . Tennessee has encroached on McDaniel's right to the free exercise of religion. "[T]o condition the availability of benefits [including access to the ballot] upon this appellant's willingness to violate a cardinal principle of [his] religious faith [by surrendering his religiously impelled ministry] effectively penalizes the free exercise of [his] constitutional liberties."[21]

The Court also observed that there was no record in American history in which a clergyperson had been less observant of the separation of church and state while holding public office than his or her unordained counterparts. Consequently, no unit of government may forbid a minister or other religious leader to hold public office. This case is very similar to *Torcaso v. Watkins*, an Establishment Clause case described in chapter 7.

THE MILITARY AND PRISONS

The following cases related to the military and prisons were heard before *Smith*, and mark the beginning of the constriction of religious liberty by the Reagan Court, the Court made up mostly of justices appointed by Ronald Reagan or sympathetic to his conservative judicial philosophy. Given that the Court, in these cases, refused to explicitly apply the compelling state interest test and consistently decided in favor of the government, *Smith* is not so surprising, though no less shocking. The first of these cases was *Goldman* v. *Weinberger*,[22] which involved an Orthodox Jewish psychiatrist serving in the Air Force. Orthodox Jewish practice mandates that males cover their heads in the presence of God as a sign of respect to God. Many Jews, reasoning that one is always in God's presence, choose to wear a skull-cap, or yarmulke, not only at worship, but at all times. The problem for Dr. Goldman was an Air Force regulation that prohibited one in uniform from wearing a head covering indoors. When he persisted in wearing his yarmulke while in uniform and on duty in the base hospital, he was disciplined and threatened with a court-marshal.[23] Goldman sued, claiming that his Free Exercise Clause right should supersede Air Force regulations.

The Supreme Court decided in favor of the Air Force. Justice William Rehnquist's opinion noted that the military wants to promote both *esprit de corps* and a discipline that leads to instinctive obedience to orders. The regulations about dress are part of those efforts. The Air Force argued that the uniform subordinates personal preferences and identities (except rank) in people, and this supports the group mission of the unit and the military as a whole. This sense of group identity and subordination to authority is just as necessary in peacetime as in time of war because the military must be always at the ready, in case of national emergency. The military can allow no exceptions and still maintain the desired discipline. The Court ruled that in this special circumstance it must defer to the expertise of military authority. Freedoms that are available to the general citizen simply are not as available in the specialized environment of the military. In this context, the free exercise of religion could not prevail.

> Our review of military regulations challenged on First Amendment grounds is far more deferential than constitutional review of similar laws or regulations designed for civilian society. . . . [W]hen evaluating whether military needs justify a particular restriction on religiously-motivated conduct, courts must give great deference to the professional judgment of military authorities concerning the relative importance of a particular military interest.[24]

A virtually identical decision was reached in *O'Lone* v. *Estate of Shabazz*.[25] The issue in this case was whether minimum-security Muslim prisoners who worked on a gang outside the prison walls during the day should be brought back for Friday noon prayers, a religious obligation for Muslims. Prison authorities argued that to do so would cause too many logistical and security problems. Not all members of the work gang were Muslims. Non-Muslims would have to be left behind while the Muslims were brought back to the prison for prayers. That would result in different amounts of work being done by different members of the gang, which would create morale problems. More important for prison authorities, the procedure would require the assignment of extra guards, guards for the Muslim prisoners *and* for those who stayed behind. Bringing prisoners in and out the main gate at noon would require an extra security check. The Court decided against the prisoners, again arguing that in the special environment of a prison constitutional rights were not as broad as for regular citizens and that the Court needed to defer to the expert opinion of prison authorities.

In both these cases the Court weighed the interest of state institutions, which had specialized, out-of-the-ordinary populations, against the religious freedom of members of those populations. It determined that the state institutions had unique needs and religious freedom was the loser.

NATIVE AMERICAN CASES

The Court continued its constriction of religious freedom, a process that would culminate in *Smith*, in some cases involving Native Americans.[26] In *Bowen* v. *Roy*,[27] the Court was confronted with a member of the Abenaki tribe who objected to the Commonwealth of Pennsylvania's demand that his daughter be provided with a Social Security number to be eligible for aid under the Aid to Families with Dependent Children and food stamp programs. Roy's belief, based on his Native American religion, was that control over one's life was essential to spiritual purity and "becoming a holy person." Consequently, a number assigned specifically and uniquely to his daughter, whose name was Little Bird of the Snow, would "rob her of her spirit" and prevent her from gaining spiritual power as she grew older. That is, for Little Bird of the Snow to have a Social Security number would put her under the power and, to some degree, the control of the government. That would prevent her from growing into a unique spiritual being. Therefore Roy requested Pennsylvania to provide benefits to Little Bird of the Snow without requiring her to have a Social Security number. The state naturally declined and Roy brought suit, claiming a violation of his free-exercise rights.

The Court decided against the Native American. Although it weighed government versus individual interests and found the government's heavier in the balance, Chief Justice Warren Burger articulated another rationale for the Court's decision. He argued that Roy was asking the government to alter its procedures in order to accommodate his religious practice. But the Free Exercise Clause did not demand that the government do that.

> Never to our knowledge has the Court interpreted the First Amendment to require the Government *itself* to behave in ways that the individual believes will further his or her spiritual development or that of his or her family. The Free Exercise Clause simply cannot be understood to require the Government to conduct its own internal affairs in ways that comport with the religious beliefs of particular citizens.[28]

The Court illustrated this concept with the statement that Roy had no more
right to determine the government's use of Social Security numbers because
of his religious beliefs than he did to dictate the color of the filing cabinets
the government used.

A similar decision, based on the same rationale but this time written by
Justice Sandra Day O'Connor, was handed down two years later in *Lyng* v.
Northwest Indian Cemetery Protective Association.[29] A primary characteristic of
Native American religion is the belief in sacred lands. Land itself is regarded
as sacred, living, and having spiritual qualities. Native Americans thus perform rituals on sites that are regarded as particularly holy for the purpose of
honoring the land itself, for gaining "medicine" or spiritual power, for seeking curative powers for healing the sick, or for good luck in hunting or love.
The ceremonies that are conducive of such things require silence and an
aesthetic environment.

The issue in this case was that the Indians' sacred lands lay within a
national forest, and the United States government was building a road
through those lands. The road was primarily to facilitate logging in the
forest. In an attempt to prevent the defilement of their sacred lands, the
Indians first had obtained a court injunction that halted construction before
the road was finished. With this suit they were now trying to get the government to abandon the project, claiming that their religious practices would be
destroyed if the road were completed.

The Supreme Court decided against the Indians. The Court acknowledged that the completion of the road would be devastating to their religious
practice, and said that was regrettable. However, the Court argued that, as
with the situation of Little Bird of the Snow in *Bowen* , the Native Americans
were trying to get the government to alter its procedures to fit their religious
needs. The land, because it lay within a national forest, belonged to the
government. Consequently, for the Indians to try to prevent the completion
of the road was clearly an attempt to impose their religious needs on government procedures. The Free Exercise Clause does not allow that.

> However much we might wish that it were otherwise, government simply
> could not operate if it were required to satisfy every citizen's religious
> needs and desires. . . . Whatever rights the Indians may have to the use of
> the area, however, those rights do not divest the Government of its right to
> use what is, after all, *its* land.[30]

SOLICITATION IN PUBLIC PLACES

Another free exercise issue was solicitation for donations in public places
by religious groups. Bearing some resemblance to some of the Jehovah's
Witnesses cases of an earlier generation, these cases had to do with the
question of how religious groups can solicit funds in public places. *Heffron* v.

International Society for Krishna Consciousness (ISKCON)[31] involved the attempts of the Hare Krishnas, as they are more commonly called, to solicit funds at the Minnesota State Fair. Hare Krishna has a doctrine, *sankirtan*, which expects its members to evangelize the population by distributing or selling literature and soliciting donations for the support of the group. For them, *sankirtan* is a religious obligation and thus protected under the Free Exercise Clause. The Minnesota State Fair had a rule that all groups that wanted to exhibit, distribute, or sell materials had to do so from a booth on the fairgrounds. The rationale for the rule was that it would be disruptive to crowd movement and crowd control for representatives of groups to be able to wander through the crowds distributing their literature and soliciting funds. So groups were confined to booths on the fairgrounds, although they could wander freely in areas adjoining the fairgrounds and solicit as they pleased. The Krishnas argued that the rule was unnecessary and restrictive of their free-exercise and free-speech rights.

Justice Byron White, in his opinion for the majority of the Court, did not reach the constitutional issues of whether ISKCON's religious and speech freedoms were violated. The Court conceded, as did the Minnesota State Fair, that the group was entitled to exercise those freedoms. The real issue was whether or not the State Fair could impose reasonable time, place, and manner restrictions on the First Amendment activity. The Court found that such restrictions were appropriate. The fairgrounds were a special environment. Unlike movement on a public thoroughfare, at the fair all the people had to go through gates and were concentrated within the grounds. The Court ruled that the fair officials had a reasonable basis for requiring that solicitation take place from booths—crowd safety and traffic control made it necessary. The fair had not prevented distribution of literature or solicitation, nor had it placed different restrictions on ISKCON than on others. Consequently, the State Fair's time, place, and manner rules did not violate the free-exercise or free-speech rights of anyone.

Some religious groups have seen airports as a potentially lucrative location to do solicitation. Airports have tried to inhibit such activity, on the basis that the solicitors were a nuisance to travelers. An important case in 1987 was *Airport Commissioners of Los Angeles* v. *Jews for Jesus*.[32] Airport officials had passed a resolution prohibiting *all* "First Amendment activities." On challenge from an evangelical Christian group, Jews for Jesus, the Supreme Court struck down the airport's prohibition as being entirely too broad. Noting that the rule had the potential effect of banning talking, reading, and wearing symbolic clothing or campaign buttons, the Court said that it violated the free-speech provision of the First Amendment.

In 1992 the Court considered a more sophisticated nonsolicitation rule than the one from Los Angeles Airport. In *International Society for Krishna Consciousness* v. *Lee*,[33] the Court ruled that religious groups may distribute literature in the concourses of airports but may not solicit funds. Again, as in *Heffron*, constitutional rights were not addressed, but rather the time, place, and manner in which those rights could be exercised. The Court reasoned that the traffic of an airport concourse was such that the distribution of literature was not disruptive. Even people hurrying to their planes could take the literature on the fly and read it later. But if someone stopped them to solicit money, it would disrupt the traffic of the concourse. Solicitees might stand for some time listening to the "pitch" of the solicitor, they might want to explain why they did not want to contribute, or, conversely, they might set down luggage to get money out of their wallets or purses. In any case, solicitation would be more intrusive into the normal flow of airport terminal activity than the mere distribution of literature, so much so that airports could reasonably ban it.

Since 1963 the Court's view of the scope of the Free Exercise Clause, and consequently the amount of religious freedom available to the American people, has varied. For most of the period, when the "*Sherbert* test" was the principle for interpreting the clause, Americans enjoyed a large amount of freedom for religious practice. Those in specialized environments like the military did not enjoy the full range of this freedom, but decisions in these areas had little implication for the general population. Religious groups that tried to solicit in public places with large concentrations of people were restricted by considerations of how the solicitation would impact the movement of people. But with the decisions that government procedures were not required to be sensitive to religious practices, in spite of the fact that those procedures might even virtually destroy a religion, as in *Lyng*, the Court began to narrow religious freedom in ways that should raise serious concerns. With the *Smith* decision, which abandoned the "*Sherbert* test" and declared the Free Exercise Clause useless except in case of laws that specifically targeted religion, religious freedom received a virtually devastating blow. The implications of that will be explored in chapter 9.[34]

5

From Congregational Fights
to Pacifism

The Court has had to decide some cases over the years that were not specifi-cally either Establishment Clause or Free Exercise Clause cases. If it can, the Supreme Court will normally decide a case on the basis of the language of a statute rather than the Constitution, simply because a constitutional inter-pretation has broader scope and greater weight. Some of the cases described in this chapter were decided on the basis of the interpretation of statutes, although some are simply the statement of principles for adjudication. This does not mean, however, that they are any less important in setting some of the boundaries of what is permitted in church–state relations.

CHURCH PROPERTY

Unfortunately, sometimes members of church congregations quarrel among themselves and congregations fight against their denomination. Fre-quently those disagreements involve the question of who owns the property of the church, and at times they become so vituperative that the parties go to court over the ownership of the property. The Supreme Court has set some guidelines on how those issues are to be settled.

Property, Not Theology

This issue first came to the Court in the nineteenth century, as an after-math of the Civil War. A Presbyterian church in Louisville, Kentucky, had divided over the issue of slavery. The General Assembly of the Presbyterian Church in the U.S.A. had ruled that those members of the church who had supported slavery or aided in the rebellion against the Union could not be thought of as legitimate church members until they repented of their pro-slavery beliefs and/or actions. But in the congregation in Louisville, both the pro-Union and pro-Confederacy members claimed to be true Presbyterians and the rightful owners of the church property. The pro-Confederacy party, those at odds with the General Assembly, brought suit in civil court to gain control of the property. Their controversy finally made it to the Supreme Court in 1872 in *Watson* v. *Jones*.[1]

45

The Court decided not to decide on the controversy itself. This was not because of faintheartedness, but because the justices understood that the concept of separation of church and state meant that civil courts are not permitted to decide controversies when it would be necessary to make a decision based on doctrine. The litigants here were asking the Court to decide who were the true Presbyterians, in order to determine who should own the church property. That would require an investigation into theology and a judgment as to which party's theological beliefs were more correct. In our system of government, civil courts may not do that. (This is the concept we have already seen in *United States* v. *Ballard*, although *Watson* arrived at it much earlier from a different set of facts.) Justice Samuel Miller stated this for the Court in ringing language:

> In this country the full and free right to entertain any religious belief, to practice any religious principle, and to teach any religious doctrine which does not violate the laws of morality and property, and which does not infringe personal rights, is conceded to all. The law knows no heresy, and is committed to the support of no dogma, the establishment of no sect.[2]

But if civil courts may not solve church property disputes based on theological differences, how are the controversies to be decided? The Court gave some guidelines that depend on the way in which the church obtained the property, and on church governance.

1. In those circumstances where property has been given to the church through a bequest or some other instrument of donation, the civil court may make sure that the will of the donor is carried out. If there are theological stipulations to the donation, the civil court must enforce them in accord with the desires of the donor, even if the majority of the congregation now holds different theology. But in this situation, the civil court does not have to evaluate theology, only guarantee that the provisions of the donation instrument are implemented.
2. In those churches which are congregationally governed (in which there is no authority above the local congregation) the majority rules. The civil court may do no more than determine who the majority is and award the property to them. In such a situation it does not have to make a judgment about whose theology is correct.
3. In hierarchical churches, such as the one at issue in this case, the function of the civil court is not to decide, but to defer to the decision of the highest level of the church's government.

   > In this class of cases we think the rule of action which should govern the civil courts . . . is, that, whenever the questions of discipline or of faith or ecclesiastical rule, custom or law have been decided by the highest of these church judicatories to which the matter has been

carried, the legal tribunals must accept such decisions as final, and as binding on them, in their application to the case before them.[3]

The *Watson* rule was slightly modified in 1929 when the Court suggested that civil courts *might* become involved in church property disputes to determine if there had been fraudulent or arbitrary behavior on the part of ecclesiastical officials (*Gonzalez* v. *Archbishop*).[4] But the prohibition against decisions based on theology remained.

The prohibitions so far mentioned were raised to a constitutional level in 1952 in *Kedroff* v. *St. Nicholas Cathedral*.[5] This case had to do with the unusual situation in which a state legislature had taken sides in a church property controversy. There was a dispute between members of the Russian Orthodox Church in America as to who was the proper head of the church, the Patriarch of Moscow or a ruling committee formed by certain Orthodox persons in America. The committee called itself "The Russian Church in America." The New York legislature passed a law declaring that "The Russian Church in America" was the proper governing body of the Russian Orthodox churches in that state and the legitimate holder of St. Nicholas Cathedral in New York City. At the time of the legislation, the cathedral was held by those loyal to the Moscow patriarchate. It was The Russian Church in America that brought suit to regain control of the cathedral from the Moscow group, which they believed the legislation authorized them to do.

The Supreme Court ruled that neither the Establishment Clause nor the Free Exercise Clause would allow the New York legislature to designate which of the groups competing for leadership was the true Russian Orthodox Church and rightful holder of the cathedral. The Moscow patriarchate was the highest judicial body of the Russian Orthodox Church, and the state legislature had to defer to its determination of the ownership of the cathedral. Because it was decided on the basis of the Establishment and Free Exercise Clauses, *Kedroff* converted the principle of *Watson* as modified by *Gonzalez* into a constitutional rule.[6]

Neutral Principles of Law

A case very similar to *Watson* is *Presbyterian Church in the United States* v. *Mary Elizabeth Blue Hull Memorial Presbyterian Church*.[7] Two local Presbyterian churches in Georgia had decided that the parent denomination had become too liberal and no longer conformed to traditional Presbyterian faith. They initiated proceedings to separate from the denomination and keep their local church property. The General Assembly had ruled that the congregations were no longer entitled to own the property. But Georgia had a law addressing such issues, the main feature of which was a "departure from doctrine" concept. If, in a trial, a party in the controversy could convince the jury that the other party had departed from traditional church doctrine, the jury could award the property to the party that had remained true to tradition. In this case, a jury had decided that the General Assembly of the Presbyterian Church U.S. had departed from doctrine and thus could not deprive the local church of its property. However, with Justice William Brennan's opinion the Supreme Court ruled that such a law is unconstitutional and that juries may not make determinations on the ownership of church property on the "departure from doctrine" concept; civil courts simply may not delve into the theological issues:

> But First Amendment values are plainly jeopardized when church property litigation is made to turn on the resolution by civil courts of controversies over religious doctrine and practice. If civil courts undertake to resolve such controversies in order to adjudicate the property dispute, the hazards are ever present of inhibiting the free development of religious doctrine and of implicating secular interests in matters of purely ecclesiastical concern.[8]

Nevertheless, as if it were giving churches and/or denominations advice, the Court did mention in passing that instruments of church property ownership could be written in such a way that courts could solve disputes without having to consider doctrinal issues. This could be done by basing ownership on "neutral principles of law." What that means is that church charters or denominational rules could include language that specifies certain conditions under which the ownership of the church property might become disputed and what is to be done in each of those circumstances. So long as no theological interpretation was required, that procedure could be ruled on by a civil court. For example, in a hierarchical church, both the charter of the local church and the rules of the denomination could specify that if the congregation as a whole or a majority of the congregation chose to secede from the parent denomination, then local church property would automatically become the possession of the denomination. That would be a "neutral principle of law."

The Supreme Court addressed that question directly in 1979 in *Jones* v. *Wolf*.[9] The facts of the case were virtually identical to *Presbyterian Church*. A Presbyterian church wanted to leave the parent denomination and keep its property. In the process of deciding this case, the Court explicitly endorsed what had previously only been hinted at: if the church property dispute can be decided on "neutral principles of law," the civil courts may render such a decision. Although the Court still held to the principle that civil courts may not adjudicate any dispute involving theological dimensions, it did give courts more latitude than had been granted before. Justice Harry Blackmun expressed this for the Court very well. Because this issue is potentially so important to local churches, an extensive passage from the opinion is quoted here.

> The primary advantages of the neutral principles approach are that it is completely secular in operation, and yet flexible enough to accommodate all forms of religious organization and polity. The method relies exclusively on objective, well-established concepts of trust and property law familiar to lawyers and judges. It thereby promises to free civil courts completely from entanglement in questions of religious doctrine, polity, and practice. . . . Through appropriate reversionary clauses and trust provisions, religious societies can specify what is to happen to church property in the event of a particular contingency, or what religious body will determine the ownership in the event of a schism or doctrinal controversy. In this manner, a religious organization can ensure that a dispute over the ownership of church property will be resolved in accord with the desires of the members.
>
> This is not to say that the application of the neutral principles approach is wholly free of difficulty. The neutral principles method . . . requires a civil court to examine certain religious documents, such as a church constitution, for language of trust in favor of the general church. In undertaking such an examination, a civil court must take special care to scrutinize the document in purely secular terms, and not to rely on religious precepts in determining whether the document indicates that the parties have intended to create a trust. In addition, there may be cases where the deed, the corporate charter, or the constitution of the general church incorporates religious concepts in the provisions relating to the ownership of property. If in such a case the interpretation of the instruments of ownership would require the civil court to resolve a religious controversy, then the court must defer to the resolution of the doctrinal issue by the authoritative ecclesiastical body.
>
> On balance, however, the promise of nonentanglement and neutrality inherent in the neutral principles approach more than compensates for what will be occasional problems in application. These problems, in addition, should be gradually eliminated as recognition is given to the obligation of "States, religious organizations, and individuals [to] structure relationships involving church property so as not to require the civil courts to resolve ecclesiastical questions." We therefore hold that a State is constitutionally entitled to adopt neutral principles of law as a means of adjudicating a church property dispute.[10]

Four justices dissented in this case, arguing that there should not be any reliance on neutral principles of law. That is, their belief was that the *Watson* rule should be interpreted broadly and strictly: civil courts should not adjudicate church property cases. Taking the view of the dissenters and the recognition by the majority that if there was any hint of theology in the church property dispute civil courts could not proceed, plus *United States* v. *Ballard*, it is clear that it is still a basic rule that government, especially civil courts, should not become involved in the theological dimensions of religion. That is a part of the separation concept that has remained inviolable.

WORKPLACE ISSUES

In chapter 4 several cases were discussed that were clearly workplace cases decided under the Free Exercise Clause. But other workplace cases do not as obviously fall under that clause; although some do have free-exercise overtones, others have establishment dimensions, and some were decided on purely statutory grounds. Title VII of the Civil Rights Act of 1964 is the backdrop of some of these cases.

Undue Hardship

One of the provisions of the Civil Rights Act made it illegal for an employer to discriminate against an employee on the basis of religion. The 1972 amendment to the law specified that an employer was obligated to accommodate the religious practices of an employee *unless* such accommodation inflicted "undue hardship" on the employer.

The scope of the "undue hardship" provision was tested in *Trans World Airlines* v. *Hardison*.[11] Hardison became a member of the World Wide Church of God, a Sabbatarian group, while he was employed by TWA. He asked to be relieved of work assignments on his day of worship, sundown Friday until sundown Saturday. Making that accommodation became increasingly difficult for the company, especially because it had entered into labor agreements with a union. For the company to be able to accommodate Hardison's religiously based work requests meant that it would have to violate some of the seniority rules of the labor agreement, which would impact other workers. Eventually Hardison was dismissed from employment. He sued, claiming that TWA had not gone far enough to accommodate his religious practices.

The Supreme Court, in an opinion written by Justice Byron White, ruled against Hardison. An employer did not have to discriminate against some employees in order to accommodate the religious preferences of other employees. On the question of "undue hardship," the Court said that an employer should have to bear no more than minimal hardship or cost to be in compliance with the law. "To require TWA to bear more than a *de minimis* cost in order to give Hardison Saturdays off is an undue hardship."[12]

The Court seemed to confirm this ruling in *Ansonia Board of Education* v. *Philbrook*,[13] when it ruled that an employer did not need to accept the employee's preferred method in deciding how to accommodate the employee's religion. "[W]here the employer has already reasonably accommodated the employee's religious needs, the statutory inquiry is at an end. The employer need not further show that each of the employee's alternative accommodations would result in undue hardship."[14]

So, in spite of the law's prohibition against religion-based discrimination in the workplace, the Court interpreted the rule in such a way that employers seem to have the advantage over employees and religious behavior carries little weight.[15]

Permissible Discrimination on the Basis of Religion

The original nondiscrimination provision of the Civil Rights Act prohibited religious groups from discriminating in hiring on the basis of religion, except that they could discriminate when hiring for jobs involving religious activity. For example, a Baptist church could consider only Baptists for the position of pastor. But Congress amended the law to say that religious institutions could also discriminate on the basis of religion when hiring for jobs not including religious activity. For example, under the earlier law a Methodist church seeking to employ a building superintendent would be required to hire a Lutheran or even an atheist if that person were best qualified for the job among all the applicants. But religious leaders complained that this law sometimes required them to hire someone whose different or nonexistent religious belief was disruptive or at least a bad influence on parishioners. Congress amended the law to allow churches to employ people of their own religion, even in nonreligious jobs; but some contended that this discrimination on the basis of religion was a violation of the Establishment Clause.

The issue came before the Supreme Court in *Church of Jesus Christ of Latter-day Saints* v. *Amos.*[16] A person employed in a secular job by the Mormon church was dismissed because he did not qualify for a "temple recommend," that is, a certificate that he was a member of the church in good standing and thus able to worship in Mormon temples. Justice Byron White, writing for the Court, argued that such discrimination was consistent with the law and that the law did not violate the no-establishment principle. A law is not an establishment when it requires the government to get out of the way of a religious group and allow it to practice its religion more freely. A religious institution ought to have leeway to define and carry out its religious mission without having to worry about whether the government is going to agree that a particular job is religious or secular. The amended law, by allowing religious groups to hire on the basis of religion for all its jobs, avoids that problem. In this regard, the Court gave some precision on how it understands establishment:

> A law is not unconstitutional simply because it *allows* churches to advance religion, which is their very purpose. For a law to have forbidden "effects"

under *Lemon*, it must be fair to say that the *government itself* has advanced religion through its own activities and influence.[17]

So, religious institutions have the right to insist that their employee's religion be consistent with their own.

Congressional Intent

Finally, a case came up about the unionization of lay teachers in parochial schools. Some teachers' unions expressed an interest in representing lay teachers in Catholic schools in the Chicago area. The National Labor Relations Board, in accordance with its procedures to oversee unionization elections, ordered elections to be held in the schools, even though Catholic school officials insisted that the NLRB had no jurisdiction in the matter. In the elections, the teachers voted to unionize and that was duly certified by the NLRB. But the Catholic authorities refused to recognize the unions or to bargain. The NLRB ruled that the Catholic authorities, by refusing to bargain, had violated the National Labor Relations Act. At that point, Catholic school officials sued.

The Supreme Court decided the controversy in *National Labor Relations Board* v. *Catholic Bishop of Chicago*.[18] The contention of the Catholic bishop was that the action of the NLRB was a violation of the Establishment Clause, on the basis of excessive entanglement. But the Court, as it always attempts to do, was able to decide this case without having to reach the constitutional issue. It examined the debates in Congress when the National Labor Relations Act was passed and came to the conclusion that Congress had not intended for parochial schools to be covered by the legislation. Consequently, the NLRB could not compel the Catholic schools to bargain with the unions. In this particular labor dispute, the Court insulated religious institutions from interference from a government agency.

CONSCIENTIOUS OBJECTION

Historically, one of the most persistent conflicts between religion and the state has been over the question of the propriety of war. In the Judeo-Christian tradition there is a stream of thought that promotes pacifism. In the Ten Commandments one reads "You shall not kill."[19] Jesus said, "Blessed are the peacemakers, for they shall be called [children] of God," and "Do not resist one who is evil. But if any one strikes you on the right cheek, turn to him the other also."[20] These and other passages have led some to adopt the position of pacifism. This has meant, at the very least, that individuals, groups, or even nations, should not aggressively employ violence, although some hold that one might legitimately use violence in self-defense. The other position, more consistent but extreme, is nonresistance. That is, not only should one not be aggressively violent, but one should not even defend oneself against violence. This second view is the commonly accepted understanding of pacifism. Conversely, there are numerous examples in religious history of warfare having been justified with religious arguments. Indeed, as in the Crusades, warfare has even been waged in the name of God. So there is a tension about what is the proper thing for a religious person to do, wage war or be a pacifist. The one who tries to live by the pacifist tradition is virtually always in the minority. In principle, the state maintains a military on the ground that it must at least defend itself and its citizens. Sometimes, of course, the state uses its military aggressively to try to expand its power and territory through conquest. The majority of the population virtually always supports the military and its functions and thinks of the conscientious objector as at least unpatriotic, if not traitorous.

The position of the pacifist in the United States has been somewhat more problematic than the previous paragraph might suggest. The Preamble of the Constitution says that one of the purposes for that charter of government is to "provide for the common defense." Furthermore Article I, section 8, empowers Congress "To declare war," "To raise and support Armies," "To provide and maintain a Navy," and "To provide for calling forth the Militia to execute the Laws of the Union." So the nation's basic law provides for national self-defense, at the very least. Of course, the assumption is that the nation will need to call on its citizens to serve in these various military bodies. For the pacifist, a dilemma results: how to be loyal to the nation and still be obedient to the belief that God's law prohibits violence. The Supreme Court has rendered decisions that have set some boundaries about how far one can carry one's pacifism before running afoul of the state's need for military service.

The Issue of Citizenship

Strangely enough, the issue first came before the Court in the cases of pacifist aliens who applied for citizenship in the United States. The first of these, in 1929, was *United States* v. *Schwimmer*.[21] The oath of naturalization contained the phrase "I will support and defend the Constitution and laws of the United States of America against all enemies, foreign and domestic." Rosika Schwimmer was an atheist, but she was conscientiously opposed to war in any form. She declared that she would not be willing to take up arms for the nation. Even though she was both female and fifty-one years old at the time of her Supreme Court case, both of which would have disqualified her from military service, the Court denied her citizenship. Although Schwimmer said that there were other ways that one could defend the country without bearing arms—through words, for example—the Court said that the only way the country could be defended was by taking up arms. Those whose conscience would not allow them to do that could not be naturalized.

In 1931 two other similar naturalization cases were handed down, *United States v. Bland*[22] and *United States v. Macintosh*.[23] Bland, also a woman, was a Christian (Episcopalian) and opposed to all war. Macintosh, a Northern Baptist and a theology professor at Yale Divinity School, wanted to make a judgment about whether or not particular wars were morally justified before he would agree to participate; he wanted to pick and choose his wars. Despite these differences in the facts of the cases, the Court decided them the same as in *Schwimmer*. Noncitizens who were opposed to participation in war could not become United States citizens because, in the words of the naturalization law, they were not "attached to the principles of the Constitution of the United States, and well disposed to the good order and happiness of the same."[24]

There is a statement in *Macintosh* that will illuminate the latter part of this chapter. One of the arguments made by these naturalization candidates was that they ought to be awarded citizenship because the government had previously passed laws exempting native-born conscientious objectors from military service.[25] All that they were asking was that they be given the same privileges as those who were already American citizens. Macintosh's lawyer wrote in his prepared brief to the Supreme Court that it was a "fixed principle of our Constitution" that a citizen should be allowed to be a conscientious objector. The Court, Justice George Sutherland for the majority, responded to that assertion as follows:

> This, if it means what it seems to say, is an astonishing statement. Of course, there is no such principle of the Constitution, fixed or otherwise. The conscientious objector is relieved from the obligation to bear arms in obedience to no constitutional provision, express or implied; but because, and only because, it has accorded with the policy of Congress to relieve him. . . . The privilege of the native-born conscientious objector to avoid bearing arms comes not from the Constitution, but from the acts of Congress. That body may grant or withhold the exemption as in its wisdom it sees fit; and if it be withheld, the native-born conscientious objector cannot assert the privilege.[26]

The right to be exempt from military service as a conscientious objector is not a constitutional right, but comes solely from the grace of Congress.

The Will of the State, the Will of God

There is a second statement in *Macintosh*, which is somewhat parenthetical to this chapter, but which reflects an attitude that has been and still is widespread in this country: somehow America is God's favored nation. It was noted above that Macintosh was not an absolute conscientious objector; he wanted to judge the moral value of the war he was asked to serve in before he would agree to serve. In his own words,

> I do not undertake to support "my country, right or wrong" in any dispute which may arise, and I am not willing to promise beforehand, and without knowing the cause for which my country may go to war, either that I will or that I will not "take up arms in defense of this country," however "necessary" the war may seem to the government of the day.[27]

Justice Sutherland responded to Macintosh's attitude with a remarkable statement:

> When he speaks of putting his allegiance to the will of God above his allegiance to the government, it is evident . . . that he means to make *his own interpretation* of the will of God the decisive test which shall conclude the government and stay its hand. We are a Christian people according to one another the equal right of religious freedom, and acknowledging with reverence the duty of obedience to the will of God. But, also, we are a nation with the duty to survive; a nation whose Constitution contemplates war as well as peace; whose government must go forward upon the assumption and safely can proceed upon no other, that unqualified allegiance to the nation and submission and obedience to the laws of the land, as well those made for war as those made for peace, are not inconsistent with the will of God.[28]

The will of the State is essentially equivalent with the will of God! There could hardly be a clearer statement of the negative side of what some now call "civil religion." I use the phrase "negative side" because it is precisely this attitude, that "*unqualified* allegiance to the nation . . . [is] not inconsistent with the will of God," which commonly leads patriots to baptize their nations' wars, that is, to wage wars in the name of God as well as country. Because the opponents automatically become enemies of God, such an attitude historically has led to unnecessary destruction, atrocities, and a demand for total victory that often disregards the humanity or civil rights of the vanquished.

Court Reversal Rooted in Previous Dissents

Finally, in 1946, the Supreme Court reversed itself on the question of the naturalization of conscientious objectors in *Girouard* v. *United States*.[29] Girouard was a Seventh-day Adventist whose position was the same as his denomination's: he would be willing to serve in the military, but only as a noncombatant. He recognized the need of the nation to wage war sometimes, but he also felt strongly that God's will is that one should not kill. He would be willing to serve in the military, but to try to preserve life rather than take it.

The Court found in Girouard's favor. In *Schwimmer* Justice Oliver Wendell Holmes had written a strong dissent, and in *Bland* and *Macintosh* Chief Justice Charles Evans Hughes had vigorously dissented. The majority opinion in *Girouard*, written by Justice William O. Douglas, picked up many of the themes of those dissents. The principal one was that the oath of naturalization actually does not require aliens to promise to bear arms. In fact, that oath is virtually identical to that required of all native-born government officeholders, yet they are allowed to be conscientious objectors. There was simply no evidence that Congress had set a higher standard for those applying for citizenship than it did for those citizens who take the oath in order to hold some government office. Another theme was that it is certainly possible to serve the welfare of the country in ways other than by bearing arms.

> Refusal to bear arms is not necessarily a sign of disloyalty or a lack of attachment to our institutions. One may serve his country faithfully and devotedly, though his religious scruples make it impossible for him to shoulder a rifle. . . . The effort of war is indivisible; and those whose religious scruples prevent them from killing are no less patriots than those whose special traits or handicaps result in their assignment to duties far behind the fighting front.[30]

As the result of *Girouard*, the law now is that noncitizens who have objections to war based on religious training and belief may take alternative forms of the oath. One form will admit them to citizenship and allow them to serve in the military as noncombatants. The other form will permit them to avoid military service altogether, provided that they do nonmilitary work of national significance when required by law.

On the question of the relation of the state to the will of God, the Court made the following observation:

> The struggle for religious liberty has through the centuries been an effort to accommodate the demands of the State to the conscience of the individual. The victory for freedom of thought recorded in our Bill of Rights recognizes that *in the domain of conscience there is a moral power higher than the State*.[31]

Here the Court recognizes the proper relationship between the will of God and the state. In fact, *Macintosh* was the last time the Court ever articulated the Christian nation heresy.

Citizen Conscientious Objectors

The other line of conscientious objection cases taken up by the Court involves the citizen (as opposed to the applicant for naturalization) who refuses to participate in the military. As noted above, in *Macintosh* the Court clearly expressed that any exemption from military service must come from Congress; it certainly is not a constitutionally given right.[32] But, in fact,

Congress has made provision for conscientious objectors. Such laws first were passed during the Civil War. In 1864 both the Union and the Confederacy exempted from conscription those people who were members of well-recognized denominations that taught pacifism, groups such as the Society of Friends (Quakers) and the Mennonites. People not members of the "peace churches" were not eligible for the exemption. The same exemption was reenacted in the Draft Act of 1917, so long as the objection was to "war in any form." The law required that all eligible persons be inducted into the armed forces, but members of peace churches were allowed to perform non-combatant service.

In 1940 the law was revised again. Now it was not necessary to belong to a peace church, so long as one's objection to war in any form was based on "religious training and belief." Those who qualified were not inducted but allowed to perform alternative service useful to the nation. Some believed, however, that such criteria were broad enough to include intellectual or humanist objections to war. So, in 1948, Congress refined the category to say that

> religious training and belief . . . means an individual's belief in a relation to a Supreme Being involving duties superior to those arising from any human relation, but does not include essentially political, sociological, or philosophical views or a merely personal moral code.[33]

With the advent of the Vietnam War, perhaps America's most unpopular war, draft boards were deluged with applications for conscientious objector status. Some of those applications involved people who claimed to have sincere conscientious objections to participation in war, but who were not religious in a conventional sense. Not only were they not participants in some organized religious group, some did not even believe in a personal God. Did these people qualify for conscientious objector status, given the wording of the law? The Supreme Court first faced this question in 1965 in *United States* v. *Seeger*,[34] a case that actually combined the appeals of three different young men.

Redefining Religious Belief

How unconventional were these people? Seeger preferred to leave open the question of whether he believed in a personal God, rather than saying yes or no. But that did not mean that he believed in nothing whatsoever. He had a "belief in and devotion to goodness and virtue for their own sakes and a religious faith in a purely ethical creed," and cited Plato, Aristotle, and Spinoza as support for such a belief. An appellant named Jakobson said he believed in "Godness" which was "the Ultimate Cause for the fact of the Being of the Universe." He believed in a relationship to Godness in two directions, "vertically, toward Godness directly," and "horizontally, toward

Godness through Mankind and the World." He preferred the latter. The third applicant, Peter, said that for him religion was "the supreme expression of human nature; man thinking his highest, feeling his deepest, living his best." He said he supposed that one could say that such a belief was grounded in a Supreme Being or God, but "[t]hese just do not happen to be the words I use."[35] In all three cases, the young men said that the beliefs thus articulated were the basis of their sincere objection to participation in war.

The question that faced the Supreme Court in this case was whether the conscientious objection of these men resulted from "religious training and belief . . . in relation to a Supreme Being," as demanded by the statute. Justice Tom Clark, writing for the Court, began his discussion by noting that Congress had used the phrase "Supreme Being" rather than the word "God" in the statute. By making this choice of words, it intended to accommodate something broader than a traditional belief in a personal God. Taking a kind of "ultimate concern" view of religion, the Court argued that the statute did not insist on a traditional concept of God, but would be satisfied with a belief in a being or impersonal power upon which all else is dependent or to which all else is subordinate. In the light of Congress's expansive language, the three men in this case fit the category of being in "relation to a Supreme Being involving duties superior to those arising from any human relation."

The Double Sincerity Test

But was this really "religious training and belief" as required by the statute? The Court set forth a test for determining religious belief: "The test might be stated in these words: A sincere and meaningful belief which occupies in the life of its possessor a place parallel to that filled by the God of those admittedly qualifying for the exemption comes within the statutory definition."[36] This is what I call a "double sincerity test." In evaluating the application of a conscientious objector with unconventional "religious" beliefs, the officials at the draft board (or a judge) have to think of some conscientious objector with conventional religious beliefs they have known (or, if they have not known any, hypothesize about one), say, a Quaker. They are to think about the sincerity of religious belief of that person, that is, the role that a personal God plays in his or her life. Then they are to think about the unconventional applicant and try to determine if that person's unconventional beliefs are held as sincerely, or play as large a part in that person's life, as those of the Quaker. If they are parallel, then the unconventional person can be granted conscientious objector status. This is not an easy assignment.

I mentioned earlier that the government (courts) is not permitted to evaluate or determine the truth or falsity of theology under our system of separation. In general that is true. But the *Seeger* case's double sincerity test pushes at the constraints, since it asks government officials to evaluate one applicant's beliefs in comparison with more conventional beliefs. Some may argue that the procedure defies the principle. But others may argue, and the Supreme Court would agree, that it is not the content of the belief that is being evaluated, but the sincerity with which it is held. The distinction is very fuzzy. It is also a generalization that the Supreme Court has never defined religion, because of our system of separation. But *Seeger* comes as close as the Court ever has come to defining religion. And the definition is very broad.

The Result: An Elastic Law

Welsh v. *United States*[37] illustrated how broad the definition was. In terms of the statements made on his application for conscientious objector status, Welsh was even less religious, in any conventional sense, than Seeger. On the application form for conscientious objector status, the question was asked as to whether the applicant's views on war were based on "religious training and belief." Seeger had put quotation marks around "religious," but Welsh marked out the word. Although he later did say that he was religious "in the ethical sense of the word," he never thought of himself as being a religious person. He certainly had no clearly defined theological views or a belief in a personal God. He characterized his beliefs as having been formed "by reading in the fields of history and sociology."

Still, the Supreme Court upheld Welsh's qualification to be classified as a conscientious objector on the ground that he was more religious than he knew. That is, Justice Hugo Black wrote, few people knew of the broad interpretation given to the word "religious" in *Seeger*. Without knowing of that definition, they might think they fall outside the category when, in reality, they could be included.

> [V]ery few registrants are fully aware of the broad scope of the word "religious" as used in §6(j) [as interpreted in *Seeger*], and accordingly a registrant's statement that his beliefs are nonreligious is a highly unreliable guide for those charged with administering the exemption. Welsh himself presents a case in point.[38]

It should be recalled that the statute specified that one's objections to war could not be based on "essentially political, sociological, or philosophical views or a merely personal moral code." The government, which opposed Welsh's application, claimed that he fell within this forbidden territory. But the Court, having said that Welsh was actually religious under the *Seeger* definition, disagreed. It said that the exclusion mentioned in the law should not include persons who have strongly held beliefs about America's domestic or foreign policy or whose objection to war is based on considerations of public policy.

> The two groups of registrants that obviously do fall within these exclusions from the exemption are those whose beliefs are not deeply held and those

whose objection to war does not rest at all upon moral, ethical, or religious principle but instead rests solely upon considerations of policy, pragmatism, or expediency.[39]

Welsh qualified as a conscientious objector.

With these two cases, the conscientious objector provision of the draft law became the most elastic of laws, able to be stretched to include almost anyone. Furthermore, Congress did not react by rewriting the law to make it more precise, but essentially accepted the interpretation of *Seeger* and *Welsh* without a whimper. Some did wonder, however, if even these broad interpretations did not function to eliminate inarticulate applicants or those with too little education to be able to cite the likes of Plato and Aristotle or who had not read in history and sociology.

Selective Conscientious Objection

Finally, *Gillette* v. *United States*[40] is another important case. Some native-born citizens applied for conscientious objector status but were not opposed to all wars. Guy P. Gillette said that although he was opposed to the war in Vietnam, he could conceive of wars in which he would be willing to participate, such as wars of national defense or those fought under the auspices of the United Nations. He considered America's efforts in Vietnam to be unjust, however, and had conscientious objections to participation therein.

The Court made short work of this application for conscientious objector status, *Gillette* v. *United States*. Remember that the statute specified that, in order to qualify, the applicant must be "conscientiously opposed to participation in war in any form." The Court took those words literally; no elastic definition here. Indeed, the Court's opinion, written by Justice Thurgood Marshall, held that there can be only one reading of the words. Gillette did not fit the statutory requirement; thus his application must be denied. Even though the Court had been most generous in its interpretation of who could fall within the boundaries of conscientious objector status, even those who might otherwise qualify under the loose standards cannot pick and choose their wars. To the argument that this interpretation might discriminate against certain denominations, those which have just war/unjust war theories, for example, the Court disagreed. The statute is religion-neutral and is not designed to single out any religious organization or creed for special treatment or discrimination.

Now that the nation no longer has conscription, but rather relies on "voluntary" armed service, these cases are moot. We can assume that if conscription were resumed under the same statutory framework as formerly, the definitions of these cases would become operative again.

6

Aid to Church-Related Schools

The propriety of the presence of religion in public schools has been and continues to be one of the most volatile issues in the church–state decisions of the Supreme Court. Americans take education—although not necessarily its funding—very seriously. Historically, schools have been seen to be crucial to the national welfare. The education of children has been perceived as essential for a strong and vital America. The knowledge and skills that the schools give youth enable them to earn a living for themselves. But such training also is fundamental to a strong economy, which makes America the world power that it has been. Furthermore, the schools have served the important purpose of passing on American values to successive genera-tions—values such as democracy, capitalism, and, with notable exceptions, a diluted form of Protestant Christianity. The notable exceptions, of course, exist because some of those schools are operated by non-Protestant or non-Christian religious groups. There are parochial schools in this country as well as public schools. Both kinds of schools are involved in the church–state decisions of the Supreme Court.

The first educational institutions in this country were all church-related and had, as their primary objective, the education of clergy. In the early seventeenth century, once the Puritans established a colony at Massachusetts Bay, "One of the next things we longed for, and looked after was to advance Learning, and perpetuate it to Posterity, dreading to leave an illiterate Min-istry to the Churches, when our present Ministers shall lie in the Dust."[1] With this motivation they founded Harvard College in 1636. But they also founded "a fair Grammar School, for the training up of young Scholars, and fitting of them for Academical Learning."[2] Likewise, the Massachusetts School Act of November 11, 1647, declared:

> It being one chief project of that old deluder, Satan, to keep men from the knowledge of the Scriptures, . . . that learning may not be buried in the grave of our fathers in the church and commonwealth, the Lord assisting our endeavors,—
>
> It is therefore ordered, that every township in this jurisdiction, after the Lord hath increased them to the number of fifty householders, shall then

61

forthwith appoint one within their town to teach all such children as shall resort to him to write and to read.[3]

The assumption that if ignorance is the work of Satan, then education must somehow be the work of the Lord undergirds all church-sponsored education. This law established the educational pattern for the rest of the colonial period. The pattern was denominationally sponsored schools along the eastern seaboard and, later, on the frontier. Although educational goals were broadened beyond training for the ministry, the curricula of all the schools included a large component of Christianity, taught from the perspective of the sponsoring denomination.

After the country won independence, virtually all recognized that education was essential to the development of the new nation. Democracy could survive only if there were informed debate about national issues. Informed debate could take place only if the citizenry were educated. But many believed it was inappropriate for the nation to reap the benefit from something for which it did not pay. Furthermore, the various denominational schools, each perpetuating its own creed, would lead to fragmentation in the body politic. That was not good for a democratic society. So, in response to these two concerns, in the early 1830s the idea of the public school developed. Schools would be paid for by the various local and state governments. They would not teach the theology of any religious group, and thus would be free from sectarian differences and divisiveness.

One of the things a nation desires, however, is law-abiding, moral citizens. Clearly, then, the new public schools should teach civic morality along with the "reading, writing, and arithmetic." But what would be the source of this civic morality, since the public schools were to be free from sectarian religious teaching? School leaders decided it would be religious virtue, made up of those virtues common to all Judeo-Christian religions, namely, a belief in God and a life of morality based on the ethical teachings of the Bible. Surely all people could agree on those as being essential to the content of public school curricula.

But all did not agree. Some of the Protestant groups that operated schools believed the public schools, even with their "common religion" approach to morality, were not religious enough. These Protestant groups wanted more emphasis on religion, denominationally proclaimed, than the public schools were able to give. So they continued their parochial schools. The Lutherans are a major example.

Beginning in about 1830 and continuing throughout the rest of the century (the Civil War years excepted), massive waves of immigrants poured into America. Many of these people were Roman Catholic. Catholics were convinced that the public schools were purveyors of "lowest common denominator Protestantism" (which surely they were). Even though it was a watered-down Protestantism, the public schools were too Protestant for the Catholics. Consequently, the Catholic Church began a parochial school movement, into which it has poured enormous amounts of money, energy, and talent.

Given this history, the Supreme Court has had to deal with two kinds of school cases. One involves government aid to parochial schools, which I discuss in this chapter. The other is about religion in the public schools, in the form of religious instruction or devotional exercises. These cases will be discussed in chapter 7. In both instances, the Establishment Clause is involved, since that clause is the one that is especially the guardian of separation of church and state. That is, it demands that government be neutral toward religion, neither aiding nor hindering it.

GOVERNMENT AID TO PAROCHIAL SCHOOLS

Once the Roman Catholics decided to have an extensive school system, they also tried to get public funding for it. This was, after all, an immigrant church in the nineteenth century, and resources were scarce for the development and maintenance of its schools. The church's principal rationale for seeking public assistance was that the parochial schools served a public good; they contributed to the educated citizenry necessary to the democracy and also relieved population pressures on the public schools. Consequently, the church felt that it was only right that some government money should help support its schools. This effort to gain government aid began as early as the 1840s, with the efforts of Archbishop John Hughes of New York.

Before examining these aid cases, it is important that we should look at a challenge to the very existence of parochial schools. In 1922, in a fit of anti-immigrant passion, Oregon passed a law that all able-bodied and educable children had to receive their education in the public schools of the state, because private and parochial schools tended to perpetuate differences between people. That law was challenged by a parochial school and a military academy. In *Pierce v. Society of Sisters*[4] the Court ruled on the basis of the Fourteenth Amendment (the First had not yet been applied to the states). Remember that the Fourteenth Amendment contains the phrase "nor shall any State deprive any person of life, liberty, or property, without due process of law." The Society of Sisters claimed that the law impermissibly denied private and parochial schools the liberty to do business (which is essentially property), in violation of that clause. The Court agreed with that contention, and further held that Oregon's law interfered with the freedom of parents to educate their children as they wanted. States could not prohibit parochial schools from existing. The Court did say, however, that the educational standards in parochial schools had to conform to the standards of quality

demanded by the state. This case is often called the Magna Carta of parochial schools.

The Child-Benefit Theory

Given that lease on life, parochial schools continued to seek public funding. The first case challenging that funding came before the Court in 1930,
Cochran v. *Louisiana State Board of Education.*[5] Louisiana had a program by
which state-financed textbooks that were used in public schools could also be
provided for the students in parochial schools. The program was challenged
on the basis that it took private (tax) money (property) and used it for a
private (parochial school) purpose, as opposed to a public purpose. This use
of tax money was alleged to be illegal under the Fourteenth Amendment.
The Court disagreed with that contention, and in the process articulated an
important concept in church–state relations: the "child benefit theory."
The Court ruled that the state benefit went only to the children enrolled in
the parochial schools, not to the schools themselves, and certainly not to the
churches that operated the schools. Chief Justice Charles Evans Hughes
wrote, "The schools, however, are not the beneficiaries of these appropria-
tions. They obtain nothing from them, nor are they relieved of a single
obligation, because of them. The school children and the state alone are the
beneficiaries."[6] The "child benefit theory" has appeared from time to time in
subsequent cases.

A prime example of its application is the landmark case *Everson* v. *Board of
Education.*[7] Ewing Township, New Jersey, consistent with state law, passed a
regulation that permitted the parents of children attending public and Catholic schools to receive a reimbursement from public money for the expense
of having their children transported to and from school on public buses. A
taxpayer of the community sued, claiming that the program was a violation
of the Establishment Clause of the First Amendment. He argued that this
transportation program at state expense aided church schools and thus violated the neutrality between church and state demanded by that clause.

Everson is an important case for two reasons. First, it was the case in
which the Court applied the Establishment Clause to the states through
the Fourteenth Amendment.[8] Second, Justice Hugo Black, the author of the
majority opinion, wrote an expansive, strict separationist description of the
scope and power of the Establishment Clause. This paragraph, or portions
of it, have been quoted in Supreme Court decisions ever since. Because of its
clarity and importance, I quote it in full:

The "establishment of religion" clause of the First Amendment means at
least this: Neither a state nor the Federal Government can set up a church.
Neither can pass laws which aid one religion, aid all religions, or prefer

one religion over another. Neither can force nor influence a person to go to or to remain away from church against his will or force him to profess a belief or disbelief in any religion. No person can be punished for entertaining or professing religious beliefs or disbeliefs, for church attendance or non-attendance. No tax in any amount, large or small, can be levied to support any religious activities or institutions, whatever they may be called, or whatever form they may adopt to teach or practice religion. Neither a state nor the Federal Government can, openly or secretly, participate in the affairs of any religious organizations or groups and *vice versa*. In the words of Jefferson, the clause against establishment of religion by law was intended to erect "a wall of separation between church and state."[9]

This 1947 statement set the tone for Establishment Clause decisions of the Court from then to the present. The justices have wrestled with the principles and implications of this statement ever since, and, although some of them recently have wanted to modify it in certain respects, quotations from it continue to appear in decisions.

Justice Black concluded his opinion with another strict-separationist statement, which seems to echo and summarize the paragraph just quoted. He wrote: "The First Amendment has erected a wall between church and state. That wall must be kept high and impregnable. We could not approve the slightest breach. New Jersey has not breached it here."[10]

Yet, amazingly, the majority approved of the public-financed bus transportation for children going to parochial schools and agreed that the program did not violate the Establishment Clause. How could this happen, given the sentiments that form the core of the opinion?

The Court reached the conclusion it did by using a variation of the "child benefit" approach, although it did not use the phrase. Bus transportation of children to school, public and parochial, was a kind of public welfare program similar to police and fire protection or sewage lines and sidewalks. These other government services are provided to churches just as they are to all other segments of the community. They are for the purpose of providing for the public's safety. Just so with the public transportation of children to school. The purpose of the program was to protect children from the dangers of walking to school or even riding with their parents in private cars. For the city to pay for transportation to church-related schools on public buses was not aid to religion, but a way to protect children from the dangers of public thoroughfares. The child was the beneficiary, not the school or the church that operated the school.

This child-benefit approach had grounding in the religion clauses of the Constitution. (This gave the theory more weight in reference to religion than the *Cochran* decision did, since that case was decided only on Fourteenth Amendment grounds.) In a passage less frequently quoted than the one cited above, but no less important, Justice Black wrote of the First Amendment:

> That Amendment requires the state to be a neutral in its relations with groups of religious believers and non-believers; it does not require the state to be their adversary. State power is no more to be used so as to handicap religions than it is to favor them.[11]

Because the result of the decision was so anomalous with its reasoning, two strong dissents were written, joined by four justices. But none of the dissenters disagreed with either the application of the Establishment Clause to the states or the strict-separationist description of the scope of the clause. So it was left to later justices to dispute the Establishment Clause philosophy expressed in this case.

EXCURSUS 1: THE "*LEMON* TEST"
A Three-Part Test for Interpreting
the Establishment Clause

In order to be able to understand the procedures the Court used to decide post-*Everson* aid to parochial school cases and other Establishment Clause cases, it is necessary briefly to explain a test that was developed to interpret the clause. In 1963, the Court decided *Abington Township School District* v. *Schempp*,[12] a case about prayer and Bible reading in the public schools, which is examined in chapter 7.

In *Schempp* the Court generated the "secular purpose test" and the "primary effect test." In order for a law to be considered constitutional under the Establishment Clause, it must have a secular purpose and it must have a primary effect that neither advances nor hinders religion. The secular purpose test has to do with the intention of the legislative body. Was the legislature's intent to pass a law that would give aid or sanction to a religion or to religion in general? If so, the law is unconstitutional. The primary effect test has to do not with the purpose of the law, but with its implementation or enforcement. The tests are independent of each other, since it is possible to enforce a secular law in such a way as to advance or hinder religion.

In 1970 the Court handed down a decision in *Walz* v. *Tax Commission of the City of New York*,[13] a case about property tax exemptions for churches that is explained in chapter 8. In that case the Court crafted a third test for interpreting the Establishment Clause, one prohibiting "excessive entanglement." If a program or law creates more than minimal interaction between a religious institution and civil authority, then it is unconstitutional. The Establishment Clause demands that the involvement between church and state be as limited as possible. In this time of rapidly expanding government, there can be no such thing as absolute separation of church and state. But the involvement must be kept slight; anything more is a violation. The "excessive entanglement test" permits the courts to determine whether a violation has occurred.

The entanglement test was added to the other two, thereby formulating a three-part test for interpreting the Establishment Clause. The first time these tests were used together, as a unit, was in an aid to parochial school case called *Lemon* v. *Kurtzman*.[14]

In the absence of precisely stated constitutional prohibitions, we must draw lines with reference to the three main evils against which the Establishment Clause was intended to afford protection: "sponsorship, financial support, and active involvement of the sovereign in religious activity."

Every analysis in this area must begin with consideration of the cumulative criteria developed by the Court over many years. Three such tests may be gleaned from our cases. First, the statute must have a secular legislative purpose; second, its principal or primary effect must be one that neither advances nor inhibits religion; finally, the statute must not foster "an excessive government entanglement with religion."[15]

This three-part test has come to be known as the "*Lemon* test." Considerably more is said of this elsewhere in this book.

Note that the elements of the test are subjective. They are not hard-and-fast rules, but what the Court once called "no more than helpful signpost[s]."[16] They require judgment calls. What is a secular purpose as opposed to a religious one? What is a primary effect to either advance or hinder religion as opposed to, say, an indirect effect? What does it take to make entanglement excessive? All these are questions of interpretation, the sort of things on which courts are supposed to rule. But they are also issues on which people, even Supreme Court justices, disagree, which will become abundantly clear.

EXCURSUS 2: STANDING

In order to be able to understand many of the parochial school issues that follow, it is necessary to become familiar with the legal concept of "standing." Standing has to do with whether the one who files a suit has the right to do so.

I mentioned earlier that we have an adversarial system of jurisprudence in this country. Article III, Section 2 of the Constitution says that the judicial power of the government shall extend to "cases" and "controversies" between parties who have real interests in conflict with each other. One question involved in the issue of standing is whether one's interest is substantial and actually protected under the law. Furthermore, will the decision of the court make a difference to the parties in the suit—will they be affected by the outcome? If the answer to these questions is negative, then the one bringing the suit does not have standing. If one lacks standing, one cannot come to court, that is, the suit presented to the court will not be considered.

A principal example, and one pertinent to this book, is that of taxpayer suits. The best way to understand this is to look at a famous case, *Frothingham* v. *Mellon*.[17] Mrs. Frothingham filed suit in federal court challenging the constitutionality of the Maternity Act of 1921. That law provided for federal money to go to the states to improve prenatal and infant care. She claimed that this act inflicted on her the burden of paying taxes in support of an unconstitutional program. To put it another way, she had to pay taxes for a government program she believed was wrong and illegal. The Supreme Court responded to this complaint by saying that Frothingham could not raise the constitutional question about the program because she did not have standing as a taxpayer. The amount of federal taxes she paid was a minuscule part of the total federal budget. Given that only a small percentage of the federal budget actually went to fund the maternity program, her personal involvement as a taxpayer in that particular program was even smaller—infinitesimal. That small level of involvement meant that she really did not have a personal stake in the funding of the program or in the outcome of her suit. She did not have standing. Consequently, the Court never considered her constitutional challenge to the maternity law because she was not qualified to be a litigant.

The rule derived from *Frothingham* is that taxpayer suits are not permitted in federal courts. State courts, however, frequently did and do allow taxpayer suits, and occasionally the Supreme Court does accept a taxpayer suit that, although it came through a state court system, presents an important federal question, in spite of the *Frothingham* rule. Both *Cochran* v. *Louisiana State Board of Education* and *Everson* v. *Board of Education* were such cases (see pp. 64–66).

An Exception to *Frothingham*: *Flast* v. *Cohen*

The question of standing was raised in the church–state area in *Flast* v. *Cohen*.[18] In 1965 Congress passed the Elementary and Secondary Education Act, which, among other things, allowed federal money to go to church-related schools for instruction and materials. In New York seven individuals brought suit in federal court, challenging the constitutionality of the part of the law that aided religious schools. Their only qualifications to be plaintiffs was that they were payers of federal taxes. The government contended that they did not have standing and that the suit should be dismissed; the plaintiffs claimed they did have standing. The case was diverted from being a challenge to the constitutionality of the Education Act and was turned into a standing suit; that is, the Court was now to decide if a taxpayer has standing when the challenge is made to a law alleged to violate the Establishment Clause.

Chief Justice Earl Warren, writing for the majority, slightly modified the *Frothingham* rule on standing, saying that a federal taxpayer has standing if two requirements are met. First, the taxpayer has to prove that the law challenged was passed under the Taxing and Spending Clause of the Constitution (Article I, section 8).[19] That is, one may not challenge expenditures under a regulatory program of government, but may challenge legislation involving expenditures from taxation. Second, the taxpayer must show that the law challenged involves a constitutional limitation on congressional taxing and spending, such as the Establishment Clause. Because the Establishment Clause prohibits government sponsorship or sanction of religion, it is a constitutional restriction on congressional taxing and spending for religious programs. The taxpayer/plaintiff must show that such a provision is involved in the lawsuit. If both these conditions are met, the plaintiffs have standing to sue. Obviously, if either one or both requirements are not met, the suit is dismissed from court.

The importance of this case lies in the determination that taxpayers who challenge government expenditures to aid church-related schools as a violation of the Establishment Clause have met both the conditions. The *Frothingham* rule was not eliminated; generally taxpayer suits are not yet allowed in federal courts. But an important exception to the rule was created. Virtually all of the parochial school cases after 1968 were taxpayer suits and could not have been brought if it were not for *Flast* v. *Cohen*. It was clearly a landmark case in church–state relationships.

Preserving but Not Expanding on a Precedent

Although the result of *Flast* is the point of this excursus from the narrative of this chapter, given its implication for challenges to government aid to church-related schools, one other standing case is worth mentioning. In 1949 Congress passed a law that enabled the government to dispose of its surplus property for the benefit of American society. Property that is no longer useful to the government can be given to public or private entities for their use. Under that law, in 1976 the government gave a seventy-seven-acre tract of property with several buildings on it to Valley Forge Christian College, which was owned and operated by the Assemblies of God. Because the government believed that it had gotten its money's worth from the property, it was given to the college free of charge.

Sometime after the transfer, some employees of Americans United for Separation of Church and State learned of the transaction through a news release. The organization and four individual employees filed suit in federal district court, asking that the transaction be voided and that the college give the property back to the government. Their claim was that they were federal taxpayers and, furthermore, as citizens they wanted the assurance that the Establishment Clause was not being violated. The Supreme Court dealt with the complaint in *Valley Forge Christian College* v. *Americans United for Separation of Church and State*.[20]

Justice William Rehnquist, writing for the Court, rejected the objection to the government giveaway by holding that the objectors did not have standing to bring suit. Even though *Flast* v. *Cohen* had held that federal taxpayers could challenge acts of Congress when the Establishment Clause was involved, it specified that the congressional acts had to be pursuant to the Taxing and Spending Clause of the Constitution, Article I, section 8. But the congressional act challenged in *Valley Forge* was under the authority of the Property Clause of the Constitution, Article IV, section 3, clause 2. Because their challenge did not meet the narrow requirement of *Flast*, those challenging the transfer of property did not have standing. The Court preserved the precedent of *Flast*, but did not go an inch beyond it.

Thus the window of opportunity for taxpayers to sue in federal court is a small one. The challenge must be specifically targeted at how Congress spends money, and it must show that the challenge is based on a constitutional limitation on the exercise of the congressional taxing and spending power. But by preserving that holding in *Flast*, the Court still left open the possibility of taxpayer challenges to government money being spent to aid church-related schools. As noted earlier, this made possible a number of cases involving that issue.

Many of the aid cases focus on specific kinds of aid provided to church-related schools. There are several cases involved. It is prudent and will be less tedious to not look at each case in detail, telling how it came to the Court or from where it came, but rather to simply describe the services the Court has permitted and those it has forbidden, with the case name in each instance.

First, however, it is important to notice that the Court, certainly in its post-*Everson* cases if not before, assumes that a church-related school is pervasively religious. Why does a church-related elementary or secondary school exist? It exists not just to teach secular subjects, for that service can be and is supplied by public schools. Its principal reason for existence is to teach religion, and to teach it from the perspective of the sponsoring church. It can do this by having worship in the school, by teaching courses that are exclusively religious in content, and by injecting religious content or themes into secular instruction. So the Supreme Court, as it has had to make decisions on a variety of efforts to supply government aid to church-related schools, has approached the enterprise with the assumption that the schools are principally religious in nature. One statement, from *Meek* v. *Pittenger*, will illustrate this view. Speaking of the aid program to "religion-pervasive institutions" involved in that case, the Court said:

> The very purpose of many of those schools is to provide an integrated secular and religious education; the teaching process is, to a large extent, devoted to the inculcation of religious values and belief. Substantial aid to the educational function of such schools, accordingly, necessarily results in aid to the sectarian school enterprise as a whole.[21]

PERMITTED GOVERNMENT AID

Lending Textbooks

It was noted earlier that the Court has approved of providing, by the expenditure of state funds, secular textbooks to the pupils in church-related schools (*Cochran* v. *Louisiana State Board of Education*). The "child benefit theory" was developed in that case and, indeed, made possible the Court's approval of the program. The provision of books was reaffirmed later in *Board of Education* v. *Allen*.[22] What makes *Allen* different from *Cochran* is that it was decided under the Establishment Clause rather than just the Fourteenth Amendment. Although it used "child benefit" language, it also held that the loan of textbooks law had a secular purpose under the Establishment Clause. *Allen* is important because it raised the loan of textbooks to parochial school students to a higher level of constitutional approval, finding such a program constitutional under the First Amendment. Subsequently, textbooks for parochial school students were approved in two other cases, *Meek*

v. *Pittenger*[23] and *Wolman* v. *Walter*.[24] We have also seen that the Court used child-benefit or public-welfare language in approving city-financed bus rides for children going to parochial schools (*Everson* v. *Board of Education*).

Standardized Testing, Diagnostic Services, and Therapy

Some states had authorized the administration of state-prepared standardized tests to students in parochial schools, as well as the grading of those tests, at public expense. The Court held such a program constitutional (*Wolman* v. *Walter* and *Committee for Public Education and Religious Liberty* v. *Regan*[25]). The reasoning was that state-prepared tests are for subjects routinely taught in public schools and thus contain no religious content. Consequently, the administration and grading of such tests at state expense would not put the state in the posture of aiding religion.

Similar reasoning was used to approve of diagnostic services for parochial school students. The program provided examinations of students to detect speech and hearing problems; the diagnosis was done by health professionals under contract to the board of public education and was performed in parochial school buildings. The Court ruled that in the process of diagnosis by doctors and nurses, no commentary or indoctrination about religion could take place at government expense, even though the services were in the parochial school. Diagnosis is religion-neutral (*Wolman* v. *Walter*).

Diagnosis may be religion-neutral, but therapy has the potential not to be. Conversation, perhaps even in-depth interaction, takes place during therapeutic services. There is the possibility that conversation, even exhortation, about religion could take place during sessions providing speech or hearing therapy, guidance counseling, or remedial services. That would be unconstitutional if the therapy were being done by government-paid therapists. However, the Court permitted such services to be provided to parochial school students by such therapists as long as the therapy occurred in a place other than the parochial school. That is, a neutral site minimized the possibility of religious indoctrination to the satisfaction of the Court (*Wolman* v. *Walter*). "It can hardly be said that the supervision of public employees performing public functions on public property creates an excessive entanglement between church and state."[26]

Standardized testing, diagnostic services and therapy, along with lending textbooks and bus transportation and aid to handicapped students, which I discuss below, are the sum total of what the Court to date has declared to be constitutional and permissible to provide to parochial schools at government expense. But these services do not represent the total of programs and services that various states have attempted to make available to parochial schools. Several states have made vigorous efforts to provide a wide variety of other forms of aid to church-related schools, efforts which have been rejected by the Court.

PROHIBITED SERVICES

The list of services prohibited begins with the "purchase of secular educational services." What this actually means is that the state paid parochial schools for the expenses they incurred teaching secular subjects. The state recognized that it could not pay for the teaching of religion, but surely it could "purchase" secular instruction. This involved the direct reimbursement of parochial schools for teachers' salaries, textbooks, and instructional materials. The Court declared such a program unconstitutional under the "excessive entanglement" test: the surveillance required by public officials to guarantee that the state money was used only for secular education in the parochial schools would create an impermissible level of interaction between religion and civil authority (*Lemon* v. *Kurtzman*[27]).

A program to pay salary supplements from public funds to teachers in parochial schools met the same fate for the same reason. Here, although the bulk of the teachers' salaries were paid by the church-related school, the law authorized supplementary payments from public funds to bring their salary levels up to minimum standards. The law specified that the teachers could teach only those subjects offered in public schools, that is, secular subjects. Furthermore, as a condition for getting the salary supplements, teachers had to promise, in writing, not to inject any religious content into their classroom presentations. But in spite of these safeguards against the state's paying for religious instruction, the Court ruled against the program. Although it assumed the honesty and integrity of the teachers, the Court noted that they were, after all, paid by and teaching in a church school. Furthermore, many of them were members of religious orders. Given that, it would still require regular and frequent surveillance by public officials to make sure that religion did not creep into their teaching. Such surveillance was impermissible entanglement (*Lemon* v. *Kurtzman*).

New York State initiated a program to give parochial schools money to maintain and repair buildings. Under the theory that the state has an interest in the health, safety, and welfare of students in parochial as well as in public schools, the program provided money for janitorial services, provision of heat and light, necessary upkeep and renovation of buildings, and a variety of other such services. Even though this kind of program has a kind of child-benefit sound to it, the Supreme Court declared it unconstitutional (*Committee for Public Education and Religious Liberty* v. *Nyquist*[28]). The problem was that the money was not confined to the upkeep of buildings or rooms used only for secular purposes; it could be used for the school chapel as well as the gymnasium, for example. Given that lack of restriction, the Court ruled that the law had the primary effect of advancing religion with state money. "If the State may not erect buildings in which religious activities are to take place, it may not maintain such buildings or renovate them when they fall into disrepair."[29]

The funding of teacher-prepared examinations in parochial schools was also declared unconstitutional. Unlike state-prepared standardized tests, which were devoid of religious content, the content of teacher-prepared tests could not be controlled by the state. Because such tests might have religious content, to provide state money to underwrite their preparation had the primary effect of advancing religion (*Levitt* v. *Committee for Public Education and Religious Liberty*[30]).

Some states tried to aid parochial schools by supplying them with instructional materials and equipment at state expense. This material consisted of such materials as maps, globes, and film projectors. The Court held such a program to be unconstitutional because it had the primary effect of advancing religion. Because religious instruction is so intertwined with secular instruction in the church-related schools, the Court argued, it simply is not possible to believe that the equipment can be used for secular purposes only. "Even though earmarked for secular purposes, 'when it flows to an institution in which religion is so pervasive that a substantial portion of its functions are subsumed in the religious mission,' state aid has the impermissible primary effect of advancing religion."[31] This form of aid was denied parochial schools in both *Meek* v. *Pittenger* and *Wolman* v. *Walter*.

When services such as guidance counseling, speech and hearing assistance, and remedial and accelerated instruction were offered to parochial school students *on the premises*, the program was unconstitutional. Although the service providers were public employees, the fact that they rendered their services in the parochial schools at least raised the possibility that some religious instruction would take place. It would require continuing surveillance to make sure that their services remained entirely secular. That surveillance would foster excessive entanglement between government and religion, a violation of the Establishment Clause (*Meek* v. *Pittenger*).

For reasons similar to those marshaled against the loan of instructional equipment to parochial schools, the Court refused to approve instructional field trips. Although the statute at issue in the case specified that public money could be used to finance only those field trips comparable to those taken by public school students, the Court noted that such trips are still led by parochial school teachers. The teachers determine the timing of the trips, that is, how they fit with the curriculum being presented in the parochial schools, and they would be the persons who interpret the site to the students. Such trips are an integral part of the educational experience. When the educational experience is pervaded with religious themes, it is likely that the field trips are not immune from that. Consequently, the Court ruled, publicly funded field trips by church-related schools have the primary effect of advancing religion (*Wolman* v. *Walter*).

The Court has also considered programs in which public school teachers actually come to parochial schools to teach supplementary and enrichment courses or even traditional academic courses to educationally deprived children. In one case, *Grand Rapids School District* v. *Ball*,[32] some of the state-paid teachers came to the church schools to teach art, music, physical education, reading, and mathematics during the regular school day. Other teachers came after the school day to teach such things as arts and crafts, yearbook production, chess, and nature appreciation. Most of these latter teachers were parochial school teachers who were hired by the city to teach these after-school classes. The Court held that this program had the primary effect of advancing religion. State-paid teachers, many of whom were identified by their students as being their parochial school teachers, teaching in the context of the church school might indoctrinate students in religion or, at the least, symbolize state support for religion.

In another case, *Aguilar* v. *Felton*,[33] the teachers were actual public school teachers hired with money supplied by the federal government to come to the parochial schools to teach traditional subjects to educationally deprived, low-income students. The teachers were instructed not to teach religion. The Court ruled that it would take supervision to guarantee that they, in fact, did not teach religion and that supervision would create impermissibly excessive entanglement between church and state. Public school or state-paid teachers may not teach in the context of the parochial school.

States and, occasionally, the federal government have been creative in trying to find ways to provide specific programs to aid church-related schools. The Supreme Court, using particularly the primary effect and excessive entanglement tests to interpret the Establishment Clause, has taken a fairly hard line against such efforts. Although not all forms of aid through services to parochial elementary and secondary schools are unconstitutional, most are.

TUITION TAX CREDIT PLANS

In addition to trying to provide specific services to church-related schools, some states have tried to create a general funding program for them. The Court dealt with one such attempt in *Committee for Public Education and Religious Liberty* v. *Nyquist*,[34] a case about tuition supplements and tax credits. The first part of the plan tried to help low-income parents send their children to parochial schools. If a parent had an annual taxable income of $5,000 or below, for New York State income-tax purposes, the state would reimburse the family $50 for each grade school child and $100 for each high school child who attended a parochial school.[35] The program was designed to be a supplement: the grants could not exceed 50 percent of the actual amount the family paid in parochial school tuition. The second part of the plan was for those whose taxable income was over $5,000. Parents whose income was between $5,000 and $9,000 could subtract from their adjusted gross income on the state income-tax form $1,000 for each dependent up to three who was enrolled in parochial school. For those whose taxable income was above $9,000, the amount of the deduction per child decreased on a sliding scale until there was no deduction at all for families with a taxable income of $25,000 or more. The design of the plan was a variation on the child-benefit theme, a kind of a "parent benefit" concept in which the parents of children in parochial schools received either a payment from the state or a tax credit, depending on their income. Neither the church school nor the church sponsoring the school received money directly from the state. (In fact, the parents did not even have to use the money to pay parochial school tuition. They could do anything they wanted to with the money. But the fact that they had a child or children in church-related school triggered their receipt of the supplement or tax credit.)

In spite of the apparent insulation from any state money going directly to the church schools, Justice Lewis Powell, writing for the Court, found the program unconstitutional. The program had the primary effect of aiding religion in that the plans provided a state incentive for parents to send their children to parochial schools.

> The qualifying parent under either program receives the same form of encouragement and reward for sending his children to nonpublic schools. The only difference is that one parent receives an actual cash payment while the other is allowed to reduce by an arbitrary amount the sum he would otherwise be obliged to pay over to the State. We see no answer to Judge Hays' dissenting statement below that "[i]n both instances the money involved represents a charge made upon the state for the purpose of religious education." . . . Special tax benefits . . . cannot be squared with the principle of neutrality established by the decisions of this Court. To the contrary, insofar as such benefits render assistance to parents who send their children to sectarian schools, their purpose and inevitable effect are to aid and advance those religious institutions.[36]

It should be noted here, at the end of this long series of rejections of attempts to supply state aid to parochial schools, that the Court did not intend to show hostility to the schools. In fact, it now and again remarked with appreciation that the church-related schools make a significant contribution to America. But the Court is responsible for interpreting the Establishment Clause, which prohibits state sponsorship and sanction of religion. More often than not, state efforts to aid the schools have fallen on the forbidden side of the line of permissibility. That the Court has enforced that prohibition should not be interpreted as animus toward church-sponsored education. The two sides of this are illustrated by this passage from *Lemon* v. *Kurtzman*:

> Finally, nothing we have said can be construed to disparage the role of church-related elementary and secondary schools in our national life. Their contribution has been and is enormous. Nor do we ignore their economic plight in a period of rising costs and expanding need. Taxpayers generally have been spared vast sums by the maintenance of these educational institutions by religious organizations, largely by gifts of faithful adherents.
>
> The merit and benefits of these schools, however, are not the issue before us in these cases. The sole question is whether state aid to these schools can be squared with the dictates of the Religion Clauses. Under our system the choice has been made that government is to be entirely excluded from the area of religious instruction and churches excluded from the affairs of government.[37]

A decade later the Court considered a similar tax credit plan in *Mueller* v. *Allen*.[38] There was one principal difference from the plan struck down in *Nyquist*. In *Mueller* the tax deduction from Minnesota income tax was available to all parents who had children in school, be it parochial, private, *or public*. The deduction was to cover the expenses incurred in paying for tuition, textbooks, and transportation. The deduction could not exceed $500 per child in grades kindergarten through six and $700 in grades seven through twelve. The factual difference from *Nyquist* made the result different. Justice William Rehnquist, writing for the majority, said the fact that the tax deductions were available to the parents of all schoolchildren negated or avoided all church–state problems. The law creating the tax deduction has a secular purpose, namely, undergirding the creation of a well-educated citizenry. It does not have the primary effect of advancing or inhibiting religion, since the money is not aimed only at the parents of parochial school pupils. (This decision thus left *Nyquist* intact; it is still unconstitutional to have a tax law that benefits only parochial school parents.) It does not create excessive entanglement between church and state, because the decision to access the tax credit is a decision made only by the parent without any interaction with a state official.

Many believed that, after *Mueller*, many states and perhaps even the federal government might pass legislation that would provide aid to parochial school parents by provisions in the income-tax codes which would allow all parents with children in school, of whatever kind, to make a deduction. So far, that has not happened, perhaps because in difficult economic times most governments are not willing to deprive themselves of the revenue they would lose by the tax deductions. It may also be that many legislators were convinced by the vigorous dissent written by Justice Thurgood Marshall and joined by three others. Marshall argued that the idea that had bamboozled the majority, that is, that all parents were helped by this "evenhanded" tax deduction, is a fiction. The deduction is not evenhanded, he argued, because only under the most unusual circumstances do public schools charge any tuition or fees for their books. Only those parents who send their children to private or parochial schools are anything beyond minimal beneficiaries of the plan. Whatever its neutral qualities on the surface, the program was designed to provide incentives for, or to aid, parents who send their children to sectarian schools.

Aid to the Handicapped

If *Mueller* did not result in expansive plans for tax deductions for parochial schools in other states or in federal law, it did provide the basis for two other cases, in which state aid flowed to handicapped persons in parochial schools. Washington State had a statute that provided aid to the visually impaired in the form of financial assistance for vocational training. The purpose of the law was to assist persons with sight disabilities to be productively employed and to contribute to society. Larry Witters enrolled in a private Christian college with the goal of becoming a pastor, missionary, or youth minister. When he applied for state funds authorized under the law, he was denied on the ground that this use of state funds in a clearly theological educational program was improper. When he sued to obtain the funds, the Washington Supreme Court ruled that the state had properly denied him the money; using state money to support religious education violated the Establishment Clause. The United States Supreme Court reversed that decision in 1986, however, in *Witters* v. *Washington Department of Services for the Blind.*[39]

In a decision written by Justice Thurgood Marshall, the Court ruled that it was permissible for Witters to receive government money. The program for vocational assistance to the blind clearly had a secular purpose, which was the attempt to make those persons productive members of society. On the question of whether Witters's use of the money for ministerial training had the primary effect of advancing religion, the Court said it did not. The fact that state money went to a theological school was because of the choice of the recipient, not because of any decision of the state. The state money went to students because of their circumstance in life, that is, their blindness. If a recipient used it for ministerial training, it was not the state's doing. Furthermore, Witters's use of the money seemed to be an isolated incident; there was no evidence that there would be widespread use of state funds under this program for ministerial education. "[The program] is in no way skewed toward religion. . . . It creates no financial incentive for students to undertake sectarian education."[40] Consequently,

> On the facts we have set out, it does not seem appropriate to view any aid
> ultimately flowing to the Inland Empire School of the Bible as resulting

from a *state* action sponsoring or subsidizing religion. Nor does the mere
circumstance that [Witters] has chosen to use neutrally available state aid
to help pay for his religious education confer any message of state endorsement of religion.[41]

(In his opinion, Justice Marshall did not refer to *Mueller* v. *Allen*, since he
had written a vigorous dissent against it. But three other justices, in concurring opinions, specifically called attention to the fact that *Witters* followed
the reasoning of *Mueller*.)

Near the end of the Court's term in 1993, it handed down *Zobrest* v.
Catalina Foothills School District.[42] Here the issue was whether a state could
pay for a sign-language interpreter for a deaf student enrolled in a parochial
high school. The federal Individuals with Disabilities Education Act (IDEA)
provided money to be administered by states for the education of disabled
persons. James Zobrest, deaf from birth, had gone to a public middle school
in Arizona, and the state, using federal IDEA funds, had paid for a sign-
language interpreter for him. When he reached high school age, James's
parents enrolled him in a Roman Catholic school and requested that the
state continue to provide the interpreter. The state refused, on the ground
that in the parochial school environment a state subsidy for the interpreter
would violate the Establishment Clause. The Zobrest family sued and the
Supreme Court ruled in their favor, Chief Justice William Rehnquist for the
majority.

The Court relied on *Mueller* v. *Allen* and *Witters* v. *Washington Department
of Services for the Blind* as precedents. In each of those cases, state benefits (tax
deduction or vocational training) were made available to all eligible recipients, whether they utilized parochial or state educational institutions. Furthermore, the decision to use church-related schools was made by the
recipients, not by the state. The same thing was true here. IDEA was designed to facilitate education of disabled persons, regardless of where they
chose to receive that education. In this case, by allowing the parents to select
a school of their choice, the provision of a sign interpreter could not be
attributed to a decision by the state; it was the result of the private decision
of individual parents with no prior incentive from the state. The Court
concluded:

> When the government offers a neutral service on the premises of a sectar-
> ian school as part of a general program that "is in no way skewed toward
> religion," it follows under our prior decisions that provision of that service
> does not offend the Establishment Clause.[43]

There is a definite "child benefit theory" flavor in *Witters* and *Zobrest*
reminiscent of much earlier cases: *Cochran* v. *Louisiana State Board of Education* and *Everson* v. *Board of Education*. It has been a fairly consistent theme of
the Court in aid-to-parochial-school cases that if the aid flows directly to the

student rather than directly or indirectly to the school, the Establishment Clause is not violated.

GOVERNMENT AID TO
CHURCH-RELATED UNIVERSITIES

All the attempts to provide government aid to parochial schools discussed so far involve elementary and secondary schools. When the Court has pondered the question of government assistance to church-related universities, its position has been very different from its attitude about aid to lower-level schools. The best way to explain this is to look at *Tilton* v. *Richardson*,[44] a case involving various forms of federal aid to church-related universities. Title I of the Higher Education Facilities Act of 1963 authorized the federal government to provide money to colleges to construct buildings, provided that neither religious instruction nor worship was to take place there. However, there was a provision in the law to the effect that after twenty years, when the government had gotten its money's worth, the government-financed building could be used for any purpose, even a religious purpose. When some church-related colleges in Connecticut received some money to build and improve buildings on their campuses, a taxpayer suit was filed.

The Supreme Court, with Chief Justice Burger writing for the majority, found this law to be constitutional for the most part. The Act had a secular purpose, in that it aimed to help improve the quality of higher education in America. It did not have the primary effect of advancing or inhibiting religion, because the buildings were to be secular buildings (no college chapels), used for secular purposes only. At that point the Court did declare the twenty-year reversion clause of the law to be unconstitutional. At no time in its existence could a government-financed building be used for religious activities or purposes. But to strike down that provision of the law did not nullify it entirely.

When it came to the excessive entanglement test, Chief Justice Burger articulated the heart of the case. Challengers to the law argued that even if the buildings were supposed to be used for secular purposes, it would take continual surveillance to assure that they were used for such purposes. That would create impermissible excessive entanglement. The Court disagreed. Continual surveillance would not be required because of the nature of a college as compared with an elementary or secondary school. Unlike the latter, a church-related college is not pervasively religious. An indicator of this is that courses are usually taught, not for the purpose of initiating or nurturing faith, but for stimulating inquiry, seeking to draw forth critical responses from students. This is true even in courses about religion. Both students and faculty enjoy the academic freedom that is characteristic of probing inquiry. Furthermore, college students are older and less impressionable than younger students. For all these reasons, the Court determined, it is not necessary to investigate colleges to determine if they are improperly using the government-funded buildings. Thus, impermissible entanglement between church and state will not be a problem. Because of the nature of colleges, courts are able to deal with them differently than with lower-level parochial schools.

The Supreme Court took the same approach in two other cases. It upheld a law by which South Carolina had made it possible for church-related colleges to borrow money at a lower rate of interest through purchase of state-issued bonds (*Hunt* v. *McNair*[45]). The Court held that by simply issuing bonds at an interest rate lower than commercial and allowing church-related colleges to buy them, the state had no significant involvement with church-related colleges and did not advance or entangle itself with religion. This was particularly true since the colleges were not pervasively religious, as it had described in *Tilton*.

Similarly, the Court upheld a Maryland program that was broader and more beneficial to church-related universities than *Tilton*. Whereas the government money in that case was available only for building construction, there were virtually no restrictions on it in the Maryland program. The only restrictions the statute imposed on a school were that it could not offer only theological degrees (so seminaries were excluded), and it had to promise not to utilize the funds for sectarian purposes. Outside those two prohibitions, the church-related colleges could use the state funds for any purpose they wanted. The Court still found the law constitutional, in *Roemer* v. *Board of Public Works of Maryland*.[46] The law had a secular purpose in that it sought to contribute to an educated population; it did not advance or hinder religion because of the character of colleges described in *Tilton*; and it did not suffer from entanglement because the inspections required to see if the schools had kept their promises would be infrequent and brief, rather like those for reaccreditation.

It is clear that the Court has adopted a different standard for church-related colleges than for parochial elementary and secondary schools. That different standard derives primarily from the character of the students. College students are older and less impressionable than elementary and secondary school students, who, being younger, are more impressionable in reference to authority figures. In addition, the nature of the teaching at the college level makes a difference. It is more objective and fostering of critical thinking, while at the lower levels there is more faith nurturing and pervasively religious teaching. Consequently, whereas the Court has been relatively unbending in not allowing government aid to lower-level church-related schools, under the Establishment Clause, it has been rather free in approving such programs at the university level.

7

Religion in Public Schools

At the beginning of chapter 6 I noted that as public schools developed in this country, the role that religion should play in them became a subject of debate. Historian Sidney E. Mead has argued that the public schools have functioned as the established church of America.[1] Mead notes that the traditional role of an established church is to provide the civic ideology of a culture, or at least a major portion of it. In the history of Western culture, the Catholic Church and, later, the various Protestant churches in the countries where they were established articulated the moral basis for national life, for citizenship. That is the principal role of the established religious body in any culture in which there is an establishment.

But when America separated church and state by means of the First Amendment, the question arose as to who or what would supply this civic ideology. For most Americans, the public schools were the answer. The schools would instill in children, native-born and immigrant alike, the ideas of Americanism: democracy, capitalism, fair play, and respect for freedom. Sectarian religion in the public schools, as I noted earlier, became a kind of "lowest common denominator Protestantism." With the increasing pluralism of society because of immigration, the development of new religions, and, coincidentally and somewhat paradoxically, the growing secularization of the American psyche, in this century the public schools became less and less obviously religious. Even the "lowest common denominator Protestantism" has diminished. But there has been a sense of nostalgia among some for a greater presence of sectarian (or at least nondenominational Judeo-Christian) religion in the public schools. Probably, without using the terminology, some have picked up on Mead's idea of the public schools as the nation's established church, but have wished that it could be more specifically religious than it has been. There have been attempts to introduce a more overtly religious presence in the public schools, either through the teaching of religious ideas or by means of prayer and Bible reading as a required part of each school day. Many believe that only by having religion so present can the public schools fulfill their necessary role of instilling civic virtue in young American citizens. Consequently, the Supreme Court has been confronted with a variety of cases in which it has had to measure this desire for religion in the public schools against the limitations imposed by the Establishment Clause.

RELEASED TIME

Instruction inside the School Building

McCollum v. *Board of Education*[2] in 1948 presented the question of the constitutionality of "released time" as a method of teaching religion in public schools. The school board of Champaign, Illinois, invited a group of clergy to teach classes on religion in its public school buildings to students in grades four through nine. Classes were held weekly, thirty minutes for the lower grades, forty-five minutes for the higher. Students were required to have parental permission to attend the religious instruction. The classes were taught by ministers from various Protestant groups, Roman Catholic priests, and Jewish rabbis. Participating students could choose which denominational instruction to attend. Those students who did not participate were not excused from school attendance, but were required to go to some other place in the school building. During this time they were not given any academic instruction, because that would put them ahead, in their regular schoolwork, of those who attended the religion classes. One assumes they spent their time in study hall. Attendance was recorded in religious classes and reported to their regular teachers, as was that of the nonparticipants.

Mrs. Vashti McCollum, an atheist and the mother of a student in the school system, contended that the program was a violation of the Establishment Clause. The Supreme Court agreed, in an opinion written by Justice Hugo Black. There were two closely related problems with the program. First, the enterprise was unconstitutional because the religion classes were taught in rooms in a tax-supported building. Second, because students were required by truancy laws to be in school and attendance was monitored to make sure children were either in the religious classes or in study hall, the program provided what amounted to a captive audience for the clergy. The essence of the opinion is contained in the following passage:

> Pupils compelled by law to go to school for secular education are released in part from their legal duty upon the condition that they attend the religious classes. This is beyond all question a utilization of the tax-established and tax-supported public school system to aid religious groups to spread their faith. . . . Here not only are the State's tax-supported public school buildings used for the dissemination of religious doctrines. The State also affords sectarian groups an invaluable aid in that it helps to provide pupils for their religious classes through use of the State's com-

pulsory public school machinery. This is not separation of Church and State.[3]

Instruction outside the School Building

The issue of released time was not laid to rest by *McCollum*, however. In 1952 the Court decided *Zorach* v. *Clauson*.[4] The facts of the case were virtually the same as in *McCollum*. Classes were taught by clergy, parental permission was required, roll was taken, nonparticipants had to remain at school biding their time during the time of religious instruction. The *only* difference was that in *Zorach* the classes were not held in school buildings, but at locations away from the public school. For the majority, that made all the difference.

The opinion was written by Justice William O. Douglas, usually a strict separationist who in this case deviated from his normal views. Obviously no tax-supported buildings were involved in this program of religious instruction. That eliminated one factor that was a fatal flaw in *McCollum*. As to the contention that released time programs gave a captive audience to religious teachers, Justice Douglas disagreed. All the schools had done here was adjust their schedules to accommodate the desires of those who wanted to attend religious instruction. He agreed that the First Amendment commands that church and state should be separated, but, he noted, that does not mean that the state should be the adversary of religion; the amendment does not say that the separation should be absolute. Religion has had an integral part to play in American history, and this may be acknowledged in the interaction between religion and the public schools. So long as the public schools do not promote or sponsor religion but merely cooperate with it, as they did in this program, there is no problem. Justice Douglas brought these themes together in a *dictum* that is a rather eloquent statement of accommodationism, one that has been referred to frequently by accommodationists in subsequent years.

We are a religious people whose institutions presuppose a Supreme Being. We guarantee the freedom to worship as one chooses. We make room for as wide a variety of beliefs and creeds as the spiritual needs of man deem necessary. We sponsor an attitude on the part of government that shows no partiality to any one group and that lets each flourish according to the zeal of its adherents and the appeal of its dogma. When the state encourages religious instruction or cooperates with religious authorities by adjusting the schedule of public events to sectarian needs, it follows the best of our traditions. For it then respects the religious nature of our people and accommodates the public service to their spiritual needs. To hold that it may not would be to find in the Constitution a requirement that the government show a callous indifference to religious groups. That would be preferring those who believe in no religion over those who do believe. . . . But we find no constitutional requirement which makes it necessary for government to be hostile to religion and to throw its weight against efforts to widen the effective scope of religious influence. The government must be neutral when it comes to competition between sects. It may not thrust any sect on any person. It may not make religious observance compulsory. It may not coerce anyone to attend church, to observe a religious holiday, or to take religious instruction. But it can close its doors or suspend its operations as to those who want to repair to their religious sanctuary for worship or instruction. No more than that is undertaken here.[5]

The three dissents in this case are worth noting. They argued that this program still delivered a captive audience to religion teachers through the mechanism of the public school. The schools were, after all, still in session during the religious instruction and the students had to choose between going to religion classes and staying in school in study hall, cleaning erasers, or doing whatever nonacademic activity the teachers could concoct to keep them busy. The dissenters said that the schools should simply close one afternoon a week and let the students go free. It would be interesting to see how many went to religion classes in that circumstance. The fact that they either had to go to religion classes or stay in school was a stimulus for them to take religious instruction. That is unconstitutionally using the power of the state to aid religion, in the view of the dissenters. Two of the dissenters left some *dicta* worth thinking about. At the conclusion of his opinion, Justice Felix Frankfurter wrote:

The unwillingness of the promoters of this movement to dispense with such use of the public schools betrays a surprising want of confidence in the inherent power of the various faiths to draw children to outside sectarian classes—an attitude that hardly reflects the faith of the greatest religious spirits.[6]

Justice Robert Jackson wrote:

It is possible to hold a faith with enough confidence to believe that what should be rendered to God does not need to be decided and collected by Caesar.
    The day that this country ceases to be free for irreligion it will cease to be free for religion—except for the sect that can win political power. . . . We start down a rough road when we begin to mix compulsory public education with compulsory godliness.[7]

Justice Jackson had such contempt for the majority opinion that he concluded his dissent with the parting shot that the opinion would be more interesting to students of psychology than to students of constitutional law.
    The result from *McCollum* and *Zorach* is that a community may provide

religious instruction for public school students, during the school day on a released-time basis, so long as it is not done in the public school building. If such instruction is done off campus, even in a church, synagogue, or other ecclesiastical structure, it is acceptable under the law. There is nothing in these cases that would prevent the classes from being taught by clergy.

PRAYER AND TEACHING RELIGION

In the 1960s the Court was presented with a matter that became, and continues to be, one of the most volatile, emotion-laden issues of the last thirty years—prayer in the public schools. Probably no church–state issue has produced more heated debate and misunderstanding than this one.

Required Classroom Prayer

The issue first came to the Supreme Court in 1962 in *Engel* v. *Vitale*,[8] a case that involved a state-written prayer. Acting under authorization from the state legislature, the Board of Education of New Hyde Park, New York, adopted a prayer written by the State Board of Regents, which had supervisory power over the state's public schools. Apparently concerned about a perceived decline in morality among schoolchildren, the Regents had initiated a program of moral and spiritual training in the schools. The prayer they had written was part of that program. Mindful of the religious pluralism in the state, the Regents had tried to make the prayer nonsectarian and general enough so as not to offend any denomination or religious person. The prayer was: "Almighty God, we acknowledge our dependence upon Thee, and we beg Thy blessings upon us, our parents, our teachers and our Country." (One commentator called it a "To whom it may concern" prayer.) Not only was the prayer written by state education officials, but its recitation was required at the beginning of each school day in the New Hyde Park school district. Students could be excused from the prayer with a written request from their parents.

The parents of ten students enrolled in the schools filed suit in a state court, claiming that this required prayer was contrary to the religious beliefs and practices of themselves and their children. More importantly, they argued that a prayer written by state officials and said at the beginning of each school day as required by law was a violation of the Establishment Clause. Hardly anything could be a clearer example of state sponsorship than this.

The Supreme Court agreed with the plaintiffs' contention. Justice Hugo Black wrote the Court's opinion, which is short and to the point. It was clear that the state and the school district had violated the Establishment Clause by writing the prayer and imposing it on the schoolchildren and their teachers. The fact that it was nondenominational and could be avoided by children with parental excuses did not make any difference. The Establishment Clause is violated with the passage of a law authorizing such a prayer, even if there should be no compulsion to say the prayer. As is frequently the case, there are some quotable and memorable *dicta* in this opinion.

> [W]e think that the constitutional prohibition against laws respecting an establishment of religion must at least mean that in this country it is no part of the business of government to compose official prayers for any group of the American people to recite as a part of a religious program carried on by government.[9]

What is the Establishment Clause for? Why should the Court, and Americans, be so diligent in strictly maintaining the separation of church and state for which it calls?

> Its first and most immediate purpose rested on the belief that a union of government and religion tends to destroy government and to degrade religion. . . . The Establishment Clause thus stands as an expression of principle on the part of the Founders of our Constitution that religion is too personal, too sacred, too holy, to permit its "unhallowed perversion" by a civil magistrate. Another purpose of the Establishment Clause rested upon an awareness of the historical fact that governmentally established religions and religious persecutions go hand in hand.[10]

Apparently the counsel for the Board of Education had argued either in briefs, at oral argument, or both, that to declare the Regents' prayer unconstitutional would mean that the Court was hostile to religion and prayer. Justice Black vociferously stated that such a contention was not true in fact and was not the attitude of the Court. Its decision striking down the state-written required prayer should not be construed as antireligious. The Establishment Clause demands that the state should stay out of the religious lives of Americans. That is not hostility to religion; it actually shows great respect for it.

> It is neither sacrilegious nor anti-religious to say that each separate government in this country should stay out of the business of writing or sanctioning official prayers and leave that purely religious function to the people themselves and to those the people choose to look to for religious guidance.[11]

In spite of this disclaimer, *Engel* v. *Vitale* provoked strong reactions across America—most of them negative. There was considerable demagoguery in Congress. Statements were released by many religious groups and by religious leaders speaking for themselves. Some were positive, but most opposed the decision. Representative of many reactions to this case, and many other separationist decisions since then, was this by the Rev. Billy Graham: "This is another step toward the secularization of the United States. . . . The framers of our Constitution meant we were to have freedom of religion, not freedom from religion."[12]

In spite of the criticism heaped on the Court (or perhaps because of it), in the very next year it agreed to hear another school prayer case. *Engel* had been a narrow decision, involving only state-written prayers. The new case, *Abington Township School District* v. *Schempp*,[13] had a much broader scope: required prayer, including the Lord's Prayer, and Bible reading in public school classrooms.

Schempp was the combination of two cases, one from Maryland and one from Pennsylvania. The Maryland case was brought to the Court by Madalyn Murray (later O'Hair) on behalf of her son, who was enrolled in a public school. The law in Maryland mandated that in the public schools in the state, each day had to begin with the "reading, without comment, of a chapter in the Holy Bible and/or the use of the Lord's Prayer."[14] Mrs. Murray, an outspoken atheist, sued the school board in Baltimore, claiming that the requirement interfered with her and her son's First Amendment rights because it preferred religious belief over nonbelief.

The law in Pennsylvania was similar to that in Maryland. It required that the school day in every public school begin with the reading of ten verses from the Bible, without commentary. The case evidence also indicated that the Bible reading was routinely followed by a recitation of the Lord's Prayer. Mr. and Mrs. Edward Schempp, who had three children enrolled in public schools, filed suit, claiming that the religious exercises were a violation of the Establishment Clause. The Schempps were a religious family; they regularly attended worship at their local Unitarian church.[15] So their suit was motivated not by hostility to religion but rather by a concern for constitutional values and a belief that mandated religious practice tended to trivialize religion. The Supreme Court combined these two cases under one title.

The Court, in an opinion written by Justice Tom Clark, declared the religious exercises to be unconstitutional. The two states argued that the required Bible readings and prayers were not intended to be religious but rather were a way to promote moral values, combat the materialistic tendencies of our times, perpetuate American institutions, and teach literature. The states claimed that these were secular reasons for having the requirement. The Court responded that they had chosen religious means to accomplish their alleged secular purposes, which the Establishment Clause will not permit. The fact that the laws specified that the Bible be read "without comment" showed that the legislators knew that the Bible is quintessentially religious literature and they wanted to avoid sectarian interpretation. Furthermore, as Justice William Brennan wrote in a concurring opinion, the secular objectives the state sought to accomplish could just as easily have been accomplished with secular literature, for example, readings from major documents in American history. But the school board chose only religious literature and prayer, obviously a religious expression. The state's choice of these obviously religious documents/practices to the exclusion of all others belied its profession of secular goals.

The fact that students could be excused with parental permission did not minimize the Establishment Clause violation. The clause was violated by the passage of the law mandating religious exercise in the public schools; it was not necessary that coercion be shown for a violation to take place. That is, the violation occurred with the enactment of the legislation requiring the religious exercises; that students could absent themselves was irrelevant to this exercise of state power.

As noted in chapter 6, in reaching its decision the Court articulated two tests for interpreting the Establishment Clause. In order for a law to be considered constitutional under the clause, it must have (1) a secular purpose and (2) a primary effect that neither advances nor hinders religion. The first test has to do with the intention of the legislative body. The second test has to do with the implementation or enforcement of the law. A law or program must conform to both tests to be constitutional. If it fails either one, it is unconstitutional.

The prayer laws at issue in this case failed both tests. Because only religious readings and prayers were required, it was clear that the legislatures' purpose in passing the laws was religious, not secular: they wanted to instill religion in the public school students of their states. Furthermore, the laws had the primary effect of advancing religion. They were clearly religious or devotional exercises; to require them by law advanced religion by state authority. Thus the prayer and Bible reading laws were unconstitutional.

It is important to analyze this decision carefully, because there has been so much demagoguery, misunderstanding, and silliness said about it since it was announced. The Supreme Court never said, in either *Engel* or *Schempp*, that young people or their teachers cannot pray in the public school context. It struck down only devotional exercise mandated by state law. The Constitution forbids a "law respecting an establishment of religion," and any law that *requires* public school students or teachers to engage in religious exercise, whether or not they agree with it, is unconstitutional. But if students or teachers want to pray silently and individually, they have perfect freedom to do so. If a student wants to pray before or during a math exam, he or she may do so. Nothing in the Constitution or the Supreme Court's opinions prohibits it. The prayer should not be disruptive of the educational process. The student cannot pray loudly during the math test, but that is a matter of school discipline and decorum, not of constitutional law. Teachers may not lead students in prayer, or even pray audibly before them, because they are authority figures and symbolize the public schools. But if teachers want to pray in the faculty lounge or silently even in the classroom while the students are studying, that is acceptable. It is absolutely incorrect to say that the

Supreme Court "took God out of the classroom" or banned prayer from the public schools, as some journalists and more politicians have proclaimed.

Especially after the negative outcry across the country following *Engel*, the Court was very conscious that there would be critical reaction to *Schempp* as well. Apparently the counsel for the respective school boards in the case argued that if the Court found against the required prayers, it would be "establishing a religion of secularism." The Court responded to that argument by denying it and spelling out a positive role for religion in public schools.

> It is insisted that unless these religious exercises are permitted a "religion of secularism" is established in the schools. We agree of course that the State may not establish a "religion of secularism" in the sense of affirmatively opposing or showing hostility to religion, thus "preferring those who believe in no religion over those who do believe." We do not agree, however, that this decision in any sense has that effect. In addition, it might well be said that one's education is not complete without a study of comparative religion or the history of religion and its relationship to the advancement of civilization. It certainly may be said that the Bible is worthy of study for its literary and historic qualities. Nothing we have said here indicates that such study of the Bible or of religion, when presented objectively as part of a secular program of education, may not be effected consistently with the First Amendment.[16]

The Court explicitly endorsed the teaching of religion as an academic study within the public schools![17] Even though the majority of the media and the public did not notice this dimension of the opinion, the Court clearly showed that it was not hostile to religion. It offered the opportunity for the schools to help their students understand more about religion. Although it did not mention it, the Court in *Schempp* implicitly endorsed the statement by Justice Robert Jackson in his concurring opinion in *McCollum* v. *Board of Education*.

> . . . I think it remains to be demonstrated whether it is possible, even if desirable, to comply with such demands as [McCollum's] completely to isolate and cast out of secular education all that some people may reasonably regard as religious instruction. Perhaps subjects such as mathematics, physics or chemistry are, or can be, completely secularized. But it would not seem practical to teach either practice or appreciation of the arts if we are to forbid exposure of youth to any religious influences. Music without sacred music, architecture minus the cathedral, or painting without the scriptural themes would be eccentric and incomplete, even from a secular point of view. Yet the inspirational appeal of religion in these guises is often stronger than in forthright sermon. Even such a "science" as biology raises the issue between evolution and creation as an explanation of our presence on this planet. Certainly a course in English literature that omit-

ted the Bible and other powerful uses of our mother tongue for religious ends would seem pretty barren. And I should suppose it is a proper, if not an indispensable, part of preparation for a worldly life to know the roles that religion and religions have played in the tragic story of mankind. The fact is that, for good or for ill, nearly everything in our culture worth transmitting, everything which gives meaning to life, is saturated with religious influences, derived from paganism, Judaism, Christianity—both Catholic and Protestant—and other faiths accepted by a large part of the world's peoples. *One can hardly respect a system of education that would leave the student wholly ignorant of the currents of religious thought that move the world society for a part in which he is being prepared.*[18]

Fifteen years after this was written, the Court said "Amen" to its sentiment in *Schempp*. Instruction in religion is an integral part of the educational process, and in calling attention to that, the Court showed that it was not hostile to religion in its school prayer decision.

As the Court anticipated, there was great negative reaction to its opinion. To cite one example, by May of 1964 more than 145 proposed constitutional amendments had been submitted in the United States House of Representatives for the purpose of reversing *Schempp*.[19] That kind of legislative initiative has occurred in spurts to the present day, usually around election time. Some centrist-to-liberal denominations, however, began to understand that the decision was very narrow (prohibiting only state-required religious exercises) and not hostile to religion, and began to express approval of it. (Representatives of the following churches testified against a constitutional amendment mandating school prayer in the late 1960s: American Baptist, American Lutheran, Christian Church (Disciples of Christ), Episcopal, Greek Orthodox, Lutheran Church–Missouri Synod, United Church of Christ, United Methodist, and United Presbyterian.) Nonetheless, on the issue of school prayer and Bible reading there has been an emotional and political tug-of-war ever since.

A Moment of Silence in Schools

In 1985 the controversy was intensified by the Court's decision in *Wallace* v. *Jaffree*.[20] In that case the issue was a moment of silence in the public schools of Alabama. In 1978 the state had passed a law authorizing a minute of silence in public schools "for meditation." In 1981 the law was modified to authorize the minute of silence "for meditation or voluntary prayer." Soon thereafter a suit was filed that argued that the addition of the words "or voluntary prayer" made the minute of silence law unconstitutional because the activity of prayer now received state endorsement.

The Court, in an opinion written by Justice John Paul Stevens, agreed. Applying the "secular purpose" test, the Court found that the legislation that added the words "or voluntary prayer" had the sole purpose of characterizing prayer as a favored practice. For the state to do that is not consistent with the Establishment Clause.

What is interesting about *Jaffree* is that the authors of the majority opinion, two concurring opinions, and three dissents all agreed that a minute of silence at the beginning of each school day was an acceptable concept which states were perfectly free to legislate. Furthermore, all acknowledged that students and/or teachers could say silent prayers during that minute of silence if they so chose. In fact, the schoolchildren of Alabama had had that opportunity to pray after the first, 1978, legislation, if not before. So, argued the majority, the legislation adding the phrase "or voluntary prayer" was redundant. But redundancy is not a constitutional offense; giving state endorsement to prayer is. Because it was unnecessary to add those words to give young people the opportunity to pray during the moment of silence, it was clear that the only purpose of explicitly adding the words was to characterize the activity of prayer as a favored practice.

The *Jaffree* ruling is very narrow. It applies only to the addition of the words "or voluntary prayer" to legislation. But it did give the justices the opportunity to again show that they were not hostile to religion and that they had never outlawed all forms of prayer from the public schools. They were able to do this by pointing out that students or teachers may pray during the minute of silence with no constitutional problem.

Commencement Prayers

In 1992 the Court addressed the question of prayers at public school commencement exercises, in *Lee* v. *Weisman*.[21] In Providence, Rhode Island, public middle and high school principals were permitted to invite clergy to say invocations and benedictions at graduation exercises. In the particular case that stimulated the lawsuit, a principal invited a rabbi to offer prayers at commencement, gave him printed guidelines for offering prayers at public occasions, and advised him that the prayer to be offered must be nonsectarian. Although it is clear that the rabbi offered prayers that he considered to be nondenominational, they did contain references to God and to Hebrew scripture that had a Jewish character to them. Nonetheless, a Jewish student and her father filed suit, seeking a permanent injunction that would prevent similar religious expressions at future commencement exercises.

Justice Anthony Kennedy wrote the opinion, holding the commencement prayers to be unconstitutional. The center of the opinion is that when the school principal selected the person to give the prayers and offered printed guidelines and advice about their content, the state was determining the content of the prayer. That had shades of *Engel*. The state may not determine the content of prayers. But, more fundamentally, there was psychologi-

cal coercion on those who might not want to participate in the prayers
because the audience (students) were expected to rise and stand in respectful
silence while the prayers were being said. A dissenting student might perceive that acceding to the expected behavior would be perceived by others as
agreeing with the religious exercises, rather than just showing respect for
those who did agree with it. The state may not use social pressure to enforce
orthodoxy, any more than it may use direct means. Additionally, although
students were not required to attend the commencement exercises, nonetheless graduation is a once-in-a-lifetime event for which students have been
aiming during their entire school careers. It is unreasonable to put them into
the position of having to miss their graduation in order not to have to
participate in prayers with which they disagree or that they believe are
wrong in relation to the Establishment Clause. Consequently, the commencement prayers are unconstitutional. Justice Kennedy wrote a *dictum*
that illuminates the Establishment Clause and the importance of the separation of church and state.

> The First Amendment's Religion Clauses mean that religious beliefs and
> religious expression are too precious to be either proscribed or prescribed
> by the State. The design of the Constitution is that preservation and trans-
> mission of religious beliefs and worship is a responsibility and a choice
> committed to the private sphere, which itself is promised freedom to pur-
> sue that mission. It must not be forgotten then, that while concern must be
> given to define the protection granted to an objector or a dissenting non-
> believer, these same Clauses exist to protect religion from government
> interference. . . . [T]he Establishment Clause is a specific prohibition on
> forms of state intervention in religious affairs with no precise counterpart
> in the [freedom of] speech provisions. The explanation lies in the lesson of
> history that was and is the inspiration for the Establishment Clause, the
> lesson that in the hands of government what might begin as a tolerant
> expression of religious views may end in a policy to indoctrinate and co-
> erce. A state-created orthodoxy puts at grave risk that freedom of belief
> and conscience which are the sole assurance that religious faith is real, not
> imposed.
>
> The lessons of the First Amendment are as urgent in the modern world
> as in the 18th Century when it was written. One timeless lesson is that if
> citizens are subjected to state-sponsored religious exercises, the State dis-
> avows its own duty to guard and respect that sphere of inviolable con-
> science and belief which is the mark of a free people. To compromise that
> principle today would be to deny our own tradition and forfeit our stand-
> ing to urge others to secure the protections of that tradition for
> themselves.[22]

In summary, on the issue of prayer in the public schools state legislatures
or school boards are prohibited from writing and requiring prayers to be said
in the classroom and from dictating the nature of prayers or even allowing

public prayers at commencement exercises, or even expressing a preference for prayer during a minute of silence. They are prohibited from requiring Bible reading as a devotional exercise at the beginning of each school day. But schools are permitted to have a truly neutral minute of silence, which may be used for prayer if a student or teacher chooses to so use it. They may teach religion, in all its dimensions, as part of the regular curriculum of a school, so long as it is *instruction* and not evangelization. Students, further-more, are permitted to pray at any time, so long as they are not disruptive of the educational environment or process, which usually would mean that the prayers would be silent. Public schools are not to be shadow or surrogate churches, but they are not constitutionally required to be insulated from or purged of religion, either.

TEACHING EVOLUTION AND CREATION SCIENCE

From time to time the debate between evolution and conservative Protes-tant Christianity has been played out in the curriculum of the public schools. The issue first came to national prominence with the trial of John Thomas Scopes in Dayton, Tennessee, in 1925. Tennessee was one of a number of states to pass laws prohibiting the teaching of evolution in the public schools. Scopes, a high school biology teacher, was convicted of having vio-lated the law, although the conviction was later overturned by the Tennessee Supreme Court because of a legal technicality.[23]

The first time this issue came to the United States Supreme Court was in *Epperson* v. *Arkansas*.[24] An Arkansas law prohibited the teaching of the theory of evolution in its public schools, including universities. The law also banned the adoption or use of any textbooks in the public schools that contained the concept of evolution. When a high school biology teacher in Little Rock realized that her local school board had adopted a textbook that contained evolution, she was in a dilemma. She could either use the adopted book and be in violation of state criminal law and subject to dismissal, or refuse to use the book and face disciplinary action from her local school authorities. She attempted to remove the dilemma by removing the law. She filed suit, seek-ing a court's declaration that the law was void and an injunction that would prevent the state from enforcing it. (The fact that the Little Rock school board violated the law by initially adopting the book was never an issue in this case.)

When the case reached the Supreme Court in 1968, the decision was that Arkansas's law violated the Establishment Clause. The Court held that the law was passed for the purpose of forbidding the teaching of a view opposed by fundamentalist Christianity. That is, the legislature had prohibited teach-ing one concept about the origin of life because it perceived that concept to be contrary to the book of Genesis, literally interpreted. It had attempted, with this law, to preserve the biblical doctrine of creation by forbidding the teaching of evolution. The law was unconstitutional because it violated the secular-purpose part of the three-part test for interpreting the Establishment Clause (see pp. 66–67). Justice Abe Fortas wrote for the Court: "There is and can be no doubt that the First Amendment does not permit the State to require that teaching and learning must be tailored to the principles or prohibitions of any religious sect or dogma."[25]

The result of *Epperson* was that states were forbidden to prohibit the teaching of evolution in public schools. Those who were opposed to evolution for religious reasons had to devise another strategy for blunting the teaching of evolution in public education.[26]

Coincidentally with this concern came the development of "creation science," also known as "scientific creationism." Although this has its roots in the religious antievolutionism of the 1920s, it is a more sophisticated approach, which tends to discredit evolution by showing that all the alleged evolutionary data are actually in conformity with the biblical account of creation and view of the world. Creation science asserts that the universe is some ten thousand years old and that creation took place in six twenty-four-hour days. The various species of life were created as "kinds," and, although there may be some development within a "kind," there is no development in life forms from one "kind" to another. Geological data that are alleged to explain the long age of the earth can actually be accounted for by a world-wide flood. Creation science attempts to offer an alternative view to evolution by showing the various findings of modern science to be consistent with the biblical account of creation, which is taken to be literally true.

Advocates of creation science were determined to try to use it to battle the teaching of evolution in the public schools. Because *Epperson* prohibited any laws forbidding the teaching of evolution, the new approach was to pass "balanced treatment" laws. The idea was to require that creation science be taught whenever evolution was. Arkansas took the lead in this. In 1981, Act 590 mandated that in all the public schools of the state, whenever evolution was taught or included in a textbook, creation science had to be given "balanced treatment." Balanced treatment did not mean equal time. Classroom presentations did not need to match minute for minute time devoted to evolution and creation science, nor did textbooks or other materials (including library holdings) need to match line for line. But there did have to be balanced coverage of each theory in the course or the literature as a whole.

Several people, including some clergy, sued to have the Arkansas act declared unconstitutional as a violation of the Establishment Clause. That happened in a federal district court in Arkansas. The court ruled that, despite its claims to the contrary, creation science was based on religious ideas. To require its inclusion in the public school curriculum every time evolution is taught was unconstitutional.[27] Creation science advocates decided not to appeal this case, because there was another balanced-treatment law in Louisiana and another case, which they felt had a better chance of gaining approval in the Supreme Court.

Those hopes were dashed, however, when the Supreme Court handed down *Edwards* v. *Aguillard*,[28] holding that the Louisiana balanced-treatment law was unconstitutional. Louisiana claimed that the purpose of the law was to advance academic freedom by guaranteeing that every time evolution was taught creation science would be also, that is, by presenting students with more than one view of the beginnings of life. But the Court found that teachers in that state had the opportunity to present more than one view of origins before the law was passed. So, in reality, the act did nothing to advance academic freedom. The actual purpose of the law was to discredit evolution by counterbalancing it with creation science and, furthermore, to give preference to a religious doctrine that rejects the factual basis of evolution in its entirety. It was clear to the Court that the balanced treatment law violated the secular-purpose part of the three-part test for interpreting the Establishment Clause.

> [T]he Creationism Act is designed *either* to promote the theory of creation science which embodies a particular religious tenet by requiring that creation science be taught whenever evolution is taught *or* to prohibit the teaching of a scientific theory disfavored by certain religious sects by forbidding the teaching of evolution when creation science is not also taught. The Establishment Clause, however, "forbids *alike* the preference of a religious doctrine *or* the prohibition of theory which is deemed antagonistic to a particular dogma." Because the primary purpose of the Creationism Act is to advance a particular religious belief, the Act endorses religion in violation of the First Amendment.[29]

The conclusion of this line of cases is, then, that states may neither forbid the teaching of evolution in public schools nor demand that creation science be taught alongside evolution. The reason for these prohibitions is that so far both plans have been premised on fundamentalist opposition to evolution, and laws that are passed because of a religious motivation are unconstitutional.

SECULAR HUMANISM

In the early 1960s, Roy Torcaso was appointed by the Governor of Maryland to the position of notary public. When the time came to actually assume the duties of the position, he was refused a commission to serve. The Maryland constitution contained the provision that in order to hold public office one had to state "a declaration of belief in the existence of God," and Torcaso would not declare such a personal belief. Furthermore, he filed suit in a state court, claiming that the requirement in the state constitution of a declaration of belief in the existence of God as a condition for public office was a violation of both Article VI and the Establishment Clause of the federal Constitution. The case is *Torcaso* v. *Watkins*.[30]

In an opinion written by Justice Hugo Black, the Court found in favor of Torcaso. Black recalled the words he had written in *Everson* v. *Board of Education*, that under the Establishment Clause neither a state nor the federal government can force a person "to profess a belief or disbelief in any religion";[31] Maryland did just that to those who would hold public office in the state. The state argued that no one was compelled to hold public office, so the requirement of belief in God was narrow in scope. The Court responded to that argument by declaring that no one should have to sacrifice a constitutionally guaranteed liberty in order to hold public office. A state may not insist on a religious affirmation as a condition for holding public office any more than may the federal government. Consequently, the Court declared a section of a state constitution to be unconstitutional, under the Establishment Clause.

This is an important case, but why is it here in the chapter on religious activities in public schools? The reason is because of some of the *dicta* in the opinion. In stating that neither states nor the federal government can impose a test oath on officeholders, the opinion said: "Neither can constitutionally pass laws or impose requirements which aid all religions as against nonbelievers, and neither can aid those religions based on a belief in the existence of God as against those religions founded on different beliefs." As an illustration of the last point, Justice Black added a footnote: "Among religions in this country which do not teach what would generally be considered a belief in the existence of God are Buddhism, Taoism, Ethical Culture, Secular Humanism, and others."[32]

Since the mid-1970s there has been a conservative trend in American religion, both in numbers of adherents and in intensity. A principal part of the style of this theological and social conservatism is its willingness, indeed eagerness, to become involved in the political arena. Part of that effort has been to give attention to what these conservatives perceive as the dramatic decline in quality in public school education. They believe that not only are the public schools not educating young people for their future places in society, but they have abdicated their role of teaching those civic virtues so important to the survival of the nation, the civic values that nourish the soul of the nation. The public schools have surrendered this crucially important function because they have become pervaded by secular humanism, and that is being passed on to the students.

Conservatives are quick to point out that the Supreme Court has ruled that traditional, theistic religion cannot be taught or practiced in the public schools. (Actually, as we have seen, the Court did no such thing.) But they insist a religion *is* being taught in the schools: secular humanism! Why can they say that secular humanism is a religion? Because the Supreme Court said it is. For this argument they go to Justice Black's footnote 11 of *Torcaso* v. *Watkins*, quoted above. If it is unconstitutional to teach traditional religious values, it is equally unconstitutional to teach the religion of secular humanism.[33] And yet conservatives believe that it is being taught all the time. To leaders of the "New Christian Right," the promulgation of secular humanism is the root cause of the disaster the public schools have become. Not only have the schools lost most of their educational quality, but they have become war zones dominated by violence and drug dealing. Moreover, there is no respect for the authority of teachers and administrators. The reason that secular humanism has led to this sad state of affairs, they argue, is that it is relativistic. It has no absolute values, because it has no conception of God. Secular humanism is a "do what makes you feel good" ethic. That sort of ethic can only lead to chaos in the lives of individual students and certainly is not adequate to be the basis for a civic ideology.

There have been at least two reactions of the conservative Christians to what they perceive as the religion of secular humanism in the public schools.

The "Christian School" Movement

Although Protestant parochial schools are not new, their number has grown dramatically since the 1950s, when many of them opened in response to the desegregation of the public schools after the Court's decision in *Brown* v. *Board of Education*.[34] Many of those early Christian schools were segregation academies. But in more recent years the principal stimulus to the founding of these schools has been the perceived decay of the public schools brought on by the pervasiveness of secular humanism in the curriculum. They are now a major alternative to the public schools. Much of the rationale for all this is derived from the alleged declaration by the Supreme Court that secular humanism is a religion. It is likely that fundamentalist Christians would have made their humanism argument without the footnote in *Torcaso* v. *Watkins*, but they have seized on it as what they consider a powerful aid in making their point.

It is ironic that the Christian Right has relied so much on the Supreme Court statement in making this claim. They so often have maligned and reviled the Court and distorted its decisions, but when it serves their purposes, they put aside their usual contempt for the Court and assert that what it has said is certainly true. The statement, however, is only an illustration of a very different point, that a state may not prefer a religion based on a belief in the existence of God over one that does not have that belief; that is, that the state may not impose theism as a condition of employment. It may be that members of the Court thought that secular humanism is a religion; but the statement is, at most, *dictum* upon *dictum*, and does not appropriately carry the great weight the Christian Right has placed on it.

The Ten Commandments

Another attempt to deal with the impact of secular humanism, this time in the public schools, took place in Kentucky. The legislature passed a law requiring that the Ten Commandments be posted in every public school room in the state. The posters were paid for by private contributions, rather than state funds. Perhaps because they foresaw an Establishment Clause fight over the program, the legislators also required that the following notation appear at the bottom of each poster: "The secular application of the Ten Commandments is clearly seen in its adoption as the fundamental legal code of Western Civilization and the Common Law of the United States."

The legislators predicted correctly. In spite of the disclaimer at the bottom of the posters and the fact that they were paid for from private funds, a lawsuit was filed. The claim was that the posting of the Ten Commandments in the public schools was a violation of the Establishment Clause.

The Supreme Court dealt with the issue in 1980 in a rare unsigned opinion, in *Stone* v. *Graham*.[35] The Court found that the program was a violation of the Establishment Clause under the secular-purpose test. The legislature argued that the purpose articulated by the disclaimer at the bottom of the posters was a secular one, that is, its purpose was to show students the influence of the Ten Commandments on the legal structure of Western society. The Court disagreed. To be sure, the Ten Commandments prohibit murder, adultery, lying, stealing—things that are the subjects of civil law. But they also exhort persons to worship God alone, to avoid idolatry, to observe the Sabbath, and not to blaspheme God. "The pre-eminent purpose for posting the Ten Commandments on schoolroom walls is plainly religious in nature. The Ten Commandments is undeniably a sacred text in the Jewish and Christian faiths, and no legislative recitation of a supposed secular purpose can blind us to that fact."[36] The purchase of the posters by private funds did not save the program. They were in the schoolrooms because Kentucky law required that they be there. It was also not significant that the Ten Commandments were merely positioned on the walls rather than being read aloud, because minor breaches of the principle of separation are just as forbidden as major ones.

EQUAL ACCESS

Primarily as a reaction to what they mistakenly perceived the school prayer decisions to mean, and because of their resentment of the Ten Commandments decision and their fear of the perceived influence of secular humanism, some people began to wonder if there was any way at all for religion to be included in public schools. (As we have seen, the prayer decisions did not sanitize public schools from all aspects of religion; far from it.) There was the additional problem that around the country some courts had prohibited religious organizations or student clubs in public schools, under the theory that they violated the Establishment Clause; if a public school permitted religious clubs to meet, it would be impermissibly sponsoring and advancing religion. Some groups began to work in Congress for the passage of an "equal access" bill, which would give religious clubs access to school time and facilities equal to that of nonreligious clubs. In 1984 Congress passed the Equal Access Act.[37] It provided that if a high school received federal funds and if it had a "limited open forum," then it would be unlawful to deny students the opportunity to meet on the basis of the religious, political, or philosophical content of their speech at such meetings. A "limited open forum"[38] means that the school permits free discussion of ideas and issues, but that the forum is open only to its students, as opposed to the public at large. Specifically in this law, the limited open forum exists when the school allows secular student groups or clubs to use school facilities before or after its instructional day for their particular activities and when those activities are not related to the normal curriculum of the school. When those conditions are met, the school is required to allow religious clubs to use its facilities in the same way that it allows the other non-curriculum-related clubs. It is also required that the religious clubs must be voluntary, student-initiated, and student-run, with no direction from public school employees or nonschool persons.

This law was tested before the Supreme Court in 1990 in *Board of Education* v. *Mergens*.[39] The case was initiated, not by persons who wanted to challenge the Equal Access Act, but by those who wanted to utilize it. Bridget Mergens and some of her friends wanted to start a Christian club at her high school in Omaha, to meet before the beginning of regular instruction, like many other student clubs. They applied to the principal for permission and were denied, a decision later endorsed by the Board of Education. School officials based their decision on the idea that to have a religious club would put the school in violation of the Establishment Clause. But the students claimed that the school, by denying their request, was in violation of the Equal Access Act. The students brought suit in federal district court to compel the school board to comply with the act. The school board responded by claiming that the Equal Access Act did not apply to this high school and, if it did, the act was unconstitutional in relation to the Establishment Clause. This was the form of the case that reached the Supreme Court.

The Court found in favor of the students and against the school board. The first issue addressed was whether the act actually applied to the school.

The law is triggered if a school has clubs that are not related to its curriculum. That is, a school is only obligated to accommodate a religious club, which would not be related to the school's curriculum, if other student clubs are non-curriculum-related. The school in this case claimed that all its clubs were curriculum-related, and thus the act did not apply—it was not required to give permission for the formation of a religious club. The Court, in an opinion written by Justice Sandra Day O'Connor, disagreed. The school wanted to define "curriculum related" to mean anything at least remotely related to its general educational goals. The Court used a much narrower definition. A student group that is not directly related to the courses taught in the school is not curriculum-related. Under that definition, the Omaha school had several clubs that were not curriculum-related.[40] Consequently, the school had a limited open forum and the act did apply to the school. It could not deny the religious club the opportunity to organize and meet in preschool hours.

To the more substantive question of the constitutionality of the act under the Establishment Clause, the Court had a ready answer—the law was constitutional. The act had a secular purpose, because Congress intended for it to prohibit discrimination on the basis of philosophical or political speech, as well as religious speech. That is, the law did not give religious speech preferential treatment over other kinds of speech, so it did not have a religious purpose.

The school board claimed that the act had the primary effect of advancing religion, in that it compelled the school to recognize religious clubs and give them support by providing them time and place to meet. The Court disagreed, holding:

> [T]here is a crucial difference between *government* speech endorsing religion, which the Establishment Clause forbids, and *private* speech endorsing religion, which the Free Speech and Free Exercise Clauses protect. We think that secondary school students are mature enough and are likely to understand that a school does not endorse or support student speech that it merely permits on a nondiscriminatory basis.[41]

Finally, the board argued that the act created excessive entanglement between the school and religion, in that school officials, particularly teachers, would have to exercise a supervisory role over the religious clubs. The Court simply pointed out that the act forbade school officials to organize, promote, or lead the religious clubs or any particular meeting of the clubs. The act does permit teacher presence at the meetings of the clubs to maintain order and to satisfy school insurance requirements, but they are not allowed to participate in the students' religious meetings. Such custodial surveillance does not excessively entangle the public school in the day-to-day administration of religious activities. The Equal Access Act passed all three tests and does not violate the Establishment Clause. If the school meets the criterion of having a limited open forum and permits non-curriculum-related student clubs access to that forum, religious clubs initiated and led by students must be permitted equal access to school facilities. The Establishment Clause does not prohibit this government accommodation of religion.

Both *Mergens* and the Equal Access Act of which it was a test relied on a 1981 case at the university level, *Widmar* v. *Vincent*.[42] The University of Missouri in Kansas City made available meeting rooms in university buildings to a wide variety of student groups. Among those was a group of Christian students calling themselves "Cornerstone," who met for prayer, Bible reading, and discussion of religious topics. But after several years of such meetings, the university withdrew permission for Cornerstone to continue to meet in University facilities, claiming to be enforcing a rule made five years previously, that the university should not allow its facilities to be used "for purposes of religious worship or religious teachings." The university claimed that the reason for its rule and its prohibition of Cornerstone's meetings was that it did not want to violate the Establishment Clause. For it to allow Cornerstone to continue to meet would be to give state sanction and encouragement to religious activity, a breach of the no-establishment principle. The students responded that they were guaranteed the right to meet in an orderly fashion for religious activity by both the Free Exercise and the Free Speech Clauses of the First Amendment. So this case presented a classic conflict between the establishment and free-exercise principles.

The Court decided in favor of the students. Its opinion, written by Justice Lewis Powell, began with the recognition that the university had created a "limited open forum" by making its facilities available to a multiplicity of student groups for meetings. (The open forum was "limited" because it was available only to students and their invited guests, including speakers, and not to the general public.) Cornerstone must be allowed "equal access" to this limited public forum.[43] The Free Exercise Clause demands that the university must not prohibit the religious activity of the students. The Free Speech Clause mandates that the university must not discriminate against the religious content of the students' speech in their meetings, particularly since it allows many other kinds of speech in student meetings. The Court disagreed with the university's Establishment Clause argument that to accommodate the religious group would have the impermissible primary effect of advancing religion. Given the existence of the open forum, the university's allowing the students to meet simply did not have that effect.

> In this context we are unpersuaded that the primary effect of the public forum, open to all forms of discourse, would be to advance religion. . . . First, an open public forum in a public university does not confer any imprimatur of State approval on religious sects or practices. . . . Second, the forum is available to a broad class of non-religious as well as religious

speakers. . . . The provision of benefits to so broad a spectrum of groups is an important index of secular effect.[44]

The Court acknowledged that the university could impose time, place, and manner regulations on religious groups and it could exclude groups that are disruptive of the educational environment of the campus. No group has unlimited access to any and all university facilities. But the university could not deny the access of student religious groups to its facilities simply because they were religious. In this case, the Free Exercise/Free Speech argument prevailed over the Establishment Clause.

A somewhat different kind of equal access case was *Lamb's Chapel* v. *Center Moriches Union Free School District*.[45] The school district, consistent with New York State law, denied a church group access to high school facilities in nonschool hours to show a film about family issues, approached from a religious perspective. The church had requested to use the high school auditorium for several evenings to present programs, open to the public, on child rearing and discipline. The centerpiece of the programs would be films, which approached the topic from a Christian viewpoint. The request was denied as a result of a school district policy forbidding school property to be used for any religious purpose. The church claimed that the school's policy violated the Free Speech, Free Exercise, and Establishment Clauses of the First Amendment.

The Court, in an opinion by Justice Byron White, agreed with the church, basing its decision principally on free-speech grounds. In prior cases, the Court had ruled that the government may not "regulate speech in ways that favor some viewpoints or ideas at the expense of others."[46] In this specific instance, the school district would have allowed other presentations on the topic of child nurture to be presented in the school, but denied Lamb's Chapel because its material had a religious orientation. That is impermissible discrimination on the basis of content. More broadly, the school district had a rule that prohibited school facilities from being used for any religious purpose, even in nonschool hours. But it had ten other, secular purposes for which schools could be used by nonschool groups. The Court ruled that content/viewpoint discrimination was built into the policy itself. That is contrary to the principle of free speech. The school district could not forbid religious groups to use the school facilities so long as it, as a matter of policy, allowed secular groups to use them.

The Court did not directly address the Establishment Clause complaint by Lamb's Chapel. In passing, Justice White said that if the case had been decided on the basis of the no-establishment principle, permitting the religious film to be shown in the public school would have passed the three-part "*Lemon* test." Justices Scalia, Thomas, and Kennedy asserted that they would have decided the case without any reference to the Establishment Clause and criticized the "*Lemon* test."

8

Blue Laws, Bars, Taxes, and Plastic Reindeer: The Complexity of Establishment Clause Issues

Although a large proportion of the Supreme Court's Establishment Clause cases have focused on school questions, a variety of other issues have been covered as well. The issues are wide-ranging and affect American life in significant ways.

SUNDAY CLOSING LAWS

The idea of rest on the day of worship is as old as the Judeo-Christian tradition. One of the Ten Commandments is:

> Remember the sabbath day, to keep it holy. Six days you shall labor, and do all your work; but the seventh day is a sabbath to the LORD your God; in it you shall not do any work, . . . for in six days the LORD made heaven and earth, the sea, and all that is in them, and rested the seventh day; therefore the LORD blessed the sabbath day and hallowed it.[1]

Christianity changed the day of worship and rest to Sunday, in honor of Jesus' resurrection, and when Christianity became the established religion of the Roman Empire, Sunday observance became mandated by law, on March 7, 321, by decree of the Emperor Constantine.

> All judges, city-people and craftsmen shall rest on the venerable day of the Sun. But countrymen may without hindrance attend to agriculture, since it often happens that this is the most suitable day for sowing grain or planting vines, so that the opportunity afforded by divine providence may not be lost, for the right season is of short duration.[2]

Notice that an exception to the prohibition was made to accommodate activity essential to human welfare.

The observance of Sunday as a day of rest and worship continued throughout medieval times and was brought to the New World. The first Sunday law of America was promulgated in Virginia in 1610. It forbade work on Sunday so that all residents could give attention to preparing for and attending Christian worship. Later, the prohibition of the sale of merchandise on Sunday was added to the laws. All the colonies had such laws, and they were generally retained by the states well after the ratification of the First Amendment.

In 1961 the Supreme Court was asked to rule on the constitutionality of the Sunday laws. In *McGowan* v. *Maryland*[3] the laws were challenged on Establishment Clause grounds. Maryland's laws were typical of those around the country: businesses were to be closed on Sunday. However, following the precedent set as early as Constantine's law, exceptions were made to the prohibitions against doing business on Sunday. Occupations of necessity and charity were exempted, for example, hospital personnel, firefighters and police officers, and grocery store workers. But exemptions from closing were also extended to businesses that facilitated the enjoyment of the day of rest, such as ice-cream stores, swimming pools, spectator sports, amusement parks, and sellers of greases and gasoline, for those who enjoyed a Sunday drive.

The *McGowan* case was brought by some employees of a large department store, who were indicted for selling a notebook, a can of floor wax, a stapler and staples, and a toy submarine, all prohibited by the law. This list of items shows that the law had begun to target the sale of certain items, rather than just whether a business could stay open on Sunday. With the advent of the large department store, as opposed to small specialty shops, this kind of refinement of the law had begun to occur in many places. The contention of the store employees in this case was that the Sunday law was a violation of the Establishment Clause because it gave state recognition to and compelled at least minimal observance of the Christian day of worship. They had suffered economic injury because the state had forced deference to Sunday on them.

Chief Justice Earl Warren wrote the opinion in this case. The Court reached its decision by employing an argument from history. It examined the history of Sunday legislation from medieval times through the colonial period in American history. The Court readily acknowledged that the original Sunday legislation, both in Europe and in the American colonies, was religious in orientation. Just as in Constantine's legislation, the laws were designed to protect the Christian day of worship from profanation and distracting activities so that people could more faithfully observe it. But, the Court observed, at least as early as the beginning of the eighteenth century nonreligious arguments began to be heard in favor of Sunday statutes, and laws themselves began to become more secular. These more secular rationales centered on the desirability and the healthfulness of periods of rest and relaxation from the labors by which one made one's living. This line of reasoning has continued and, indeed, become more prevalent in this century. In short, the Sunday closing laws had become secularized. Their purpose was to benefit individuals and society as a whole by providing a day of rest. Sunday was regarded in the laws as a day when people could rest and recover from the work of the week past and mentally and physically prepare for the work week that approached. The laws were now no more than social-welfare legislation. In light of the evolution of Sunday closing laws, it was clear that the laws at issue in this case were not violations of the Establishment Clause. That the state's secular rest and relaxation laws happened to correspond with the Christian day of worship was of no constitutional significance. It used laws against murder, condemned by both Judaism and Christianity, as an example of legitimate secular legislation that incidentally corresponded with religious precept.

> Sunday Closing Laws, like those before us, have become part and parcel of this great governmental concern wholly apart from their original purposes or connotations. The present purpose and effect of most of them is to provide a uniform day of rest for all citizens; the fact that this day is Sunday, a day of particular significance for the dominant Christian sects, does not bar the State from achieving its secular goals. To say that the States cannot prescribe Sunday as a day of rest for these purposes solely because centuries ago such laws had their genesis in religion would give a constitutional interpretation of hostility to the public welfare rather than one of mere separation of church and State.[4]

The plaintiffs in the case also contended that the state could reach its public-welfare goal by another means, namely, by mandating that employers provide for their employees one day of rest in every seven. The Court recognized that that would be a plausible plan, but said that states were not obligated to do that. Such a plan would be much more difficult to enforce than a uniform day of rest. Furthermore, a state might want there to be a virtually uniform day of rest in order to promote family solidarity, that is, a day when all family members could be together. Because Sunday was already regarded by people of all religions and no religion as a traditional day of rest, it was only logical that a state might enforce its use with Sunday closing laws, given that it now had a secular rationale. Sunday closing laws were not a violation of the Establishment Clause.[5]

Another case, *Braunfeld* v. *Brown*,[6] argued that Sunday laws violate the Free Exercise Clause as well as the Establishment Clause. The plaintiffs in this case were Orthodox Jews who operated a business. Their religion required them to cease from work (and thus close their business) for purposes of worship on Saturday; the law compelled them to close on Sunday. They claimed that the law infringed on the exercise of their religion, in that they had to suffer economic loss and competitive disadvantage to businesses operated by nonsabbatarians; it forced them into competitive disadvantage if they practiced their religion. Furthermore, the law would likely cause the Orthodox Jewish faith to be less attractive to potential converts, knowing that converting to that faith would put them at economic risk.

One might think that this free-exercise argument would make this case harder than a purely establishment one. But actually Chief Justice Warren's opinion for the Court made short work of it. He began by reasserting that the Free Exercise Clause prohibits government from passing any law that compels the acceptance of any creed or the prohibition of any activity of worship. The Sunday closing law, even as applied to sabbatarians, had neither of those effects. "[T]he statute before us does not make criminal the holding of any religious belief or opinion, nor does it force anyone to embrace any religious belief or to say or believe anything in conflict with his religious tenets."[7] The law did not prohibit the Jews from practicing their faith, it just made it more expensive. Although that is regrettable, it does not prohibit a state from enacting a constitutional (remember *McGowan* v. *Maryland*) law that has the beneficial effects of enforcing a day of rest for the majority of the population. The Sunday closing law was not unconstitutional under the Free Exercise Clause as it applied to sabbatarians.

There were dissents from the opinions in the Sunday closing law cases. In the *Braunfeld* case, Justice Potter Stewart summed up what he saw as the flaw in the majority opinion in just five sentences.

> Pennsylvania has passed a law which compels an Orthodox Jew to choose between his religious faith and his economic survival. That is a cruel choice. It is a choice which I think no State can constitutionally demand. For me this is not something that can be swept under the rug and forgotten in the interest of enforced Sunday togetherness. I think the impact of this law upon these appellants grossly violates their constitutional right to the free exercise of their religion.[8]

Some may say that these cases are essentially moot these days. The pervasiveness of the large department store makes item-specific sales prohibitions virtually impossible to enforce. Furthermore, item-specific prohibitions are foolish, for they fail to accomplish what has been the secular rationale for Sunday closing laws—a day of rest for employees. When stores are allowed to stay open because some items may be sold while other items may not, employees still have to work. In addition, as our society has become increasingly materialistic and commercialized, there is not the sentiment in the general population for Sunday closing laws. But the cases are still worth review, if for no other reason than that they are a reminder of the religiously pluralistic nature of our society and the need for sensitivity to the beliefs of others, particularly minorities. That is the reason that Justice Stewart's dissent is mentioned, as well as the long quote being given from Justice Douglas's in note 8 (see pp. 164–65).

Twenty-four years after *McGowan* and *Braunfeld*, the Court handed down a workplace case that had Sunday law–like characteristics, *Estate of Thornton* v. *Caldor*.[9] Connecticut amended its Sunday closing law to say that no one could be required to work on his or her day of worship. One assumes that the law was passed out of free-exercise-of-religion considerations, that is, to avoid the kind of discrimination that had been upheld in *Braunfeld*. Thornton was a Presbyterian who claimed Sunday as his day of worship. His employer, the Caldor Company, opened its stores for Sunday business and expected its managers to work at least one Sunday a month. When Thornton refused, he was demoted in rank and salary. Thereupon Thornton filed a grievance with the state's arbitration service and claimed that the Caldor Company had violated Connecticut law. So far this case sounds very much like *Frazee* v. *Illinois Department of Employment Security*, described in chapter 4 (pp. 34–35). As in that case, one would expect that Thornton would win on Free Exercise Clause grounds. But Caldor Company responded with the contention that the law violated the Establishment Clause, in that it gave employees the absolute right to impose their day of worship on employers and fellow employees. That controversy worked its way through the state courts to the U.S. Supreme Court.

The Court decided for Caldor. Chief Justice Warren Burger made short work of the case. He began with a pithy and true statement: "Under the Religion Clauses, Government must guard against activity that impinges on religious freedom, and must take pains not to compel people to act in the name of religion."[10] The problem with Connecticut's law was that it did compel people to act in the name of religion. It forced employers and employees to conform their business practices and their own schedules to the religious practices of any employee who wanted to observe her or his particular day of worship.

> The State thus commands that Sabbath religious concerns automatically control over all secular interests in the workplace. . . . The employer and others must adjust their affairs to the command of the State whenever the statute is invoked by an employee.[11]

Consequently, the law had a primary effect of advancing religion in violation of the Establishment Clause. Workplace laws may not give employees an absolute right to impose their Sabbath requirements on their employers.

LEGISLATIVE CHAPLAINS

There is a long-standing practice in this country, at both the state and federal levels, of having state-paid chaplains for legislative bodies. The chaplains perform a variety of functions, such as counseling with individual legislators about personal problems, and may even conduct an occasional wedding or funeral for legislative personnel. But their most visible activity is opening legislative sessions with prayer. Such an obviously religious activity conducted at state expense in the very seat of government has caused many to question its constitutionality. The issue was raised at the Supreme Court level in *Marsh* v. *Chambers*.[12]

Marsh came out of the state of Nebraska. The challenge was raised by a member of the legislature, so it was clear that he had standing. The chaplaincy program was attacked in three ways. It was claimed that, first, the state funding of the chaplain violated the Establishment Clause. Second, the legislature had employed the same chaplain, a Presbyterian, for sixteen years. Employment of that length was alleged to be impermissible preferential treatment for one religion over others. Third, the chaplain's prayers were distinctly Judeo-Christian in content, again said to be showing preference for one tradition over others.

The Court, in an opinion by Chief Justice Burger, began its response to the challenges by pointing out that there was a long history of legislative chaplains in the country. Most specifically to the point, the precedent was begun by the Continental Congress. In April and May 1789, the Senate and House elected chaplains and, on September 22, 1789, they passed a law to pay them from federal funds. Just three days later, the Congress finalized the language of the religion clauses of the First Amendment. The Court concluded that if those who wrote the Establishment Clause did not think that providing governmentally paid chaplains for the legislative bodies was a violation, it must not be. There was the further evidence that the national Congress has had chaplains for two hundred years, and many states have a long history of the practice as well. Nebraska had had legislative chaplains for over one hundred years.

> In light of the unambiguous and unbroken history of more than 200 years, there can be no doubt that the practice of opening legislative sessions with prayer has become part of the fabric of our society. To invoke Divine guidance on a public body entrusted with making the laws is not, in these circumstances, an "establishment" or a step toward establishment; it is simply a tolerable acknowledgement of beliefs widely held among the people of this country.[13]

This argument using history was enough to deal with the three challenges to the program. Paying a chaplain with state funds was not unconstitutional. The historical evidence that was the centerpiece of this opinion showed that. That the legislature had hired the same chaplain for sixteen years simply showed that they were satisfied with his work, not that they preferred Presbyterianism. (In fact, the chaplain had invited ministers of other religious groups to give prayers before the legislature.) The content of the prayers, predominantly Judeo-Christian, was not a violation of the Constitution so long as the prayers were not used to proselytize. There was no evidence of that in this case.

Although the three-part *"Lemon* test" for interpreting the Establishment Clause had been formulated by the time *Marsh* v. *Chambers* was decided, the test was not used in this case. I believe there was at least one reason for that, perhaps two. First, it may be that Chief Justice Burger believed an argument from history was sufficient to reach the conclusion he thought was correct and so it was not necessary to apply the three-part test, although this was the first case in which some aspect of it had not been applied since it was formulated. Second, the chief justice might have realized that the program of legislative chaplains could not be affirmed if the three-part test were applied. Both the court of appeals below and two of the three dissenters in the case argued that legislative chaplains failed all three parts of the test, and that therefore legislative chaplains were clearly unconstitutional under the Establishment Clause. At any rate, the test was not applied.

Marsh v. *Chambers* marks the beginning of what strict separationists feel has been an erosion of a strict (and correct) interpretation of the Establishment Clause. As the more accommodationist approach to the clause has evolved, both in the nation and on the Court (a process discussed in chapter 9), *Marsh* v. *Chambers* has been seen as a bellwether and model of what that accommodationism should look like. But its immediate and obvious result was that state-paid legislative chaplains, even of one denomination year after year, are constitutional.

There are other chaplaincy programs that are alleged to raise constitutional questions, although the Supreme Court has not dealt with any of them. Many have argued that for the federal government to provide chaplains to the military at government expense, and for the federal government or the various state governments to provide chaplains to prisoners in their respective prisons, is a violation of the Establishment Clause. But the counterargument (and this is the position the various governments have taken) is that if a government did not provide chaplains for military personnel or prisoners, they would be denied their Free Exercise Clause rights. The government takes military personnel and prisoners out of their home environments and compels them to go somewhere else. In their new locations the religious among them do not have the opportunity to practice their religion as they did at home. For the government not to provide any religious services to them would be an unconstitutional establishment of secularism and a denial of their free exercise of religion. Of course, the government does not compel the persons to utilize the services. Consequently, although providing chaplains with government funds might appear to violate the Establishment Clause, the Free Exercise Clause requires government to supply the opportunity for religious activity, thus justifying the "violation."[14]

A CHURCH AS GOVERNMENT AGENT

Larkin v. *Grendel's Den*[15] is a strange case. Cambridge, Massachusetts, had an ordinance that prohibited the licensing of a place of business to sell alcoholic beverages if the place was within five hundred feet of a church or school and if the governing body of the church or school protested its presence. Grendel's Den, a restaurant that was located ten feet from Holy Cross Armenian Catholic Church, applied for a liquor license. Holy Cross Church protested the granting of the license, as it was entitled to do under the law, and the License Commission voted to deny Grendel's Den's application. The restaurant then sued the License Commission in federal district court, claiming that the statute violated the Establishment Clause.

The Supreme Court, in an opinion written by Chief Justice Warren Burger in 1982, decided in favor of Grendel's Den. The rationale was that the law allowed churches to exercise governmental authority, so that it was the protest of the church that triggered the enforcement of the law. Without church action, the statute would not be activated in reference to the application for a liquor license. Consequently, the church functioned in a governmental manner. No greater intermixing of church and state could occur. The ordinance had the primary and principal effect of advancing religion, a violation of the second part of the "*Lemon* test."

> [T]he core rationale underlying the Establishment Clause is preventing "a fusion of governmental and religious functions." The Framers did not set up a system of government in which important, discretionary governmental powers would be delegated to or shared with religious institutions.[16]

The Court emphasized that it had no objection to the intent of the law in question; it is perfectly acceptable to have zoning laws that prohibit the sale of alcoholic beverages within a close distance to schools and churches. But the enforcement of such laws must be triggered by a true governmental agency such as a city council or a zoning commission, not by a church, synagogue, or mosque.

UNEQUAL GOVERNMENT TREATMENT

Chapter 4 discussed cases concerning the regulation of solicitation of funds by religious groups. *Larson* v. *Valente*[17] is a solicitation case with an Establishment Clause dimension. An issue that has risen occasionally in the last three decades has been concern over "cults." A widespread perception exists, fed by media hunger for sensationalist headlines, that such groups are heretical, sinister, fraudulent, and rapacious in their search for money. As a result of this image, governments have sometimes taken measures to try to inhibit controversial religious groups, or, at least, to keep them under close surveillance. That seems to have been Minnesota's motivation when it amended its charitable solicitation law in 1978. Prior to then, the law required organizations soliciting funds in the state to submit forms telling the percentage of income spent on administrative costs. If the amount rose above 30 percent, organizations were forbidden to solicit funds in the state. Religious groups were exempt from the requirement. In 1978 a provision was added to the law which stated that a religious group that raised more than 50 percent of its revenue from its own membership would continue to be exempt from the solicitation law. If more than 50 percent of its revenue came from nonmembers, however, the organization would have to register with the state, file financial disclosure forms, and be subject to state scrutiny. Right after the change in the law, state officials wrote to the Unification Church, the leader of which is the Rev. Sun Myung Moon, saying that it was now required to register. The church initiated a lawsuit, claiming that the law discriminated among religious organizations, a violation of the Establishment Clause.

The Supreme Court found in favor of the Unification Church. Justice William Brennan's opinion began with the recognition that Minnesota had a significant interest in protecting its citizens from fraudulent charitable organizations. But, he wrote, it is also clear that the Establishment Clause commands that the state cannot prefer one denomination over another—and that was what the law effected in this case. It was clear that the law targeted for stricter state scrutiny those religious groups which solicited funds in airports, parks, or shopping centers, as opposed to those which received most of their funds from the Sunday morning collection plate. The 50 percent rule treated religious groups differently, and the no-establishment principle would not allow this. The Unification Church could not be compelled to register and report under that provision of the statute.

The larger lesson, of course, is that governments may not pass laws that enable them to inflict greater surveillance and regulation on controversial religious groups.

TAXES

The question of the taxation of religious institutions has been a vexing one over the years. Many have argued that churches should not be exempt from either income or property taxes. Frequently, when the country is in economic hard times, such as the late 1980s and early 1990s, and governmental units are searching frantically for new sources of revenue, the argument is made that if the religious institutions were taxed, the economic problems of America would be over. Not only is that too optimistic a statement, but it also fails to recognize that there are strong constitutional arguments for the exemption of religious institutions from taxation. The Supreme Court has dealt with several different dimensions of the question of the taxation of religious institutions.

Property-Tax Exemptions

One of the earliest tax issues taken up by the Supreme Court was that of property-tax exemptions for religious institutions. In *Walz* v. *Tax Commission of the City of New York,*[18] in 1970, a challenge was made against tax exemptions for buildings used exclusively for worship. The case was a narrow one. It did not involve parsonages, education buildings, camps, or other properties religious institutions might own. The Supreme Court has never dealt with exemptions for those kinds of properties. But on the question of tax exemptions for sanctuaries, the Court has spoken clearly. The allegation in *Walz* was that property-tax exemptions are a violation of the Establishment Clause, because they amount to government support of religion. Religious institutions are obviously relieved of an expenditure because of the exemptions, which allows them to spend that money for religious programming. Furthermore, those who do pay property taxes indirectly make contributions to religious institutions. That is, church properties are the beneficiaries of government services (for example, police and fire protection) for which they do not pay. Because those services are funded, at least in part, by those who do pay property taxes, those taxpayers are indirectly compelled to make a contribution to religious organizations, in violation of the Establishment Clause.

The Court, in an opinion written by Chief Justice Burger, decided that property-tax exemptions do not violate the Establishment Clause. It used three arguments to support its finding. One was a historical argument. Tax exemptions for religious properties are nothing new in American history. The Court found examples in the colonial period and in other times since the Revolutionary War. It concluded that even though there is a long history of such tax exemptions, there is no evidence that the practice has ever created even "the remotest sign of leading to an established church or religion."[19]

A second rationale was what may be called a "charitable class argument." Religious properties were part of a larger class of eleemosynary institutions (from the Greek *eleēmosynē*, "mercy") such as schools, museums, libraries, and hospitals, all of which were exempt from property taxes, and thus were not singled out for special government favor.

A third argument raised the issue of "excessive entanglement." The Establishment Clause was designed to minimize interaction between church and state. If governments were allowed to collect property taxes from religious institutions, that would have the effect of raising the level of interaction between churches and civil authority. But to continue to exempt religious properties from taxation would keep the entanglement of church and state at a lower, and acceptable, level.

> Either course, taxation of churches or exemption, occasions some degree of involvement with religion. Elimination of exemption would tend to expand the involvement of government by giving rise to tax valuation of church property, tax liens, tax foreclosures, and the direct confrontations and conflicts that follow in the train of those legal processes.

Granting tax exemptions to churches necessarily operates to afford an indirect economic benefit and also gives rise to some, but yet a lesser, involvement than taxing them.[20]

(As described earlier, this argument became the third "prong" of the "*Lemon* test" for interpreting the Establishment Clause.)

These three arguments combined made it very clear that property-tax exemptions for places of worship do not violate the Establishment Clause.

The class argument is an effective answer to those who would take away the tax exemptions of religious institutions, whether for property or income taxes. Given that there is a broad class of exempt organizations, to eliminate the exemptions of religious organizations only would single them out for special, negative treatment. That is arguably unconstitutional as a violation of the Establishment Clause. Only the most radical enemy of exemptions would be willing to eliminate them for all charitable organizations, given the variety of beneficial services those organizations render to society. But that would be the only way to remove the exemptions for religious organizations without running afoul of the Constitution.

Social Security Taxes

Social Security taxes were the subject of *United States* v. *Lee*.[21] The case has to do with the Old Order Amish and their attitudes toward interaction with government. The Amish have a strong belief in hard work and self-sufficiency and, because of that, prefer to care for their own sick or aged. They also regard this as a religious obligation in response to 1 Timothy 5:8: "If any one does not provide for his relatives, and especially for his own family, he has disowned the faith and is worse than an unbeliever" (RSV). They thus believe that to pay Social Security taxes and receive benefits therefrom is to acknowledge that the government has a responsibility to care for the aged and infirm—and that is to deny the faith. So the Amish petitioned Congress for an exemption from participating in the Social Security program. They based their petition on Free Exercise Clause grounds. Congress granted an exemption for the self-employed among the Amish and any other religious groups with theological objections to Social Security from paying the taxes and receiving the benefits of the program.[22]

The *Lee* case arose when an Amish employer of Amish employees failed to file required Social Security tax forms for them, withhold the tax from the employees' paychecks, and pay the employer's share of the Social Security tax. Eventually the IRS presented Lee with a bill for back taxes. Instead of paying, Lee sued, claiming that his free exercise of religion rights exempted him from making the required payments and submitting the required forms. He argued that this was especially true in light of the exemption Congress had granted the Amish from participation in the Social Security program.

Chief Justice Warren Burger wrote the 1982 opinion for a unanimous Court. Although the justices accepted the fact that the Amish had religiously based conscientious objection to participation in Social Security, they ruled that there were two reasons why Lee could not win his contention. First, the exemption from Social Security granted by Congress was only for self-employed Amish, not Amish employers, even when their employees were also Amish. The Court was not willing to, indeed could not, go beyond the narrow exemption provided by the law. Second, although Lee's request was based on sincerely held religious belief, his free-exercise argument could not prevail in this circumstance. "Not all burdens on religion are unconstitutional. The state may justify a limitation on religious liberty by showing that it is essential to accomplish an overriding governmental interest."[23] The essential governmental interest in this case was preserving the integrity of the Social Security tax system. The system is huge, with multiple millions of participants. To begin to have to grant exemptions beyond what Congress had already authorized would put a strain on the system.

> The tax system could not function if denominations were allowed to challenge the tax system because tax payments were spent in a manner that violates their religious belief. Because the broad public interest in maintaining a sound tax system is of such a high order, religious belief in conflict with the payment of taxes affords no basis for resisting the tax.[24]

Congress had earlier provided the Amish a narrow exemption from Social Security taxes. That was all they were to have.

Sales Tax

The Court has also dealt with the question of religious exemptions from sales-tax collection. A Texas law exempted from its sales tax periodicals that promoted the teaching of religious faith and books that were writings sacred to a religious faith. Nonreligious periodicals and books were not exempt from the sales tax. A secular magazine, *Texas Monthly*, filed suit, claiming that the exemption for religious publications was discriminatory and a violation of the Establishment Clause, because it gave preferential treatment to the religious publications.

The Supreme Court dealt with the issue in *Texas Monthly* v. *Bullock*,[25] in which in 1989 it decided against the State of Texas. Justice William Brennan's opinion began with the observation that the Establishment Clause does not forbid government policies or programs that incidentally aid religion, that is, when the secular, nonsectarian aims of government and those of religion overlap. The primary way to tell whether the government aid to religion is actually incidental to religion is to determine whether the aid is widely distributed to nonreligious organizations as well. Texas's tax exemption was not available to publications generally; it was available only to those magazine subscriptions and books that had religious content and, indeed, *promulgated* the teachings of religious faiths. To not require the buyers of such publications to pay sales tax clearly was a government aid to their sale. The Court concluded that the tax exemption was state sponsorship of religious belief and consequently banned by the Establishment Clause.

Texas tried to make its case by arguing that if it were not allowed to exempt religious publications, it would be infringing on the Free Exercise Clause rights of their publishers. In making this argument, it relied on *Murdock* v. *Pennsylvania*,[26] a Jehovah's Witness case in which the Court ruled that a city could not impose a flat tax on a religious activity *for the privilege of engaging in that activity*. Texas's theory was that the sales tax exemption was necessary to avoid the kind of tax forbidden in *Murdock*. The Court rejected that argument, saying that there was no evidence that the payment of a sales tax by subscribers would inhibit the religious activity of the publishers. Conversely, Texas also argued that to uphold *Murdock* would suggest that government may never tax religious publications, and that would be a violation of the Establishment Clause. The Court rejected that argument, as well. It pointed out that the *Murdock* rule held that while the government may not tax a minister *for the privilege of preaching*, it may tax the income of the minister, just as it taxes the income of people in other professions, as a part of a general taxation program.

Consequently, the Court held that a state may exempt the sale of all books and subscriptions to magazines, including those with religious content, from its sales tax. On the other hand, it may tax the sale of all books and subscriptions to magazines, including those containing religion. But it may not exempt religious publications only, for that is a violation of the Establishment Clause.

Another case involving sales taxes was *Jimmy Swaggart Ministries* v. *Board of Equalization of California*.[27] California requires retailers to pay a sales tax on the items they sell. There is also a use tax, which is a sales tax paid by the residents of California for the items they buy from out-of-state retailers. In both cases, the tax is collected by the seller at the time of sale.

Between 1974 and 1981 Jimmy Swaggart Ministries conducted twenty-three evangelistic crusades in California. During those meetings, religious and nonreligious items were sold to those who attended. The Ministries also published a magazine, sold nationwide by subscription. The magazine carried advertisements and order forms for items that could be purchased from the Ministries' headquarters in Baton Rouge, Louisiana. Among those who made mail-order purchases were residents of California.

In 1980 the California Board of Equalization informed Jimmy Swaggart Ministries that its sales were subject to both the sales and use taxes. The Board calculated how much had been bought in in-state crusades and through the mail-order process and sent the Ministries a bill for back taxes, interest, and a penalty for a total of $166,145.10. The Swaggart organization did not protest the taxes on merchandise such as T-shirts, mugs, bowls, plates, pen and pencil sets, all with the logo of the Ministries on them. But it did contest the taxes on religious items such as books, tapes of sermons, and Bibles, and on religious music in the form of songbooks, tapes, and records. The Swaggart organization argued that a tax on religious materials violates both the Free Exercise and Establishment Clauses.

The Free Exercise challenge was that the taxes inhibited the exercise of the Ministries' religion. Swaggart based his challenge on *Murdock* v. *Pennsylvania*, claiming that that case forbids a state from imposing a tax on the sale of religious items used for evangelistic purposes by a religious organization. The Court, in an opinion written by Justice Sandra Day O'Connor, rejected that argument. Noting that *Murdock* had held only that a state may not put a tax on a religious activity as a precondition to engaging in that activity (that is, the tax could not be a prior restraint), the Court held that California's tax did not have that function. The tax was not restricted to sales of religious items only, but rather applied to all retail sales made in the state. It in no sense was a prior restraint. That is, it was not collected from the seller as a payment for the privilege of conducting sales in the state, but from the buyer only as the item was sold. Furthermore, there was no evidence that the tax violated the religious beliefs of those engaged in the ministry. The Court concluded that the Free Exercise Clause did not require the state to grant the Ministries an exemption from its sales and use taxes.

Swaggart Ministries also claimed that the taxes violated the Establishment Clause because they created excessive entanglement between government and the religious organization. The Court disagreed, claiming that the collection and payment of sales and use taxes creates hardly any entanglement at all. Indeed, a general tax, which does not exempt sales of religious articles, actually lessens the possibility of entanglement between government officials and religious groups. If religious items were exempt from taxation, government officials would have to determine what is religious, and so qualifies for the exemption, and what is not. That would entangle the activities of government and the religious organization more than a tax that applied to all sales of all items. (This is virtually identical to one of the Court's arguments in the property-tax exemption case *Walz* v. *Tax Commission*.) Consequently, the California sales and use taxes did not create excessive entanglement between church and state and were not unconstitutional as they applied to the sales of religious items.

Federal Income Tax

Finally, in the area of taxation, there is a line of cases involving religion and federal income taxes. Section 501(c)(3) of the Internal Revenue Code is the law that describes the categories of institutions and organizations that are exempt from federal income tax. The law exempts, in pertinent part:

> Corporations, and any community chest, fund, or foundation, organized and operated *exclusively* for religious, charitable, scientific, testing for public safety, literary, or educational purposes, . . . *no part* of the net earnings of which inures to the benefit of any private shareholder or individual, *no substantial part* of the activities of which is carrying on propaganda, or otherwise attempting, to influence legislation . . . , and which does not participate in, or intervene in (including the publishing or distributing of statements), any political campaign on behalf of any candidate for public office.[28]

In order for a religious organization, either a denomination or a local congregation, to be exempt from federal income tax, it must conform with the restrictions contained within this section of the law. Furthermore, the law on deductibility, section 170 of the code, contains language that is virtually identical to section 501(c)(3). So, if an organization loses its tax exemption, it also loses deductibility; that is, those who donate to the now nonexempt organization cannot deduct their contributions from their personal income taxes. Because many people make contributions to religious organizations as much to get the tax deduction as because they believe in the theology or work of the group, for the organization to lose its tax exemption would be a double blow. Not only would it now have to pay taxes on income, but its donors and potential donors would lose a primary incentive to make donations.

A case that vividly illustrates how this works is *Christian Echoes National Ministry* v. *United States*.[29] This case was not decided by a Supreme Court opinion, but it is included because it has such relevance to denominations and local churches. Christian Echoes National Ministry was organized by Dr. Billy James Hargis in 1951; in 1953, it was recognized by the IRS as a 501(c)(3) organization. The Ministry was fundamentalist in theology and vehemently opposed to Communism. "Its mission [was] a battle against Communism, socialism and political liberalism, all of which [were] considered arch enemies of the Christian faith."[30] In 1964 the IRS revoked the Ministry's tax exemption (and thus its deductibility). The reason for the revocation was that through its publications and radio broadcasts, which were the bulk of its activities, the Ministry had encouraged people to write to their congressional representatives in support of conservative causes: to support the Becker and Dirksen amendments (both attempts to amend the Constitution to restore prayer to the public schools after *Abington Township School District* v. *Schempp*); withdraw from the United Nations; outlaw the Communist Party in the United States; and stop federal aid to education, socialized medicine, and public housing, among a long list of political concerns. In

addition, the Ministry endorsed the candidacy of Barry Goldwater in the
1964 presidential election. In the face of the IRS's action, the Ministry paid
the back taxes, interest, and penalty and sued in federal court to recover its
money and restore its exemption.

The court of appeals found in favor of the government. I quote a fairly
long passage from the opinion, because it spells out the rationale for exempting charitable organizations and also the rationale for removing exemptions
because of political activity by charitable organizations.

> The exemption to corporations organized and operated exclusively for
> charitable, religious, educational or other purposes carried on for charity is
> granted because of the benefit the public obtains from their activities and
> is based on the theory that: " . . . the Government is compensated for the
> loss of revenue by its relief from financial burden which would otherwise
> have to be met by appropriations from public funds, and by the benefits
> resulting from the promotion of the general welfare." H.R. Rep. No. 1860,
> 75th Cong., 3d Sess. 19 (1939). Tax exemptions are matters of legislative
> grace and taxpayers have the burden of establishing their entitlement to
> exemptions. The limitations in Section 501(c)(3) stem from the Congres-
> sional policy that the United States Treasury should be neutral in *political
> affairs and that substantial activities directed to attempts to influence legislation
> or affect a political campaign should not be subsidized.*[31]

The court concluded that the IRS was correct in removing the Ministry's
exemption on the ground that a substantial amount of its time and resources
had been devoted to legislative initiatives and the support of specific candidates. But Christian Echoes National Ministry vigorously argued that such
activity was protected by the Free Exercise Clause because it was religiously
motivated. The Ministry and its followers had religious convictions about
the welfare of the nation and its citizens, and it was for that reason that it
had become involved in the political arena. To remove the tax exemption was
an attack on free-exercise rights and a discrimination against religion.

The court answered that argument by essentially ignoring it. The IRS
and the court explicitly acknowledged that Christian Echoes engaged in the
political activities because of religious motivations. They said that the Ministry could engage in whatever political activity it wanted, for even religious
motivations; it just could not do so *and* have a tax exemption.

> A religious organization that engages in substantial activity aimed at influ-
> encing legislation is disqualified from tax exemption, whatever the motiva-
> tion. . . . The free exercise clause of the First Amendment is restrained
> only to the extent of denying tax exempt status and then only in keeping
> with an overwhelming and compelling Governmental interest: That of
> guarantying [*sic*] that the wall separating church and state remain high and
> firm. . . . The taxpayer may engage in all such activities without restraint,
> subject, however, to withholding of the exemption or, in the alternative,

the taxpayer may refrain from such activities and obtain the privilege of exemption.[32]

In essence, your religious organization can be political *or* you can have tax exemption and deductibility; but you cannot have the tax benefits if you believe that religion places an obligation on you to be involved in the social/ political arena and you use a "substantial" amount of time and resources to do it. The United States Supreme Court subsequently denied certiorari to the *Christian Echoes* case.[33]

One of the most celebrated and bitterly fought cases of the late 1970s and early 1980s was *Bob Jones University* v. *United States*.[34] In 1970, based on its interpretation of the Civil Rights Act of 1964, the IRS announced that henceforth institutions that discriminated on the basis of race could no longer be section 501(c)(3) and section 170 institutions. Bob Jones University, a fundamentalist Christian institution, believed that the Bible clearly teaches that interracial dating and marriage are forbidden. At that time, the University had a policy of not admitting black students. In 1971 it changed its policy, to admit black people married within their race, but to continue to exclude unmarried black people. After 1975 it admitted unmarried black students, but continued to have strict rules against interracial dating, the penalty for violation being expulsion from the school. After some preliminary notification, in 1975 the IRS revoked the tax exemption of Bob Jones University because it was not in conformity with congressionally established public policy. The school had not violated any of the specific provisions of section 501(c)(3), but its racial policies were not consistent with national policy on that issue. The university responded with a suit in federal court, claiming that the IRS action denied its free exercise of religion and that the IRS had acted improperly, in that it had assumed a role that belonged only to Congress.

The Supreme Court seemed to think that this was not a difficult case. Chief Justice Burger's opinion began with the assertion that there are essentially two dimensions to income-tax exemption. One dimension is the specifications of the law itself. Obviously an institution must conform to those to maintain exempt status. The second dimension is public policy; an institution must be consistent with that to be exempt, as well. The rationale behind exempting organizations is that they perform charitable services the government otherwise would have to perform at taxpayer expense. Thus, an exempt institution must serve a public purpose and not be contrary to public policy established by Congress. Because the Civil Rights Act of 1964 had made racial discrimination contrary to public policy, Bob Jones was not in compliance. Consequently, although the university had not specifically violated any of the provisions of section 501(c)(3), the IRS had acted properly in revoking its tax exemption and deductibility.

[I]t cannot be said that educational institutions that, for whatever reasons, practice racial discrimination, are institutions exercising "beneficial and stabilizing influences on public life," or should be encouraged by having all taxpayers share in their support by way of special tax status. . . . Whatever may be the rationale for such private schools' policies, and however sincere the rationale may be, racial discrimination in education is contrary to public policy. Racially discriminatory educational institutions cannot be viewed as conferring a public benefit within the "charitable" concept . . . or within the Congressional intent underlying §170 and §501(c)(3).[35]

To the university's allegation that the IRS had assumed for itself a role only appropriate to Congress, the Court disagreed. Congress had created the agency to implement and enforce the tax laws and gave to the agency the authority to do so. This authority included making the kind of rulings being attacked in this case. Congress can change IRS rules and procedures if it considers either one wrong, but until that happens, the agency has the authority to implement public policy. The Court was unwilling to step in here.

On the more important constitutional question of whether the IRS's action had denied Bob Jones University freedom of religion, the Court's answer was almost curt. It asserted that religious freedom is subject to limitation, if the limitation is necessary for the government to accomplish a major interest. The government interest here—the elimination of racism in America—was compelling. Consequently, the university was not entitled to its tax exemption. The IRS action did not interfere with the university's freedom of religion. The university could still believe, on the basis of sincerely held theology, that racial intermixing was wrong. It just could not implement such a belief *and* have an income-tax exemption.

Denial of tax benefits will inevitably have a substantial impact on the operation of private religious schools, but will not prevent those schools from observing their religious tenets.

The governmental interest at stake here is compelling. . . . [T]he government has a fundamental, overriding interest in eradicating racial discrimination in education. . . . That governmental interest substantially outweighs whatever burden denial of tax benefits places on petitioners' exercise of their religious beliefs.[36]

So, religious groups stand in danger of losing their income-tax exemption and their deductibility either by becoming substantially involved in the political arena or by beliefs or practices that are contrary to established public policy.

Charitable Contributions

Two cases have dealt with the issue of what *is* a charitable contribution under section 170 of the IRS code. One of those, *Hernandez* v. *Commissioner of Internal Revenue*,[37] decided in 1989, may have significant implications for local congregations. It involved the deductibility from personal income taxes of payments made for services received from the Church of Scientology.

Scientology is a psychologically oriented organization, whose members are expected to undergo a procedure known as "auditing." Auditing is designed to identify and eliminate a person's spiritual and/or psychological difficulties. An auditor (counselor) asks a series of probing questions to bring psychic stress to a person's consciousness in order to discuss the stress, identify it for what it is, and thereby purge it. The goal of Scientology is to help a person to reach the condition of "clear." Roughly equivalent to salvation, clear is the state of being free of all psychological/spiritual malfunctions. Given that a person may have a multitude of such problems, accumulated not only from the earlier years of his or her present life but from previous lives, the process of auditing may be long, requiring many sessions.

In addition to auditing, Scientology offers doctrinal courses, known as "training." The primary function of this instruction is to prepare people to become auditors. The training courses, like auditing sessions, are provided in sequential levels. Scientologists believe that spiritual gains result from participation in such courses.

Scientology charges fees for both auditing and training. It calls these charges a "price," a "fixed donation," or a "fixed contribution." Furthermore, there is a schedule with a set price for each level of each service. The payments are based on a central concept of Scientology, the "doctrine of exchange." This is the idea that anytime one receives something, one must pay something back. Under this doctrine, the revenue generated from auditing and training are Scientology's primary source of income.

The plaintiffs in *Hernandez* had deducted the payments they had made for auditing and training from their federal income tax, claiming that they were a section 170 charitable contribution. The IRS disallowed the contributions, saying that because they were payments for specific services and made in response to a specific fee schedule, they were not real *contributions*. The plaintiffs sued to restore the deductibility of their contributions.

The Supreme Court, like the lower courts, denied their request. The Court, in an opinion by Justice Thurgood Marshall, asserted that Congress, in passing the charitable contribution section of the law, said that payments made in return for goods or services are not contributions. " 'The *sine qua non* of a charitable contribution is a transfer of money or property *without adequate consideration.*' "[38]

The plaintiffs argued that they were entitled to the deductions because a quid pro quo analysis is not appropriate when the benefit the taxpayer receives is completely religious in nature. Furthermore, any payment made in order to be able to participate in a religious service should be automatically deductible.

The Court was not persuaded by these arguments: the language of section 170 would not support them. Congress has restricted deductibility to only gifts or contributions. Payments to religious organizations are not in a separate category. Furthermore, the Scientologists' theory would increase the entanglement between church and state. That is, the IRS and ultimately the judiciary would have to differentiate between religious benefits and secular ones. That would be impermissible under the Establishment Clause. Accordingly, the Court held that payments for auditing and training, made on the basis of a quid pro quo fee schedule, were not deductible.

The Scientologists argued that the law created a denominational preference by erecting a harsher standard of deductibility for religious groups that raise funds by imposing fixed costs for participation in some religious practices. The Court disagreed. The law does not discriminate between denominations. If the payment is a gift or contribution, it is deductible. If it is given with the expectation of a quid pro quo return, it is not deductible. Those provisions of the law are true in reference to all religions. Section 170 bears no animus to religion in general or Scientology in particular. As for entanglement, while it is true that ascertaining whether a payment to a religious institution is a quid pro quo transaction may require the IRS to obtain pertinent information from the religious group, that involves neither inquiry into religious doctrine nor close administrative contact between the IRS and the religious group in question. Also, section 170 does not require the government to put a monetary value on a religious service.

The Scientologists also argued that the denial of deductibility of these payments to the church violated their free-exercise rights by deterring adherents from engaging in auditing and training sessions, and that it interfered with the observance of the "doctrine of exchange."

The Court responded by saying that the doctrine of Scientology does not forbid the payment of taxes generally or, specifically, in connection with auditing or training. At most, the denial of deduction may mean that adherents have less money available to use for auditing and training. The same is true with the doctrine of exchange. But *any* taxing program reduces one's discretionary money; it does not make that tax unconstitutional.

The Scientologists continued their fight with the IRS, however, and on November 1, 1993, the Court's decision became academic for them when the IRS reversed its position and granted tax exemption and deductibility.

A similar case was *Davis* v. *United States*.[39] Some Mormon parents wanted to deduct the payments they had made to their sons who were engaged in missionary work on behalf of the church. The money was sent to the missionaries, who had discretion over how it was to be spent, rather than to the church. Even though the missionaries were acting on behalf of the church and had used the money for expenses directly related to their missionary work, the IRS would not allow the deductions. The reason was that the contributions were not "for the use of" the church and were not in the control of the exempt organization, as required by the statute. The Supreme Court upheld the IRS's ruling.

The "bottom line" of all this is that no payment to a religious organization, national or local, is deductible from federal income taxes if it is given in expectation of a specific return, or in payment, according to a set price, for goods or services already rendered. If money is given in such a way that the exempt organization does not have control over its use, it likewise is not deductible under section 170.

RELIGIOUS SYMBOLS ON PUBLIC PROPERTY

One of the more interesting problems to come before the Court in the last decade has been the question of the constitutionality of religious symbols, sometimes financed by public funds, on public property. The issue first came before the Supreme Court in 1984, in a case from Pawtucket, Rhode Island, *Lynch* v. *Donnelly*.[40] The city each Christmas erected a display, a nativity scene surrounded with other paraphernalia of Christmas—a wishing well, reindeer, candy-striped poles, a Christmas tree, Santa Claus, and his house. Some residents of the community sued, claiming that the display, owned and maintained by the city, which contained the scene of the birth of Jesus, was clearly city sponsorship of religion, a violation of the Establishment Clause.

The Supreme Court disagreed with that contention. Chief Justice Warren Burger wrote for the Court that the Establishment Clause does not demand strict separation between church and state. In fact, he said, it demands accommodation between the two. In this case, it was clear that the city did not intend to promote Christianity with its display, nor did it. Analogous to religious paintings hanging in the National Gallery of Art, the crèche with Jesus, Mary, and Joseph appeared with many secular symbols of Christmas that communicated that it is really just a festive season. "The crèche in the display depicts the historical origins of this traditional event long recognized as a National Holiday."[41] Given the visual impact of the total display, the city had not singled out a specifically religious symbol for display for the winter holiday season, and thus had not violated the Establishment Clause. There was no reason for the city not to continue to use the display.

The key to the decision in *Lynch* is that the nativity scene was surrounded by a multitude of secular symbols of the season. This has been referred to as the "plastic reindeer rule." After the decision was handed down, legal scholars wondered what the Court would decide if there were a city-sponsored nativity scene standing alone.

Allegheny County v. *ACLU of Pittsburgh*[42] in 1989 enabled them to find out. There were two religious symbols involved in this case. One was a nativity scene that stood on the "grand staircase" of the Allegheny County Courthouse. The staircase was in a prominent place in the courthouse and readily observable by all who came into the building. The crèche included the figures of the holy family, some animals, shepherds, and Wise Men, and a manger. Positioned above the scene was an angel bearing a banner with the inscription "Gloria in Excelsis Deo!" There were small evergreen trees and poinsettia plants on the periphery of the display, as well as a sign stating "This Display Donated by the Holy Name Society." The display was essentially a standing-alone nativity scene.

The other display was a block away, at a building jointly owned by the city and the county. There was displayed an eighteen-foot Hanukkah menorah, donated by a group of Lubavitcher Hasidim, an ultra-orthodox branch of Judaism. Alongside the menorah was a forty-five-foot Christmas tree. At the foot of the tree was a sign bearing the mayor's name and the motto "Salute to Liberty." Beneath the motto the sign stated: "During this holiday season, the City of Pittsburgh salutes liberty. Let these festive lights remind us that we are the keepers of the flame of liberty and our legacy of freedom."

The Pittsburgh chapter of the ACLU and some local residents filed suit, claiming that the displays violated the Establishment Clause because they gave government endorsement to religion. The task of the Supreme Court was to determine whether the crèche and the menorah, in their particular settings, had the effect of endorsing religious beliefs.

The Court, in Justice Harry Blackmun's opinion, declared the nativity scene, standing alone in the courthouse, to be unconstitutional. Unlike the crèche in *Lynch* v. *Donnelly*, there was nothing to detract from its religious message. Furthermore, it was located on the grand staircase of the county courthouse, which communicated the message of government approval and support.

> Thus, by permitting the display of the crèche in this particular physical setting, the county sends an unmistakable message that it supports and promotes the Christian praise to God that is the crèche's religious message. . . . [T]he Establishment Clause does not limit only the religious content of the government's own communications. It also prohibits the government's support and promotion of religious communications by religious organizations. . . . In sum, *Lynch* teaches that government may celebrate Christmas in some manner and form, but not in a way that endorses Christian doctrine. Here, Allegheny County has transgressed this line. It has chosen to celebrate Christmas in a way that has the effect of endorsing a patently Christian message: Glory to God for the birth of Jesus Christ.[43]

When the Court turned to the question of the menorah, it reached a different conclusion. The menorah was accompanied by both a Christmas tree and a sign in praise of liberty. Justice Blackmun recognized that the menorah is a religious symbol of Judaism, although it is the symbol of a holiday that has both religious and secular dimensions, as is the Christmas tree. To have the two in juxtaposition is to recognize that they represent two holidays, not one. That, by itself, would not save them from Establishment Clause stricture. If the city celebrates two religious holidays it still violates the clause. But, if it celebrates them as secular holidays, then the clause is not violated. The Court concluded that the two symbols together showed that the city did not want to endorse either religion, but

> rather simply recognizes that both Christmas and Chanukah are part of the same winter-holiday season, which has attained secular status in our society. . . . [I]t is not "sufficiently likely" that residents of Pittsburgh will perceive the combined display of the tree, the sign, and the menorah as an "endorsement" or "disapproval . . . of their individual religious choices."[44]

So, in the matter of religious symbols either financed with public money or sponsored by the government, the rule seems to be that if the symbol stands alone, it is a violation of the Establishment Clause. But if a display combines the symbols of several religions and is accompanied by some secular object, if it passes the "plastic reindeer rule," or if the holiday clearly has a cultural as well as a religious dimension, the display merits constitutional approval.

9

Flash Points and the Future

In the preceding chapters the decisions of the Court have been described with only occasional notice taken of dissenting opinions and with little commentary. That should not suggest that everything is tranquil or positive or unanimous in the area of church–state relationships. In fact, the contrary is true. In this area, as in so many other areas of American social and political life, things are in turmoil. In this chapter I note some of the areas of greatest concern to those who, like me, believe that the maximum amount of religious liberty is consistent with the Constitution and best for religious groups and American life in general.

THE RISE OF THE CHRISTIAN RIGHT

Since the late 1970s the Christian Right has attracted the attention of the media, religious folk, and observers of church–state relations. The movement began primarily for secular reasons. Several members of the leadership of the secular political right wing recognized that evangelical/fundamentalist Christians, and perhaps conservatives of other religions, were a great, untapped market for their political philosophy. In an attempt to reverse the influence of both moderate and liberal lawmakers at every level of government, particularly national, these political operatives persuaded conservative Christians to become involved in the political arena. One of the earliest of these conservative Christians to make the change from being antipolitical (or at least apolitical) to political activism was Jerry Falwell, pastor of the Thomas Road Baptist Church in Lynchburg, Virginia, who in the late 1970s founded the Moral Majority, the first and most famous of the organizations of the Christian Right. This movement fit into the larger phenomenon of the turn to the right in America. Beginning in the late 1970s and continuing until now, there has been both a growing nostalgia for earlier, simpler times and much greater political conservatism. The results of this include the election of Ronald Reagan to the presidency of the nation for two terms and George Bush for one.

The Christian Right has performed a positive service for the country. After its secular political beginnings, it has been able to maintain vitality because an increasing number of people have become concerned about what they consider the moral decline in the nation. This issue, the moral corruption in every stratum of society, became the stock-in-trade of the Christian Right. Its advocates have performed a service for society by raising the issue of morality—in politics, in personal and family life, and in the media—and by stimulating national discussion. Unfortunately, the discussions have often yielded more heat than light, because Christian Right advocates themselves have often taken intractable positions that have tended to polarize society. Nonetheless, to have had these issues raised so that people had to think about them and so that a national debate has taken place is better than if the issues had not been raised at all. A democratic society is designed to thrive and progress on the basis of robust debate about political and moral issues. In many ways, society is the better and stronger for having had the Christian Right in its midst raising issues, some of which are of transcendent importance.

What has been more problematic about the movement, from the church–state point of view, is its political efforts to remake the country in its own image. Not content with simply raising the issues of public morality for public debate, the Christian Right has attempted to correct the problems it identified by trying to vote out of office those who did not pass its muster and to vote into office those who were more acceptable from a conservative religious point of view. Of course, nothing in the Constitution prevents citizens from acting in the political arena from a religious perspective. Indeed, the Free Exercise Clause guarantees people the right to participate in politics, as candidates, as voters, and as lobbyists, because of religious motivation. As Christian Right leaders are wont to say, "The First Amendment was designed to separate church from state, not religion from government." Although the statement covers up many complexities, it is essentially correct. So, in the 1980s and 1990s, adherents of the Christian Right, both at rank-and-file and leadership levels, have tried to improve this country by voting their religious convictions at the ballot box. One student of the movement summarizes the motivation as follows:

> The leadership of the movement will always be dedicated toward achieving an effective working relationship between national piety and national patriotism so that the two might function as harmonizing collaborative teammates in the pursuit of the common good. The movement remains committed to synthesizing selected Christian theological judgments with specific conceptions of how a democracy ought to function. In working toward this objective, the New Right believes that it carries the authority of both the Bible and the guiding philosophical principles of the nation's Founding Fathers.[1]

So far, so good. But there is that very first mention of religion the authors of the Constitution included in Article VI: "[N]o religious Test shall ever be required as a Qualification to any Office or public Trust under the United States." To vote people in or out of office because of their adherence or lack thereof to a theological standard is to violate the spirit, if not the letter, of Article VI. Some of the more ardent advocates of the Christian Right have argued vociferously for the creation of a "Christian America," which they mistakenly think was the posture of the nation in its first generation. To make this nation Christian it is necessary to put into office born-again Christians or those sympathetic to their views. But the Constitution prohibits any sort of religious litmus test for being qualified for public office.

Furthermore, to try to impose specifically theological ideas on the nation through legislation is contrary to the Establishment Clause, which requires that the government be religiously neutral. This means that the government not be hostile to religion, however. It does not mean that religious values may not be injected into the body politic by the religiously concerned. What the concept of separation prohibits is religious groups, singly or in concert, trying to legislate the relation of people to God. Such concepts or procedures would be narrowly theological and inappropriate. But it is entirely legitimate to legislate the social principles of religion, as long as (1) there is a broad public consensus on the desirability of such moral tenets and (2) the laws are grounded on public policy considerations.

So, the rise of the Christian Right has both raised interesting issues for the church–state (and the broader moral) debate and, at the same time, placed great stress on the concept of separation. Nowhere is this stress more apparent regarding the Supreme Court on church and state than the election of Ronald Reagan and, later, George Bush, to the presidency. It certainly cannot be said that the Christian Right was wholly responsible for electing either of these men, but there is evidence that it contributed significantly to that result. There is no doubt that both candidates courted the Christian Right and identified with it, at least for purposes of being elected. In part to appease the Christian Right, both these Presidents adhered to the philosophy that the justices of the Court were to be "strict constructionists" and judicial passivists (not pacifists). The idea of strict construction is that those who judge must do so on the basis of the original meaning of the constitutional text. This is also known as judging on the basis of the "original intent" of the authors of the Constitution. This philosophy is especially applicable to adjudicating under the Establishment Clause, and will be discussed shortly. The idea of a passivist as opposed to an activist judiciary is frequently expressed in the saying that judges "are to interpret law, not make law." A judicially passive Court would defer to the other branches of government as much as possible, especially the legislative branch.

In their appointments to the High Court, Presidents Reagan and Bush adhered to their philosophy, with the possible exception of Justice David Souter, whose concurring opinions in *Lee* v. *Weisman* and *Church of the*

Lukumi Babalu Aye v. *City of Hialeah* suggest that he may not fit the mold. Presidents also have the responsibility of appointing the judges for the federal district courts and courts of appeals. The two men appointed hundreds of federal judges, filling the vast majority of positions available.[2] From the viewpoint of their critics, of whom there were many, their philosophy and appointments turned back the cultural and judicial clock. There is no doubt that in the area of church–state relationships, the justices appointed by Presidents Reagan and Bush have made a dramatic change in the Court. The Supreme Court has changed direction in its understanding of the Religion Clauses. In what follows below, I argue that the approach of the Court has put religious freedom in the greatest peril.

THE FREE EXERCISE CLAUSE

To understand the assault on religious freedom from the free-exercise side, it is necessary to quickly review what was said in chapter 4 about the "compelling state interest test." It is commonly accepted that the Free Exercise Clause is not absolute; the clause does not mean that "anything goes" in the area of religious behavior. From the time of Jefferson's "Bill for Establishing Religious Freedom," through *Reynolds* v. *United States*, to *Cantwell* v. *Connecticut* it was assumed that the government has the right to interfere with religious action. The question was, how much latitude does the government have to prevent or hinder religious freedom? The *"Sherbert* test," a most satisfactory answer to the question, was given in *Sherbert* v. *Verner*. This "compelling state interest test" says that the government may not interfere with religious endeavors *unless* it has a compelling interest that the religious action violates. Furthermore, it may not prevent or inhibit the expression of religious freedom if it has an alternative way to accomplish its legitimate goals without interference with religion. So, the compelling state interest test has meant that religious freedom is the rule, government interference is the exception.

This important principle was seriously undermined by *Employment Division of Oregon* v. *Smith*.[3] Justice Antonin Scalia wrote the opinion, in which he said that the compelling state interest test was no longer available in most free exercise of religion cases. His reasoning was that the test should not apply to laws of general applicability. The Court held that if a law targets religion specifically, that is, if it bans religious acts or compels acts that religious conviction forbids, then that law can be struck down under the Free Exercise Clause. However, if a law has application across the board, that is, if it does not single out religion, then the compelling state interest test cannot be used to adjudicate the concerns of a religious plaintiff. For example, in *Smith* the law in question was a law prohibiting the use of drugs on the state's list of forbidden drugs. It was a law of general applicability, in that it was a law prohibiting a wide range of drugs, including peyote. Consequently, the Court was not willing to apply the Free Exercise Clause to the worship of the Native American Church, which uses peyote as its sacrament. So the law of general applicability took precedence over the free exercise of the Native Americans in this case. Justice Scalia was not willing to apply the compelling state interest test to the issue. Furthermore, and this is one of the most important parts of this case, he generalized to say that henceforth the compelling state interest test should never be used on laws of general applicability, except in unemployment compensation cases.

But that was not all. The majority ruled that the Free Exercise Clause itself does not apply to laws aimed at general behavior, except in certain circumstances. The Free Exercise Clause can be used to adjudicate a law of general application considered to be burdensome to religion *if* it is used *in combination with* other constitutional principles such as free speech, freedom of the press, or the rights of parents.[4] This means that the Free Exercise Clause is powerless unless it is supported by some other constitutionally guaranteed right. It is no longer a freestanding, independent constitutional freedom. It is no longer one of the principal freedoms that historically have made this country unique—and great.

In some of the cases of the 1940s, religious freedom, guaranteed by the Free Exercise Clause, was called by the justices a "preferred freedom."[5] Now, after the opinion of Justice Scalia, joined by Chief Justice Rehnquist and Justices Kennedy, Stevens, and White, in the majority opinion in *Smith*, it was not even a discrete freedom.

As a result of *Smith*, neither the compelling state interest test nor the Free Exercise Clause itself could be used as a defense against laws of general application, no matter how burdensome they may be to the practicing of religion. In fact, Justice Scalia wrote that the solicitude for religious freedom, which originally was the reason for existence of the compelling state interest test, is a "luxury" which "we cannot afford."[6] This means that government, at whatever level, except in the most narrow of circumstances, no longer had to show that it had a strong interest to justify its burden on religious exercise. Whereas before *Smith*, religious freedom was the rule and government interference was the exception, now just the opposite was true. Whereas before, government was of limited power in reference to religious behavior, now government had virtually unlimited power. Essentially the only limit to that power was that it could not pass a law specifically targeting religion for hostile government action. But if the law was one of general applicability, no matter how burdensome it was to religion, government would have its way under the *Smith* doctrine.

The previous paragraph must be nuanced slightly. Justice Scalia pointed out that legislatures could carve out exceptions for religion in their laws of general applicability. (For example, at the time of *Smith*, twenty-three states and the federal government had made exemptions, in their laws prohibiting drugs, for the sacramental use of peyote by the Native American Church.) They *could* carve out such exceptions—they were not constitutionally required to. But the possibility of legislative exceptions was small consolation for the small, obscure, or unpopular religious group. Such groups were at a decided disadvantage in trying to win recognition of their religious freedom needs as exceptions to general laws. Legislatures are not likely to be supportive of the practices of religious groups that cannot produce many votes or that are thought of as being odd or out of favor with the majority. Justice Scalia acknowledged that fact but said that this kind of disadvantage for the minority religious group is just an "unavoidable consequence of democratic government."[7]

I would argue that Justice Robert Jackson, a generation earlier, was more on target than Justice Scalia. Justice Jackson recognized that there are certain liberties that are not subject to majority rule, as essential as that is to democracy.

> The very purpose of a Bill of Rights was to withdraw certain subjects from the vicissitudes of political controversy, to place them beyond the reach of majorities and officials and to establish them as legal principles to be applied by the courts. One's right to life, liberty, and property, to free speech, a free press, freedom of worship and assembly, and other fundamental rights may not be submitted to vote; they depend on the outcome of no elections.[8]

What the Court did in *Smith*, having forgotten the sound constitutional principle articulated by Justice Jackson, was to adopt a position of "majoritarianism" or "statism." That is, it embraced the view of the sovereignty of the majority or of the state. One might ask, What is wrong with that? In a democratic country, the majority rules. That is what a democracy is all about. That is so, but American government is a system of checks and balances. The very concept of checks and balances recognizes that unfettered power by any branch, or by the majority over the minority, is tyranny. Specifically, the founders of the nation recognized that the state, governed by the majority, might assume to itself unlimited power. James Madison, a principal author of the Constitution, wrote in his famous "Memorial and Remonstrance": "True it is, that no other rule exists, by which any question which may divide a Society, can be ultimately determined, but the will of the majority; but it is also true that the majority may trespass on the rights of the minority" (see Appendix A). The power of the state, arrayed against the individual or minority groups, is awesome. Recognizing this potential for raw power, the founders created a government in which none of the branches could assume dominant power over the other two. That system is a symbol for the larger concept that the state, the majority, must recognize the rights of the weak: minority groups and individuals. State power must be kept in check. To do that, the founders enacted the Bill of Rights. Those ten amendments to the Constitution are all designed in some way to protect the minority, the powerless, the accused against the power of the majority acting through the mechanisms of the state.[9] To turn specifically to the freedom of religion, Peter Berger argues that

> *Religious freedom is fundamental because it posits the ultimate limit on the power of the state.* . . . [R]eligion limits the power of the state because it refuses to recognize the state's sovereignty as ultimate; religion posits *another* sovereignty beyond and indeed over that of the state. . . . [T]he state that guarantees religious liberty does more than acknowledge another human right: It acknowledges without knowing it, that its power is less than ultimate. . . . [D]emocracy, whose very essence is the limitation of state power, is always in need of firm guarantees of religious liberty.[10]

Whether or not the authors of the Constitution were fully aware of this insight, they wrote the First Amendment as a limitation on the power of the state to have its way with the people in the matter of religion. As Justice Sandra Day O'Connor insisted in her strong dissent from the rationale in *Smith*, the First Amendment was

> enacted precisely to protect the rights of those whose religious practices are not shared by the majority and may be viewed with hostility. . . . The compelling interest test reflects the First Amendment's mandate of preserving religious liberty to the fullest extent possible in a pluralistic society. For the Court to deem this command a "luxury," is to denigrate "[t]he very purpose of a Bill of Rights."[11]

The religion clauses of the First Amendment, particularly the Free Exercise Clause, are supposed to protect the minority from the tyranny of the majority. The judiciary, particularly the Supreme Court, is the branch of government to best serve that role.[12] But the Court, in *Smith*, in the name of judicial passivity, abdicated its role as defender of minority or unpopular religious groups by abandoning the compelling state interest test, relegating the Free Exercise Clause to the extreme margin of constitutionally guaranteed liberties, and exposed minority religions to the vagaries of legislative bodies—majoritarianism with a vengeance.[13]

It would have been bad enough if the Supreme Court had taken this position for itself alone. But, of course, the Supreme Court establishes the ultimate precedents for the adjudication of law by courts, federal and state, all over the country. So all the courts began to interpret free-exercise cases along the lines laid down in *Smith*. Within a few months, cases began to appear all over the country in which the free exercise of religion was curtailed, if not prohibited, in ways that never would have been possible when the compelling state interest test was applied.[14] The bottom line of all this is that religious freedom in this country was, for a time, in extreme jeopardy. As the result of the Reagan-Bush Court's decision in *Smith*, along with the growth of government, majoritarianism/statism put religious freedom at significant risk.

After the *Smith* decision, the sense of alarm about its disastrous effects on religious freedom was high. My concern was shared by so many that in response to the decision the Religious Freedom Restoration Act was introduced into Congress. Its sole purpose was to restore the compelling state interest test as a principle of adjudicating laws. It was a law that would require courts to compel the government, at whatever level, to demonstrate that it had a legitimate public-good interest of great importance that could be accomplished in no other way before it could curtail or prohibit religious activity by individuals or groups. Who would ever have thought the American people would have to petition Congress to restore what the founders of the country thought they had guaranteed through the Free Exercise Clause? But that was exactly the situation after Justice Scalia and four of his colleagues dismantled the Clause in *Smith*. The bill had the support of religious groups from across the theological spectrum, including groups of the Christian Right. So even those who had aided Presidents Reagan and Bush to get elected and insisted that they appoint conservative jurists to the federal courts, and especially to the Supreme Court, were having second thoughts in the area of religious liberty. They saw that the position taken by the Court in *Smith* was devastating to religious liberty in this country.

The Religious Freedom Restoration Act became law in November 1993.[15] Courts, including the Supreme Court, again are obligated to use the compelling state interest test when deciding Free Exercise Clause cases. Religious liberty is presumably secure again. I say "presumably" because it is not presently clear how the Court will implement the "*Sherbert* test." Justices who were willing to weaken this freedom are still on the Court[16] and it is not yet known if they will find another way to circumvent the traditional understanding of the Free Exercise Clause.

THE ESTABLISHMENT CLAUSE AND ORIGINAL INTENT

The question of the meaning and interpretation of the Establishment Clause is a flash point, as well. The controversy centers on the "original intent" of the authors of the Constitution. The position of many strict constructionists is that it is possible for later generations to know the minds of those who wrote the Constitution and that it is imperative that judges use this original intent in their interpretation of that document. Regarding the Establishment Clause, strict constructionists argue that the founders intended only to prohibit the creation of a national church. That is, all they intended with the no-establishment principle was to prohibit the government from picking one church or denomination to be the established church of the nation. The implication, then, is that they did not intend strict separation, but rather wanted to create a system in which nondiscriminatory government aid to religion was permissible. Thus, government can aid religion so long as it does so in an evenhanded way that does not show preference for one religion over another. To use terms mentioned earlier, this approach is "nonpreferentialism" or "accommodationism." In fact, according to this understanding, the government must affirmatively aid religion in order to avoid being hostile to it. This accommodationist view was articulated by Chief Justice Burger in *Lynch* v. *Donnelly*:

> "It has never been thought either possible or desirable to enforce a regime of total separation. . . . " Nor does the Constitution require complete separation of church and state; it affirmatively mandates accommodation, not merely tolerance, of all religions, and forbids hostility toward any. Anything less would require the "callous indifference" we have said was never intended by the Establishment Clause.[17]

This original intent concept was argued at length by then Justice William Rehnquist in his dissenting opinion in *Wallace* v. *Jaffree*. He summarized his argument as follows:

> The Framers intended the Establishment Clause to prohibit the designation of any church as a "national" one. The Clause was also designed to stop the Federal Government from asserting a preference for one religious denomination or sect over others. Given the "incorporation" of the Establishment Clause as against the States via the Fourteenth Amendment in *Everson*, States are prohibited as well from establishing a religion or discriminating between sects. As its history abundantly shows, however, nothing in the Establishment Clause requires government to be strictly neutral between religion and irreligion, nor does that Clause prohibit Congress or the States from pursuing legitimate secular ends through nondiscriminatory sectarian means.[18]

Based on this view, the concept of strict separation between church and state, so forcefully stated in *Everson* v. *Board of Education*, which had been the predominant view of the Court, is wrong. "The 'wall of separation between church and State' is a metaphor based on bad history, a metaphor which has proved useless as a guide to judging. It should be frankly and explicitly abandoned."[19]

However, I believe that what is *really* "bad history" and wrong is the entire "original intent" viewpoint, with its accommodationist ramification. The attempt to discern the intent of the authors of the First Amendment (to take only the part of the Constitution most relevant to our study) is flawed, if for no other reason than because there were so many consenting to its language. We know that there were some who were enthusiastic supporters of adding the amendments to the Constitution as guarantees of fundamental rights to American citizens. There were others, however, who were philosophically opposed to a Bill of Rights, but who went along with the enterprise because otherwise some states might not have ratified the Constitution. Did enthusiastic advocates and reluctant supporters of the First Amendment have the same ideas in mind when they voted for it? We cannot know. Did all the members of the Constitutional Convention understand the terms "establishment" and "free exercise" in the same way? We cannot know. An eminent scholar of the Constitution, Laurence Tribe, speaks directly to these kinds of questions:

> The nagging doubt prompted by inquiries like these is that no collective body—be it the Congress or the Constitutional Convention or the aggregate of state legislatures—can really be said to have a *single*, ascertainable "purpose" or "intent." And even if such a mythical beast could be captured and examined, how relevant would it be to us today? Should the peculiar opinions held, and the particular applications envisioned, by men who have been dead for two centuries *always* trump contemporary insights into what the living Constitution means and ought to mean? . . . But the constitutional text is not enough—we need to search for, and explain our selection of, the *principles behind* the words.[20]

Interpretation of the Constitution cannot proceed on the basis of a slavish, literalistic reading of the text. But that does not mean that judges can decide anything they want. They are, after all, supposed to interpret the Constitution. But, as Professor Tribe says, the interpretation must express "the principles behind the words." What the Court must do is to find and apply the great, living truths of the Constitution.[21] One of those great truths is the idea that government is to be limited government.[22] In chapter 2 I argued that not only did the founders believe in limited government, but they also were much aware of multiple establishments, because that system existed in several of the colonies. The historical fact is that they were familiar with the very same kind of nonpreferential, nondiscriminatory government aid to religion that Justice Rehnquist and other accommodationists argue for. Yet they wrote in the First Amendment "Congress shall make *no law respecting* an establishment of religion, . . . " The word "respecting" means "about," "concerning," or "regarding." They knew of nondiscriminatory aid for religion, but said "no law!" So, based on history, the principle behind the Establishment Clause that must be applied to the present is that the government should refrain from extending itself into religion, neither hindering it *nor aiding it, even if that aid can be given in a nondiscriminatory, evenhanded way.* That is what the separation of church and state, no establishment, means.

Just as there has been a conservative attack on the concept of separation, there has also been an attack on the "*Lemon* test,"[23] the method by which the Establishment Clause has been interpreted. There is no doubt that the application of this three-part test has usually led to strict separationist decisions by the Court. It is also clear that these decisions have been opposed by those of a more accommodationist understanding of separation of church and state. Consequently, the conservative justices on the Court have tried to modify or even remove the test for interpreting the Establishment Clause. There was the opinion in *Marsh* v. *Chambers*, the legislative chaplains case, in which Chief Justice Burger refused to use the test in order to come down on the accommodationist side (see pp. 107–9). Justice Rehnquist, in the "original intent" argument just reviewed, came to the conclusion that the three-part test should be abandoned.[24]

Justice Sandra Day O'Connor, who I believe has written the most thoughtful and creative church–state opinions of any of the justices in the last decade, concurred with the majority in *Lynch* v. *Donnelly*. She agreed with the constitutionality of the nativity scene, surrounded with secular symbols of the winter holiday season, on public property. In the process, she suggested a modification of the "*Lemon* test." She suggested that the function of the "secular purpose" part of the test is to inquire whether the government intends to convey a message of endorsement or disapproval of religion. The "primary effect" part of the test is to determine whether government action does actually communicate a message of endorsement or disapproval of religion. That is, the effects test is the inquiry into whether government has operated in such a way as to make religion relevant to an individual's or a group's status in the political community.

> The purpose prong of the *Lemon* test asks whether government's actual purpose is to endorse or disapprove of religion. The effect prong asks whether, irrespective of government's actual purpose, the practice under review in fact conveys a message of endorsement or disapproval. An affirmative answer to either question should render the challenged practice invalid. . . . Endorsement sends a message to nonadherents that they are outsiders, not full members of the political community, and an accompanying message to adherents that they are insiders, favored members of the political community. Disapproval sends the opposite message.[25]

The third part of the test, "excessive entanglement," tries to determine whether or not government has interfered with the independence of religious institutions, given religious groups access to government or government power to the exclusion of nonadherents to the religion, or created political alignments defined along religious lines.[26]

The effect of this reformulation of the "*Lemon* test" was to move somewhat toward accommodationism. Government could either advance or in-hibit religion, so long as it did not intend to or actually endorse it or disapprove of it. Justice O'Connor's modification of the three-part test gained some favor on the Court. In fact, it was referred to with approval in the majority opinions in *Wallace* v. *Jaffree* and *Allegheny County* v. *ACLU of Pittsburgh*.

But not all the justices were happy with Justice O'Connor's reformulation of the test.[27] Justice Anthony Kennedy, in a sharply worded dissent in *Allegheny County* v. *ACLU of Pittsburgh*, denounced both the original "*Lemon* test" and Justice O'Connor's restatement of it, strongly rejecting the latter. In Kennedy's view, both tests, as they had been applied, were too hostile to religion; they did not allow enough government accommodation of religion. The endorsement understanding of the test is totally unacceptable to him because it is too broad. Because it asks whether government practice makes nonadherents to a religion feel like outsiders in the political community, Kennedy said few government acknowledgments of religions would not have that result. National days of prayer, the phrase "under God" in the Pledge of Allegiance, or the statement "In God We Trust" on our currency could surely make some feel like outsiders in the political community, yet all those are acceptable accommodations of religion.

What did Justice Kennedy propose as a proper test for interpreting the Establishment Clause to allow for the proper government accommodation of religion? One should look to American history. Since the founding of the nation, government has recognized the religious inclinations of the people in a variety of ways, such as those mentioned in the previous paragraph. The Establishment Clause must be interpreted so as to be sympathetic to that tradition.

> Whatever test we choose to apply must permit not only legitimate prac-tices two centuries old but also any other practices with no greater poten-tial for an establishment of religion. . . . A test for implementing the protections of the Establishment Clause that, if applied with consistency, would invalidate longstanding traditions cannot be a proper reading of the Clause.[28]

The test that Justice Kennedy recommended to accomplish the proper government accommodation of religion is what has come to be called the "coercion test." Government may interact with religion in whatever way it chooses so long as it does not coerce people to be religious or to adopt religious practices. The government may not tax the population to benefit a state-sponsored faith, exert direct compulsion to religious practice, "or gov-ernmental exhortation to religiosity that amounts in fact to proselytizing." The "bottom line" is that, for Justice Kennedy, government coercion to observance and direct benefits are all that are forbidden. Any other sort of government aid or abetment of religion is permitted. This is accommodationism with a vengeance.[29]

IMPLICATIONS OF RECENT DECISIONS

Readers at this point are likely asking themselves, "Who cares?" or, "All this is just lawyer squabbles. What difference does it make?" It makes considerable difference. From both the free-exercise and establishment sides, religious freedom is under such serious attack that it is in grave danger. Presidents Reagan and Bush, goaded by the Christian Right, appointed justices to the Supreme Court who placed religious freedom at risk by relegating the Free Exercise Clause virtually to the ash heap and by eviscerating the separation of church and state with various accommodationist schemes.[30] One may ask, what is so wrong with the government's aiding religion? Surely religion is a good thing for the welfare of the American people, and for the government to give it aid and comfort cannot hurt and might help. There are several answers to that position.

The phrase "aid and comfort" can help to elucidate the problems with government aid to religion. The Constitution mandates that government should and must give comfort to religion. The Free Exercise Clause requires that government must allow religion the maximum amount of freedom. This freedom does not include the right to operate contrary to the public good, in ways that would be harmful to persons, groups, or to the society as a whole. But the freedom of religion does mean that religious individuals or groups have the right to worship, evangelize, try to influence public opinion on matters of civic importance, aid the hurting, comfort the sorrowing, and so on, in ways that are consistent with their theology. How can the government best give "comfort" to these religious activities? By keeping its distance from religion. By not trying to aid religion. When government sets out to accommodate[31] religion, religion usually suffers, in a variety of ways.

When government gives money, government control is not far behind. That is the way it should be. The government at whatever level should expect some accountability in the use of its resources. But if government money is given to religious institutions, even if it is given in a nondiscriminatory way to agencies sponsored by a variety of religious groups, then the religious institutions find themselves under government supervision. One of the facts of life in America since World War II has been the expansion of government. Government is big and getting bigger, both in terms of the regulations it imposes on Americans and in the number of government employees enforcing the regulations. Consequently, there is likely to be rather significant government intrusiveness into those programs in which government money is involved, including religious programs. Those who lust after government aid for religion invite that government involvement. They should ask themselves whether they really want supervision from government, telling them how to operate their religious enterprises. An example of this kind of government intervention is found in *Grand Rapids School District v. Ball* (see p. 74). In that case parochial school classrooms were leased by the city's public schools to teach community service courses. During the time the rooms were used for that purpose, all religious symbols had to be removed from the rooms, and they had to display a sign stating that they were "public school classrooms." In short, during the time they were receiving government aid they had to disavow their religious affiliations and loyalties. Are churches and related institutions willing to submit to the government regulation that is always appended to government aid?

In terms of the Establishment Clause, the third part of the "*Lemon* test," which has to do with "excessive entanglement," is supposed to deal with problems of government intervention with and supervising of religious activities. But the accommodationist justices also want to get rid of the excessive entanglement part of the test. They will do religious institutions no service if this happens.

A variation on that theme is the trivialization of religion when it seeks government aid or sponsorship. It is clear to all under our system that government may not sponsor sectarian or denominational religion. Consequently, when groups seek public funds they have to divest themselves of sectarian or even distinctively religious characteristics. This has the effect of compromising their religion for the purpose of gaining the public aid and/or sponsorship they desire. Five examples come to mind.

In *McGowan* v. *Maryland* and *Braunfeld* v. *Brown*, examined in chapter 8, Christians might have considered it a victory when the Court decided that it was constitutional for states to have Sunday closing laws if they chose. But we should remember that the Court was able to reach that decision only by declaring that the laws were contemporaneously devoid of religious meaning, in spite of their clearly theological content at the time of their origin. The laws could stand only because they were completely secularized! This was no victory for Christian theology, even though churches did/do indirectly benefit from the fact that some of their members do not have to be at work on Sunday mornings.

Similarly, one thinks of the issues of religious symbols on public property, litigated in *Lynch* v. *Donnelly* and *Allegheny County* v. *ACLU of Pittsburgh*, described in chapter 8. The Court decided that religious symbols on public property did not violate the Establishment Clause, but only because they were surrounded by other paraphernalia that were not distinctively religious—the "plastic reindeer rule." Furthermore, Christmas, which was the holiday that caused the religious symbols to be placed on public ground, was described as a festive season, a winter holiday season devoid of any specifically religious content. The problem with that was rather flamboyantly expressed by Russell H. Dilday, Jr., then president of Southwestern Baptist Theological Seminary, in a speech to the Southern Baptist Convention.

> Call on Big Brother in Washington to help you witness and worship, and Big Brother will trivialize your Lord, sanctioning his sacred birth as nothing more than a folk festival, giving Bethlehem's manger no more significance than Rudolf's red nose. Ask the Supreme Court to endorse your Christian faith, and they will relegate the virgin-born Jesus, the only begotten of the Father, the King of Kings and Lord of Lords, to the company of Santa Claus, Frosty the Snowman and Alvin the Caroling Chipmunk.[32]

Western Maryland College, a Methodist school, was one of the colleges involved in *Roemer* v. *Board of Public Works of Maryland*, a case about state aid to church-related colleges. Apparently the college thought it might lose its state funds if the state lost this case, so it completely withdrew from Methodist sponsorship, that is, completely secularized itself, so that it would be eligible for state funds no matter how the case came out.[33] The majority opinion upheld the constitutionality of the law granting state funds to the church schools. Justice John Paul Stevens wrote a short dissent, one sentence of which is particularly pertinent: "I would add emphasis to the pernicious tendency of a state subsidy to tempt religious schools to compromise their religious mission without wholly abandoning it."[34] Western Maryland College *did* wholly abandon its religious identity in its desire to receive state funds.

A very recent example of this same phenomenon is the change of policy by Liberty University, founded and headed by Jerry Falwell. Since its inception, the university was clearly based on conservative theology and was pervasively religious. As part of that distinctively Christian character, both students and faculty had to adhere to explicitly fundamentalist doctrine, faculty were not allowed to publish anything that did not meet the approval of the school's administration, and students were required to attend chapel or church six times a week. But those charged with administering Virginia's Tuition Aids Grant Program, which provided state aid to students attending Liberty, threatened to withdraw those funds. Their reason was that a program that discriminated on the basis of religion did not fit the state's college aid law. At that point, Liberty changed its policy and discontinued basing the admission of students and the hiring of faculty on their adherence to a theological position, agreed to grant academic freedom to professors, and ended mandatory chapel for students.[35] Once again, the desire and need for state funds diluted the religious mission and distinctiveness of an institution.

One of the main items on the agenda of the Christian Right in the last decade or so has been to get "balanced treatment" laws passed so that "creation science" would be taught in public schools any time evolution was taught. (See the discussion of *McLean* v. *Arkansas* and *Edwards* v. *Aguillard* in chapter 7.) When such a law was challenged in court in Arkansas, the state submitted a pretrial brief to the court, laying out its case. A passage from the brief of the state's lawyers shows how much the traditional Christian concept of God had been disposed of in order to try to make creationism winnable in court.

> There is nothing inherently religious about the terms "creator" or "creation," as used in the context of Act 590. Act 590 is concerned with a non-religious conception of "creation" and "creator," not the religious concepts dealt with in the Bible or religious writings. . . . Assuming *arguendo* that a "creator" and "creation" are consistent with some religions, this does not make them inherently religious. The entity which caused the creation hypothesized in creation-science is far, far away from any conception of a god or deity. All that creation-science requires is that the entity which caused creation have power, intelligence, and a sense of design. There are no attributes of the personality generally associated with a deity, nor is there necessarily present in the creator any love, compassion, sense of justice, or concern for any individuals. Indeed, under creation-science as defined in Act 590, there is no requirement that the entity which caused creation still be in existence.[36]

Christians (or Jews or Muslims) with any sense of what their religion is about should be offended by that. One wonders how many fundamentalist Christians are aware of how much had to be given up to try to defend the inclusion of creation science into the public schools by law.

Accommodationists should realize that another problem with asking the government to aid religion is that every taxpayer is consequently required to pay for what he or she does not believe. One may respond that there is precedent for that. Taxpayers may not believe in public education, or air traffic controllers, or a public highway system, or standing armies, but they still have to pay for them. But the difference is that in the area of religion, there are constitutional principles involved. The Establishment Clause guarantees Americans freedom of conscience to believe or disbelieve as they choose and to be free from government-mandated funding of the advancement of religion different from their own or of any religion. Thomas Jefferson said it best, in his famous "Bill for Establishing Religious Freedom," which became law in Virginia in 1786 and was one of the principal influences on the writing of the First Amendment.

> [T]o compel a man to furnish contributions of money for the propagation of opinions which he disbelieves, is sinful and tyrannical; that even the forcing him to support this or that teacher of his own religious persuasion, is depriving him of the comfortable liberty of giving his contributions to the particular pastor whose morals he would make his pattern, and whose powers he feels most persuasive to righteousness.[37]

Requiring a person to support a minister (or religious institution) with whom or which that person agrees, much less one with which he or she disagrees, is to deprive that person of the freedom to support religion as conscience guides. An example, of course, of requiring someone to pay for that which they disbelieve is government aid to parochial schools. The Court has repeatedly made the observation that what distinguishes a church-related school from a public school is its religious content and mission. Why do religious schools exist, particularly at the elementary and secondary level? They exist primarily to propagate the religious views of the sponsoring church. They have the perfect constitutional right to do that (*Pierce* v. *Society of Sisters;* see chapter 6). But to require taxpayers of any or no religion to pay for the propagating of those religious beliefs through programs of government aid is sinful and tyrannical, in Jefferson's words, because the program demands that they pay for what they disbelieve. So, programs of government aid, accommodation, deprive the religious institutions receiving the aid of freedom from government supervision and deprive the taxpayers of the constitutionally guaranteed right to be free from coercion in matters of religion.

Furthermore, accommodation leads to the irrelevance of the church (or synagogue, mosque, or shrine). What happens if government promotes religion in public life? It may well take over some of the functions of religious institutions. The more government does the work of the church, the less relevant the church is in our society. Of course, the classic example is prayer in the public schools. Not only does the requirement of nonsectarian prayer trivialize religion in the manner of the "To whom it may concern" prayer of *Engel* v. *Vitale*, but it requires the public school to assume one of the principal activities of the church: prayer and worship. That clearly is a violation of the Establishment Clause, as the Court said in *Abington Township School District* v. *Schempp*. But more to the point here, it makes the church increasingly irrelevant as an institution. I do not understand why many church leaders, not to mention innumerable laypeople, particularly among the Christian Right, insist on a constitutional amendment to require "voluntary" group prayer in public schools.[38] Many of them wonder why the church is not so important in people's lives as it used to be, why secularism seems to be invading the church itself, and yet, in the next breath, they will ask the government to take over the work of the church in terms of prayer or government-financed religious education. Government accommodation and promotion of religion is the enemy of a vibrant, creative church.

What is wrong with government aid to religion? I have tried to argue that several things are wrong with it. All of this has been from the Establishment Clause side of the religious freedom issue. Those justices of the Supreme Court who argue the accommodationist position, either from the "original intent" or from the "practices of history" perspective, apparently are doing so out of sympathy for the role of religion in American life. I believe that if this accommodationism is successful, it will not help religion but will have the opposite effect. Religious freedom in our time is in great peril.

From the Free Exercise Clause side, we should remember a scary three years in our constitutional history. The decision in *Employment Division of Oregon* v. *Smith*, eliminating the "compelling state interest test" and shunting the Free Exercise Clause to the position of being the most minimal of constitutional freedoms, endangered religious freedom to the maximum degree. In free-exercise disputes between government and religious individuals or groups, government at any level no longer had to show that it had a legitimate interest of great importance before it could interfere with the religious behavior at issue. The Free Exercise Clause could not be used to adjudicate laws of general application unless it was used in tandem with some other First Amendment principle or if a law targeted religious behavior only. This great freedom, which has contributed mightily to make this nation so attractive to residents and foreigners alike, was eviscerated by the Supreme Court of the United States. Although these dire consequences were reversed with the passage of the Religious Freedom Restoration Act in 1993, they are indicative of an attitude abroad in the land (and among some justices still on the Court), which should remind those who cherish religious freedom of the wisdom of the maxim that "eternal vigilance is the price of liberty."

The claim is often made by accommodationists, especially those from the Christian Right, that separation of church and state is equivalent to hostility to religion. Just the opposite it true. Strict separation is not hostility to religion. Strict separation is necessary for religious freedom. The Religion Clauses of the Constitution demand that government remain distant from religion so religion may flourish. Separation prevents government from meddling in matters of religion. It guarantees the free exercise of religion. Separation is better for the government and better for religion. It is better for government because it prevents government from assuming roles that it was not intended to serve, such as involving itself in matters of conscience, persons' relationship with what they perceive as the Divine, or finding meaning for life. It is better for government because it reminds government of its limited nature. Separation is better for religion because it allows religion to grow and prosper as it will, dependent only on its own vitality and persuasiveness.

To those who insist that accommodationism is the best way to understand the relationship between church and state in this country, I close with two statements that say the same thing. The first is from James Madison, when he was arguing against the bill that would support the Christian religion in Virginia through a government tax:

It [the bill] is moreover to weaken in those who profess this Religion a pious confidence in its innate excellence and the patronage of its Author;

and to foster in those who still reject it, a suspicion that its friends are too conscious of its fallacies, to trust it to its own merits.[39]

The second statement is from Justice Robert Jackson:

It is possible to hold a faith with enough confidence to believe that what should be rendered to God does not need to be decided and collected by Caesar.[40]

Epilogue

For the last several years the Court has handed down at least one church–state case a year, sometimes as many as three or four. Given the "hotness" of this topic, I anticipate that activity by the Court will continue. The church–state relationship, even confined to only Supreme Court decisions, is a moving target and a "growth industry." But, by having read this far, you have been exposed to most of the major issues and the procedures the Court uses to arrive at its decisions. You are better equipped to understand decisions that may come down from the Court in the future. Search out the best information available to you and keep up with what the Court does. Some of the journals listed in the Bibliography may be very helpful to you. It is my hope that you have become a better-informed consumer of information about the Court and the decisions it makes. It is also my strong hope that this book has given you greater appreciation for our great heritage of religious liberty.

As to the question that is part of the title of the book: Is the Supreme Court godless or not? As in so many things in life, even important things, the answer must be that it depends on who you talk to. There are multitudes, particularly those on the political and theological right, who believe that it is a godless Court. They see its decisions upholding a strict separation between church and state as being somehow harmful to religion. I have argued in chapter 9 that in its more recent decisions, especially those which appear on the surface to be most accommodating to religion, the Court has put religion in the greatest danger, that of being either corrupted by too close association with the state or destroyed by too much deference to the state.

Of course, neither answer to the question is completely true. The Court, by its very nature, is neither godly nor godless. It is, rather, an institution of a secular state. To say that the American system of government is secular is not to slander it, even from a conservative Christian perspective. It is instead to argue that the founders showed the greatest respect for religion by mandating that it should be neither an enemy nor a servant of the state. Believing in the inalienable rights of human beings, they created a system of government by which those rights could be actualized. Among those was the right

145

to respond to what one perceived to be the Divine if one chose to and as one chose to, without interference from the powers that be. The Supreme Court has the responsibility to maintain that relationship between church and state, a relationship by which the state maintains the most benevolent attitude toward religion by keeping its distance from it. That may appear to the hyper-pious to be "godlessness," but in reality it is the best for religion in all the forms it has taken in the fertile minds of men and women. As Justice Hugo Black wrote in *Engel* v. *Vitale*:

> [The separation of church and state] stands as an expression of principle on the part of the Founders of our Constitution that religion is too personal, too sacred, too holy, to permit its "unhallowed perversion" by a civil magistrate.[1]

Amen and Amen.

Appendix A

Memorial and Remonstrance against Religious Assessments

To the Honorable the General Assembly of the Commonwealth of Virginia, A Memorial and Remonstrance

We, the subscribers, citizens of the said Commonwealth, having taken into serious consideration, a Bill printed by order of the last Session of General Assembly, entitled "A Bill establishing a provision for Teachers of the Christian Religion" and conceiving that the same, if finally armed with the sanctions of a law, will be a dangerous abuse of power, are bound as faithful members of a free State, to remonstrate against it, and to declare the reasons by which we are determined. We remonstrate against the said Bill,

1. Because we hold it for a fundamental and undeniable truth, "that Religion or the duty which we owe to our Creator and the Manner of discharging it, can be directed only by reason and conviction, not by force or violence." The Religion then of every man must be left to the conviction and conscience of every man; and it is the right of every man to exercise it as these may dictate. This right is in its nature an unalienable right, It is unalienable; because the opinion, of men, depending only on the evidence contemplated by their own minds, cannot follow the dictates of other men: It is unalienable also; because what is here a right towards men, is a duty towards the Creator. It is the duty of every man to render to the Creator such homage, and such only, as he believes to be acceptable to him. This duty is precedent both in order of time and degree of obligation, to the claims of Civil society. Before any man can be considered as a member of Civil Society, he must be considered as a subject of the Governor of the Universe: And if a member of Civil society, who enters into any subordinate Association, must always do it with a reservation of his duty to the general authority; much more must every man who becomes a member of any particular Civil Society, do it with a saving of his allegiance to the Universal Sovereign. We maintain therefore that in matters of Religion, no man's right is abridged by the institution of Civil Society, and that Religion is wholly exempt from its cognizance. True it is, that no other rule exists, by which any question which may divide a Society, can be ultimately determined, but the

Written by James Madison. Quoted in *Everson* v. *Board of Education* 330 U.S. 1 at 63–72 (footnotes omitted).

will of the majority; but it is also true, that the majority may trespass on the rights of the minority.

2. Because if religion be exempt from the authority of the Society at large, still less can it be subject to that of the Legislative Body. The latter are but the creatures and vicegerents of the former. Their jurisdiction is both derivative and limited: it is limited with regard to the coordinate departments, more necessarily is it limited with regard to the constituents. The preservation of a free government requires not merely, that the metes and bounds which separate each department of power may be invariably maintained; but more especially, that neither of them be suffered to overleap the great Barrier which defends the rights of the people. The Rulers who are guilty of such an encroachment, exceed the commission from which they derive their authority, and are Tyrants. The People who submit to it are governed by laws made neither by themselves, nor by an authority derived from them, and are slaves.

3. Because, it is proper to take alarm at the first experiment on our liberties. We hold this prudent jealousy to be the first duty of citizens, and one of [the] noblest characteristics of the late Revolution. The freemen of America did not wait till usurped power had strengthened itself by exercise, and entangled the question in precedents. They saw all the consequences in the principle, and they avoided the consequences by denying the principle. We revere this lesson too much, soon to forget it. Who does not see that the same authority which can establish Christianity, in exclusion of all other Religions, may establish with the same ease any particular sect of Christians in exclusion of all other Sects? That the same authority which can force a citizen to contribute three pence only of his property for the support of any one establishment, may force him to conform to any other establishment in all cases whatsoever?

4. Because, the bill violates that equality which ought to be the basis of every law, and which is more indispensable, in proportion as the validity or expediency of any law is more liable to be impeached. If "all men are by nature equally free and independent," all men are to be considered as entering into society on equal conditions; as relinquishing no more, and therefore retaining no less, one than another, of their natural rights. Above all are they to be considered as retaining an *"equal* title to the free exercise of Religion according to the dictates of conscience." Whilst we assert for ourselves a freedom to embrace, to profess and to observe the Religion which we believe to be of divine origin, we cannot deny an equal freedom to those whose minds have not yet yielded to the evidence which has convinced us. If this freedom be abused, it is an offence against God, not against man: To God, therefore, not to men, must an account of it be rendered. As the Bill violates equality by subjecting some to peculiar burdens; so it violates the same principle, by granting to others peculiar exemptions. Are the Quakers and

Menonists the only sects who think a compulsive support of their religions unnecessary and unwarrantable? Can their piety alone be intrusted with the care of public worship? Ought their Religions to be endowed above all others, with extraordinary privileges, by which proselytes may be enticed from all others? We think too favorably of the justice and good sense of these denominations, to believe that they either covet preeminencies over their fellow citizens, or that they will be seduced by them, from the common opposition to the measure.

5. Because the bill implies either that the Civil Magistrate is a competent Judge of Religious truth; or that he may employ Religion as an engine of Civil Policy. The first is an arrogant pretension falsified by the contradictory opinions of Rulers in all ages, and throughout the world: The second an unhallowed perversion of the means of salvation.

6. Because the establishment proposed by the Bill is not requisite for the support of the Christian Religion. To say that it is, is a contradiction to the Christian Religion itself; for every page of it disavows a dependence on the powers of this world: it is a contradiction to fact; for it is known that this Religion both existed and flourished, not only without the support of human laws, but in spite of every opposition from them; and not only during the period of miraculous aid, but long after it had been left to its own evidence, and the ordinary care of Providence: Nay, it is a contradiction in terms; for a Religion not invented by human policy, must have pre-existed and been supported, before it was established by human policy. It is moreover to weaken in those who profess this Religion a pious confidence in its innate excellence, and the patronage of its Author; and to foster in those who still reject it, a suspicion that its friends are too conscious of its fallacies, to trust it to its own merits.

7. Because experience witnesseth that ecclesiastical establishments, instead of maintaining the purity and efficacy of Religion, have had a contrary operation. During almost fifteen centuries, has the legal establishment of Christianity been on trial. What have been its fruits? More or less in all places, pride and indolence in the Clergy; ignorance and servility in the laity; in both, superstition, bigotry and persecution. Enquire of the Teachers of Christianity for the ages in which it appeared in its greatest lustre; those of every sect, point to the ages prior to its incorporation with Civil policy. Propose a restoration of this primitive state in which its Teachers depended on the voluntary rewards of their flocks; many of them predict its downfall. On which side ought their testimony to have greatest weight, when for or when against their interest?

8. Because the establishment in question is not necessary for the support of Civil Government. If it be urged as necessary for the support of Civil Government only as it is a means of supporting Religion, and it be not necessary for the latter purpose, it cannot be necessary for the former. If

Religion be not within [the] cognizance of Civil Government, how can its legal establishment be said to be necessary to Civil Government? What influence in fact have ecclesiastical establishments had on Civil Society? In some instances they have been seen to erect a spiritual tyranny on the ruins of Civil authority; in many instances they have been seen upholding the thrones of political tyranny; in no instance have they been seen the guardians of the liberties of the people. Rulers who wished to subvert the public liberty, may have found an established clergy convenient auxiliaries. A just government, instituted to secure and perpetuate it, needs them not. Such a government will be best supported by protecting every citizen in the enjoyment of his Religion with the same equal hand which protects his person and his property; by neither invading the equal rights of any Sect, nor suffering any Sect to invade those of another.

9. Because the proposed establishment is a departure from that generous policy, which, offering an asylum to the persecuted and oppressed of every Nation and Religion, promised a lustre to our country, and an accession to the number of its citizens. What a melancholy mark is the Bill of sudden degeneracy? Instead of holding forth an asylum to the persecuted, it is itself a signal of persecution. It degrades from the equal rank of Citizens all those whose opinions in Religion do not bend to those of the Legislative authority. Distant as it may be, in its present form, from the Inquisition it differs from it only in degree. The one is the first step, the other the last in the career of intolerance. The magnanimous sufferer under this cruel scourge in foreign Regions, must view the Bill as a Beacon on our Coast, warning him to seek some other haven, where liberty and philanthropy in their due extent may offer a more certain repose from his troubles.

10. Because, it will have a like tendency to banish our Citizens. The allurements presented by other situations are every day thinning their number. To superadd a fresh motive to emigration, by revoking the liberty which they now enjoy, would be the same species of folly which has dishonored and depopulated flourishing kingdoms.

11. Because, it will destroy that moderation and harmony which the forbearance of our laws to intermeddle with Religion, has produced amongst its several sects. Torrents of blood have been spilt in the old world, by vain attempts of the secular arm to extinguish Religious discord, by proscribing all difference in Religious opinions. Time has at length revealed the true remedy. Every relaxation of narrow and rigorous policy, wherever it has been tried, has been found to assuage the disease. The American Theatre has exhibited proofs, that equal and compleat liberty, if it does not wholly eradicate it, sufficiently destroys its malignant influence on the health and prosperity of the State. If with the salutary effects of this system under our own eyes, we begin to contract the bonds of Religious freedom, we know no name that will too severely reproach our folly. At least let warning be taken

at the first fruits of the threatened innovation. The very appearance of the Bill has transformed that "Christian forbearance, love and charity," which of late mutually prevailed, into animosities and jealousies, which may not soon be appeased. What mischiefs may not be dreaded should this enemy to the public quiet be armed with the force of a law?

12. Because, the policy of the bill is adverse to the diffusion of the light of Christianity. The first wish of those who enjoy this precious gift, ought to be that it may be imparted to the whole race of mankind. Compare the number of those who have as yet received it with the number still remaining under the dominion of false Religions; and how small is the former! Does the policy of the Bill tend to lessen the disproportion? No; it at once discourages those who are strangers to the light of [revelation] from coming into the Region of it; and countenances, by example the nations who continue in darkness in shutting out those who might convey it to them. Instead of levelling as far as possible, every obstacle to the victorious progress of truth, the Bill with an ignoble and unchristian timidity would circumscribe it, with a wall of defence, against the encroachments of error.

13. Because attempts to enforce by legal sanctions, acts obnoxious to so great a proportion of Citizens, tend to enervate the laws in general, and to slacken the bands of Society. If it be difficult to execute any law which is not generally deemed necessary or salutary, what must be the case where it is deemed invalid and dangerous? and what may be the effect of so striking an example of impotency in the Government, on its general authority?

14. Because a measure of such singular magnitude and delicacy ought not to be imposed, without the clearest evidence that it is called for by a majority of citizens: and no satisfactory method is yet proposed by which the voice of the majority in this case may be determined, or its influence secured. "The people of the respective counties are indeed requested to signify their opinion respecting the adoption of the Bill to the next session of Assembly." But the representation must be made equal, before the voice either of the Representatives or of the Counties, will be that of the people. Our hope is that neither of the former will, after due consideration espouse the dangerous principle of the Bill. Should the event disappoint us, it will still leave us in full confidence, that a fair appeal to the latter will reverse the sentence against our liberties.

15. Because, finally, "the equal right of every citizen to the free exercise of his Religion according to the dictates of conscience" is held by the same tenure with all our other rights. If we recur to its origin, it is equally the gift of nature; if we weigh its importance, it cannot be less dear to us; if we consult the Declaration of those rights which pertain to the good people of Virginia, as the "basis and foundation of Government," it is enumerated with equal solemnity, or rather studied emphasis. Either then, we must say, that the will of the Legislature is the only measure of their authority; and that in

the plentitude of this authority, they may sweep away all our fundamental rights; or, that they are bound to leave this particular right untouched and sacred: Either we must say, that they may control the freedom of the press, may abolish the trial by jury, may swallow up the Executive and Judiciary Powers of the State; nay that they may despoil us of our very right of suffrage, and erect themselves into an independent and hereditary assembly: or we must say that they have no authority to enact into law the Bill under consideration. We the subscribers say, that the General Assembly of this Commonwealth have no such authority: And that no effort may be omitted on our part against so dangerous an usurpation, we oppose to it, this remonstrance; earnestly praying, as we are in duty bound, that the Supreme Lawgiver of the Universe, by illuminating those to whom it is addressed, may on the one hand, turn their councils from every act which would affront his holy prerogative, or violate the trust committed to them: and on the other, guide them into every measure which may be worthy of his blessing, may redound to their own praise, and may establish more firmly the liberties, the prosperity, and the Happiness of the Commonwealth.

Appendix B

An Act for Establishing Religious Freedom, Passed in the Assembly of Virginia in the Beginning of the Year 1786

Well aware that Almighty God hath created the mind free; that all attempts to influence it by temporal punishments or burdens, or by civil incapacitations, tend only to beget habits of hypocrisy and meanness, and are a departure from the plan of the Holy Author of our religion, who being Lord both of body and mind, yet chose not to propagate it by coercions on either, as was in his Almighty power to do; that the impious presumption of legislators and rulers, civil as well as ecclesiastical, who, being themselves but fallible and uninspired men have assumed dominion over the faith of others, setting up their own opinions and modes of thinking as the only true and infallible, and as such endeavoring to impose them on others, hath established and maintained false religions over the greatest part of the world, and through all time; that to compel a man to furnish contributions of money for the propagation of opinions which he disbelieves, is sinful and tyrannical; that even the forcing him to support this or that teacher of his own religious persuasion, is depriving him of the comfortable liberty of giving his contributions to the particular pastor whose morals he would make his pattern, and whose powers he feels most persuasive to righteousness, and is withdrawing from the ministry those temporal rewards, which proceeding from an approbation of their personal conduct, are an additional incitement to earnest and unremitting labors for the instruction of mankind; that our civil rights have no dependence on our religious opinions, more than our opinions in physics or geometry; that, therefore, the proscribing any citizen as unworthy the public confidence by laying upon him an incapacity of being called to the offices of trust and emolument, unless he profess or renounce this or that religious opinion, is depriving him injuriously of those privileges and advantages to which in common with his fellow citizens he has a natural right; that it tends also to corrupt the principles of that very religion it is meant to encourage, by bribing, with a monopoly of worldly honors and emoluments, those who will externally profess and conform to it; that though indeed these are crimi-

Written by Thomas Jefferson. Quoted in *The Writings of Thomas Jefferson*, ed. Andrew A. Lipscomb (Washington, D.C.: The Thomas Jefferson Memorial Association, 1904), 300–303. Sometimes referred to as Jefferson's "Bill for Establishing Religious Freedom."

nal who do not withstand such temptation, yet neither are those innocent who lay the bait in their way; that to suffer the civil magistrate to intrude his powers into the field of opinion and to restrain the profession or propagation of principles, on the supposition of their ill tendency, is a dangerous fallacy, which at once destroys all religious liberty, because he being of course judge of that tendency, will make his opinions the rule of judgment, and approve or condemn the sentiments of others only as they shall square with or differ from his own; that it is time enough for the rightful purposes of civil government, for its offices to interfere when principles break out into overt acts against peace and good order; and finally, that truth is great and will prevail if left to herself, that she is the proper and sufficient antagonist to error, and has nothing to fear from the conflict, unless by human interposition disarmed of her natural weapons, free argument and debate, errors ceasing to be dangerous when it is permitted freely to contradict them.

Be it therefore enacted by the General Assembly, That no man shall be compelled to frequent or support any religious worship, place or ministry whatsoever, nor shall be enforced, restrained, molested, or burthened in his body or goods, nor shall otherwise suffer on account of his religious opinions or belief; but that all men shall be free to profess, and by argument to maintain, their opinions in matters of religion, and that the same shall in nowise diminish, enlarge, or affect their civil capacities.

And though we well know this Assembly, elected by the people for the ordinary purposes of legislation only, have no power to restrain the acts of succeeding assemblies, constituted with the powers equal to our own, and that therefore to declare this act irrevocable, would be of no effect in law, yet we are free to declare, and do declare, that the rights hereby asserted are of the natural rights of mankind, and that if any act shall be hereafter passed to repeal the present or to narrow its operation, such act will be an infringement of natural right.

Notes

1. THE COURT AND ITS PROCEDURES

1. "Statistical Recap of Supreme Court's Workload During Last Three Terms," *United States Law Week* 61 (August 11, 1992): 3098; ibid., 62 (August 17, 1993): 3124.

2. Max Radin, *Radin Law Dictionary* (Dobbs Ferry, N.Y.: Oceana Publications, 1970), 50.

3. William Howard Taft, testimony, in *Hearings before the Committee on the Judiciary: House of Representatives, on H.R. 10479,* "Jurisdiction of Circuit Courts of Appeals and United States Supreme Court," 67th Congress, 2d session, March 30, 1922, at 2.

4. Harry W. Jones, "Church–State Relations: Our Constitutional Heritage," in *Religion and Contemporary Society,* ed. Harold Stahmer (New York: Macmillan Co., 1963), 168. Unfortunately, Jones does not identify the justice or when and where he made this statement.

5. An extreme example, but one illustrative of the use of *amicus curiae* briefs, is the Missouri abortion case, *Webster v. Reproductive Health Services* 492 U.S. 490 (1989). In that case there were 20 *amicus* briefs urging reversal of the lower court opinion, 21 urging affirmance, and 34 other *amici* arguing some aspect of the case, for a total of 75 different briefs. Because organizations often share in the responsibility and cost of preparing an *amicus* brief, those 75 briefs represented hundreds of different interest groups and individuals.

6. Occasionally the Court considers a case so important that it *must* achieve unanimity and will take extra time to do so. An example is *Brown v. Board of Education* 347 U.S. 483 (1954), the case declaring "separate but equal" education to be unconstitutional.

7. David M. O'Brien, *Storm Center: The Supreme Court in American Politics* (New York: W. W. Norton & Co., 1986), 124–35.

8. 310 U.S. 586 (1940); Robert T. Miller and Ronald B. Flowers, *Toward Benevolent Neutrality: Church, State, and the Supreme Court,* 4th ed. (Waco, Tex.: Baylor University Press, 1992), 82. (Hereafter referred to as Miller and Flowers.)

9. 319 U.S. 624 (1943); Miller and Flowers, 87.

2. BACKGROUND OF CONSTITUTIONAL PRINCIPLES

1. "Dale's Laws," in *American Christianity: An Historical Interpretation with Representative Documents,* ed. H. Shelton Smith, Robert T. Handy, and Lefferts A. Loetscher, vol. 1 (New York: Charles Scribner's Sons, 1960), 41–44.

2. John Winthrop, "A Model of Christian Charity," in *American Christianity,* 100.

3. Nathaniel Ward, "The Simple Cobbler of Aggawam," in *American Christianity*, 127.

4. Among those were the famous Anne Hutchinson and Roger Williams.

5. There is a statue of Mary Dyer in front of the State Capitol building in Boston, bearing the inscription: "Mary Dyer, Quaker; Witness for Religious Freedom; Hanged on Boston Commons 1660; 'My Life Not Availeth Me in Comparison to the Liberty of the Truth.' Sylvia Shaw Judson—Sculptor."

6. Edwin S. Gaustad, *A Religious History of America*, rev. ed. (San Francisco: Harper & Row, 1990), 56.

7. Sidney E. Mead, *The Lively Experiment: The Shaping of Christianity in America* (New York: Harper & Row, 1963), 62.

8. Quoted in Leo Pfeffer, *Church, State, and Freedom*, rev. ed. (Boston: Beacon Press, 1967), 122. See pp. 121–24.

9. Leonard W. Levy, "The Original Meaning of the Establishment Clause of the First Amendment," in *Religion and the State: Essays in Honor of Leo Pfeffer*, ed. James E. Wood, Jr. (Waco, Tex.: Baylor University Press, 1985), 61.

3. DEFINING THE SCOPE OF
RELIGIOUS FREEDOM: PRIOR TO 1963

1. 95 U.S. 145 (1879); Miller and Flowers, 49.

2. 98 U.S. 145 at 164; Miller and Flowers, 51.

3. The Court subsequently handed down two other cases in which the offense was not practicing polygamy, but advocating a religious belief in polygamy. Even here what was prohibited was the proclamation of the belief, not the belief itself, although the laws affirmed by the Court criminalized membership in an organization that taught polygamy. So, in essence, to be a Mormon was a crime. *Davis* v. *Beason* 133 U.S. 333 (1890); Miller and Flowers, 52, and *Church of Jesus Christ of Latter-day Saints* v. *United States* 136 U.S. 1 (1890). However, the criminalization of belief has never had the same weight as precedent as the belief/action distinction of *Reynolds*. In 1890 the church blunted the government's campaign against it by discontinuing the practice of plural marriage. See Leo Pfeffer, *Church, State, and Freedom* (Boston: Beacon Press, 1967), 645–50.

4. One scholar has made this important point this way: "It is the nuts, or those so regarded by the rest of us, on whom government restraint or censorship are brought to bear. When they resolutely defend their constitutional liberties, the nuts are surrogates for the freedom of us all." Harry W. Jones, "Church–State Relations: Our Constitutional Heritage," in *Religion and Contemporary Society*, ed. Harold Stahmer (New York: Macmillan Co., 1963), 178.

5. 310 U.S. 296 (1940); Miller and Flowers, 60.

6. 310 U.S. 296 at 303–4; Miller and Flowers, 61.

7. 310 U.S. 296 at 307; Miller and Flowers, 62.

8. 319 U.S. 105 (1943); Miller and Flowers, 74.

9. 312 U.S. 569 (1941); Miller and Flowers, 96.

10. See *Niemotko* v. *Maryland* 340 U.S. 268 (1951), and *Fowler* v. *Rhode Island* 345 U.S. 67 (1953).

11. 321 U.S. 158 (1944); Miller and Flowers, 99.

12. This is known as the *parens patriae*, literally "parent of the country," power of the state. The state has the power to legislate for the public welfare of citizens,

especially those less likely to be able to care for themselves, such as the aged, the mentally incompetent, or children.

13. 321 U.S. 158 at 170; Miller and Flowers, 101.

14. See Genesis 9:3–4; Leviticus 17:10–12; Acts 15:19–21. Although these passages refer only to the eating of blood, the Witnesses make the point that in the ancient world consuming blood was the only way to take it into the body. Modern technology has made ingesting blood possible through transfusion, and that is equally prohibited by God's law. Ingesting blood, i.e., life, is the issue, not the methodology.

15. See *Jehovah's Witnesses* v. *King County Hospital* 278 F.Supp 448 (1967), affirmed without argument 398 U.S. 598 (1968). The "F.Supp" in the first citation refers to the *Federal Supplement*, the series of volumes used to report decisions of the U.S. District Courts since 1932.

16. Of course, this principle has even more impact on those groups which refuse medical care altogether. For example, in the late 1980s and early 1990s there were several cases brought against Christian Scientists, accusing them of criminal behavior because they dealt with their children's illnesses with prayer and spiritual healing rather than taking them to doctors.

17. See Exodus 20:3–6; Luke 4:8; 1 John 5:21.

18. 310 U.S. 586 (1940); Miller and Flowers, 82.

19. 310 U.S. 586 at 595–96; Miller and Flowers, 83.

20. 319 U.S. 624 (1943); Miller and Flowers, 87.

21. 319 U.S. 624 at 641; Miller and Flowers, 90.

22. 319 U.S. 624 at 642; Miller and Flowers, 90–91. This case played an indirect role in the 1988 presidential campaign. Governor Michael Dukakis of Massachusetts, the Democratic candidate, had been asked to get the opinion of the Massachusetts attorney general about whether that state's public schools could require the pledge of allegiance to the flag. The attorney general responded in the negative, citing *Barnette*. Dukakis made this report public. During the campaign then Vice-President Bush shamefully impugned Dukakis's patriotism, claiming that he was against the pledge of allegiance, never once mentioning that this was not Dukakis's position or that it was the law of the land that one cannot be compelled to salute the American flag.

23. 322 U.S. 78 (1944); Miller and Flowers, 16.

24. Jones, "Church–State Relations: Our Constitutional Heritage," 182. Professor Jones, on p. 184, expands on this concept in words worth remembering:

> When we get down to the hard cases, we are forced, however unwillingly, to the conclusion that the free exercise of religion means and must mean both "true" and "untrue" religion, must include the extravagances of the false prophet as well as the witness of the genuinely inspired.
>
> The best test of truth, for constitutional purposes if for no other, is the power of an idea to get accepted. . . . We may choose the "truth," as God gives us to see the truth, but government and the officials of government must not be empowered to pass on questions concerning the truth or sincerity of religious professions. In a genuinely free society, the forum of choice is in the intellect and conscience of the individual, not in the jurisdiction of a judge, jury, postmaster, or licensing official. The American prophet, however venal or misguided, is not without freedom in his own country.

25. 322 U.S. 78 at 86–87; Miller and Flowers, 18.

26. 322 U.S. 78 at 94–95; Miller and Flowers, 20. Justice Jackson was dissenting, not because he disagreed with the majority opinion, but because he thought that the Court should not have taken the case at all, given the potential of judicial intrusion into religious belief.

4. THE UNCERTAIN STATUS OF RELIGIOUS FREEDOM: 1963–1990

1. 374 U.S. 398 (1963); Miller and Flowers, 148.

2. See Genesis 2:1–3; Exodus 20:8–11.

3. 374 U.S. 398 at 406; Miller and Flowers, 149. The Court quoted *Thomas* v. *Collins* 323 U.S. 516 at 530 (1945).

4. 374 U.S. 398 at 406; Miller and Flowers, 149.

5. 406 U.S. 205 (1972); Miller and Flowers, 234.

6. 406 U.S. 205 at 215; Miller and Flowers, 236.

7. Jehovah's Witnesses have, more often than not, been conscientious objectors to war, primarily in obedience to God's commandment, "You shall not kill," Exodus 20:13. However, as this case shows, not all members understand this to extend to a prohibition against manufacturing munitions.

8. 450 U.S. 707 (1981); Miller and Flowers, 161.

9. 450 U.S. 707 at 715–16; Miller and Flowers, 162–63.

10. 450 U.S. 707 at 717–18; Miller and Flowers, 163.

11. 480 U.S. 136 (1987); Miller and Flowers, 166.

12. 480 U.S. 136 at 144; Miller and Flowers, 168.

13. 489 U.S. 829 (1989); Miller and Flowers, 169.

14. As its name implies, the Native American Church is a trans-tribal religious group organized by and for American Indians. Although it was first legally incorporated in 1918 in Oklahoma, its origins are in the nineteenth century. However, at the time of its beginning it incorporated a practice of Indians of North America that seems to go back some 400 or 500 years—the use of peyote as an inducer of spiritual experience. The use of peyote is the central, but not the only, characteristic of Native American Church worship. Its role is to heighten the spiritual sensitivity of the worshiper, to help him or her experience God. The church teaches that peyote itself is a sacred substance and must be properly used, which means that it should never be abused. Consequently, believers are never to use peyote outside worship. Some congregations will expel members who do use it improperly, that is, as a "recreational drug." Virtually all states include peyote on their lists of prohibited drugs. But because of the discipline on its use imposed by the Native American Church, at the time the issue came before the Supreme Court in 1990 in the *Smith* case, 23 states and the federal government had exempted peyote from prosecution when it is used in worship. Texas, which is the only place in the United States where the peyote cactus grows, has laws that regulate, but permit, its growth, harvesting, and distribution for religious purposes. Also, going into the *Smith* litigation, there was some case law that permitted the use of peyote for worship purposes. The leading case was decided by the California Supreme Court, *People* v. *Woody* 394 P.2d 813 (1964). (The "P.2d" in the citation refers to the *Pacific Reporter*, second series, which is the official reporting document for cases of the California Supreme Court and other courts of that region.)

15. 494 U.S. 872 (1990); Miller and Flowers, 171.

16. 113 S.Ct. 2217 (1993); Miller and Flowers 1993 Supplement, 7.

17. 113 S.Ct. 2217 at 2225; Miller and Flowers 1993 Supplement, 9–10, quoting *Thomas* v. *Review Board of Indiana* 450 U.S. 707 at 714 (1981); Miller and Flowers, 162.

18. 113 S.Ct. 2217 at 2231; Miller and Flowers 1993 Supplement, 13.

19. 113 S.Ct. 2217 at 2234; Miller and Flowers 1993 Supplement, 14.

20. 435 U.S. 618 (1978); Miller and Flowers, 188.

21. 435 U.S 618 at 626; Miller and Flowers, 190, quoting *Sherbert* v. *Verner* 374 U.S. 398 at 406; Miller and Flowers, 149.

22. 475 U.S. 503 (1986); Miller and Flowers, 195.

23. Actually, the regulation had not been enforced against Dr. Goldman for several years. But after he testified for the defense in a court-marshal, wearing his yarmulke but not his service cap, his commanding officer, apparently in retribution for his testimony, began to enforce the regulation.

24. 475 U.S. 503 at 507; Miller and Flowers, 196.

25. 482 U.S. 342 (1987); Miller and Flowers, 213.

26. As noted earlier, *Smith* involved Native Americans too. But it was actually an unemployment compensation case. The cases now under review focused more centrally on behavior characteristic of Native American religion.

27. 476 U.S. 693 (1986); Miller and Flowers, 203.

28. 476 U.S. 693 at 699 (emphasis in original); Miller and Flowers, 205.

29. 485 U.S. 439 (1988); Miller and Flowers, 221.

30. 485 U.S. 439 at 452–53 (emphasis in original); Miller and Flowers, 224–25.

31. 452 U.S. 640 (1981); Miller and Flowers, 276.

32. 482 U.S. 569 (1987).

33. 112 S.Ct. 2701 (1992).

34. In the months after *Smith*, courts all across the country were deciding cases in such a way as to restrict religious freedom, a decidedly different trend from decisions before the *Smith* decision.

5. FROM CONGREGATIONAL FIGHTS TO PACIFISM

1. 13 Wallace 679 (1872); Miller and Flowers, 10. Before the *United States Reports* became the official record of Supreme Court decisions, the Court records were named after the court reporter who compiled the reports, thus the "Wallace" in the citation of this case.

2. 13 Wallace 679 at 728; Miller and Flowers, 14. In fact, the last sentence of this statement was quoted 72 years later in *United States* v. *Ballard* 322 U.S. 78 at 86; Miller and Flowers, 18.

3. 13 Wallace 679 at 727; Miller and Flowers, 13.

4. 280 U.S. 1 (1929).

5. 344 U.S. 94 (1952); Miller and Flowers, 20.

6. For a similar, later case, see *Serbian Eastern Orthodox Diocese* v. *Milivojevich* 426 U.S. 696 (1976); Miller and Flowers, 28.

7. 393 U.S. 440 (1969); Miller and Flowers, 26.

8. 393 U.S. 440 at 449; Miller and Flowers, 28.

9. 443 U.S. 595 (1979); Miller and Flowers, 39.

10. 443 U.S. 595 at 604; Miller and Flowers, 41. The Court quoted from *Presbyte-*

rian Church in the U.S. v. *Mary Elizabeth Blue Hull Memorial Presbyterian Church* 393
U.S. 440 at 449; Miller and Flowers, 28.

11. 432 U.S. 63 (1977); Miller and Flowers, 153.

12. 432 U.S. 63 at 84; Miller and Flowers, 158.

13. 479 U.S. 60 (1986).

14. 479 U.S. 60 at 68.

15. A lawyer who practices workplace/religion law regularly described the hardship rule after *Hardison* and *Philbrook*: "Undue hardship is anything that violates a union contract or other seniority agreement, anything resulting in more than a very minor cost or the diminishment of efficiency or productivity, or anything that violates the rights of other workers. Congress built a substantial protective fence around religious observance in the workplace, but the Court cut the fence down to a height so low that most employers can step over it with ease." Letter from Mitchell A. Tyner, Associate General Counsel, General Conference of Seventh-day Adventists, to Ronald B. Flowers, February 1, 1993.

16. 483 U.S. 327 (1987); Miller and Flowers, 395.

17. 483 U.S. 327 at 337 (emphases in original); Miller and Flowers, 397.

18. 440 U.S. 490 (1979); Miller and Flowers, 389.

19. Exodus 20:13 (RSV).

20. Matthew 5:9, 39 (RSV); see also verses 21–22.

21. 279 U.S. 644 (1929); Miller and Flowers, 109.

22. 283 U.S. 636 (1931).

23. 283 U.S. 605 (1931); Miller and Flowers, 112.

24. 8 United States Code, § 382. *Schwimmer* and *Macintosh* were cited as precedents in a case in which the Court denied the request of conscientious objector students, who were Methodists, to be exempted from the requirement of a state university to take R.O.T.C. courses; *Hamilton* v. *Regents of the University of California* 293 U.S. 245 (1934); Miller and Flowers, 118.

25. These laws will be reviewed later in the chapter.

26. 283 U.S. 605 at 623–24; Miller and Flowers, 114.

27. 283 U.S. 605 at 618; Miller and Flowers, 113. Macintosh had been a chaplain in the Canadian army in World War I and served in areas of combat.

28. 283 U.S. 605 at 625 (emphasis in original); Miller and Flowers, 114–15. For an earlier expression by the Court of the Christian nation idea, see *Church of the Holy Trinity* v. *United States* 143 U.S. 457 at 470 (1892).

29. 328 U.S. 61 (1946); Miller and Flowers, 121.

30. 328 U.S. 61 at 64–65; Miller and Flowers, 122.

31. 328 U.S. 61 at 68 (emphasis added); Miller and Flowers, 123.

32. Some have argued that the Establishment Clause contains the right to conscientious objection exemptions from military service. In fact, in 1917 the Selective Service Act was attacked as a violation of that clause. The Supreme Court brushed aside that argument as "unsound" and not worthy of discussion; Selective Draft Law Cases (*Arver* v. *United States* 245 U.S. 366 at 389 [1918]). Then there was the Court's emphatic statement in *Macintosh*. Since that time the Establishment argument has been mentioned occasionally, but with no success.

33. 50 United States Code App. § 456(j) (1958 ed.).

34. 380 U.S. 163 (1965); Miller and Flowers, 124.

35. 380 U.S. 163 at 166 (Seeger), 168 (Jakobson), 169 (Peter); Miller and Flowers, 125–26.

36. 380 U.S. 163 at 176; Miller and Flowers, 128.
37. 398 U.S. 333 (1970); Miller and Flowers, 132.
38. 398 U.S. 333 at 341; Miller and Flowers, 133.
39. 398 U.S. 333 at 342–43; Miller and Flowers, 134.
40. 401 U.S. 437 (1971); Miller and Flowers, 137.

6. AID TO CHURCH-RELATED SCHOOLS

1. "New England's First Fruits," in *American Christianity: An Historical Interpretation with Representative Documents*, ed. H. Shelton Smith, Robert T. Handy, and Lefferts A. Loetscher, vol. 1 (New York: Charles Scribner's Sons, 1960), 124.
2. Ibid.
3. Lawrence A. Cremin, *American Education: The Colonial Experience, 1607–1783* (New York: Harper & Row, 1970), 181.
4. 268 U.S. 510 (1925); Miller and Flowers, 623.
5. 281 U.S. 370 (1930); Miller and Flowers, 625.
6. 281 U.S. 370 at 375; Miller and Flowers, 625.
7. 330 U.S. 1 (1947); Miller and Flowers, 626.
8. Although *Cantwell* v. *Connecticut* mentioned the Establishment Clause, it really was only a Free Exercise Clause case and only applied that clause to the states through the Fourteenth Amendment.
9. 330 U.S. 1 at 15–16; Miller and Flowers, 628.
10. 330 U.S. 1 at 18; Miller and Flowers, 629.
11. 330 U.S. 1 at 18; Miller and Flowers, 629.
12. 374 U.S. 203 (1963); Miller and Flowers, 516.
13. 397 U.S. 664 (1970); Miller and Flowers, 317.
14. 403 U.S. 602 (1971); Miller and Flowers, 645.
15. *Lemon* v. *Kurtzman* 403 U.S. 602 at 612–13; Miller and Flowers, 647, quoting *Walz* v. *Tax Commission of the City of New York* 397 U.S. 664 at 668, 674; Miller and Flowers, 317, 319.
16. *Hunt* v. *McNair* 413 U.S. 734 at 741.
17. 262 U.S. 447 (1923).
18. 392 U.S. 83 (1968); Miller and Flowers, 292.
19. "The Congress shall have Power . . . [t]o lay and collect Taxes, Duties, Imposts and Excises, to pay the Debts and provide for the common Defense and general welfare of the United States; but all Duties, Imposts and Excises shall be uniform throughout the United States."
20. 454 U.S. 464 (1982); Miller and Flowers, 300.
21. 421 U.S. 349 at 366; Miller and Flowers, 685.
22. 392 U.S. 236 (1968); Miller and Flowers, 639.
23. 421 U.S. 349 (1975); Miller and Flowers, 682.
24. 433 U.S. 229 (1977); Miller and Flowers, 701.
25. 444 U.S. 646 (1980); Miller and Flowers, 710.
26. 433 U.S. 229 at 248; Miller and Flowers, 705.
27. 403 U.S. 602 (1971); Miller and Flowers, 645.
28. 413 U.S. 756 (1973); Miller and Flowers, 669.
29. 413 U.S. 756 at 777; Miller and Flowers, 673.
30. 413 U.S. 472 (1973).
31. *Meek* v. *Pittenger* 421 U.S. 349 at 366; Miller and Flowers, 685, quoting *Hunt*

v. *McNair* 413 U.S. 734 at 743. Interestingly, this is exactly contrary to the argument made in *Board of Education* v. *Allen* 392 U.S. 236 (1968); Miller and Flowers, 639. There the Court held that the religious and secular parts of parochial education are easily separable, so that it is possible to guarantee that schoolbooks loaned to parochial school students are really used for secular instruction. That was a major rationale for approving the loan of schoolbooks to students in church-related schools, which was done in *Allen* and two subsequent cases.

32. 473 U.S. 373 (1985); Miller and Flowers, 732.

33. 473 U.S. 402 (1985); Miller and Flowers, 723.

34. 413 U.S. 756 (1973); Miller and Flowers, 669.

35. The dollar amounts in this case make more sense if one remembers that the legislation was passed in 1972.

36. 413 U.S. 756 at 791, 793; Miller and Flowers, 676.

37. 403 U.S. 602 at 625; Miller and Flowers, 651.

38. 463 U.S. 388 (1983); Miller and Flowers, 717.

39. 474 U.S. 481 (1986); Miller and Flowers, 473.

40. 474 U.S. 481 at 488; Miller and Flowers, 474.

41. 474 U.S. 481 at 488–89; Miller and Flowers, 474.

42. 113 S.Ct. 2462 (1993); Miller and Flowers 1993 Supplement, 26.

43. 113 S.Ct. 2462 at 2467; Miller and Flowers 1993 Supplement, 27, quoting *Witters* 474 U.S. 481 at 488; Miller and Flowers, 474.

44. 403 U.S. 672 (1971); Miller and Flowers, 662.

45. 413 U.S. 734 (1973).

46. 426 U.S. 736 (1976); Miller and Flowers, 693.

7. RELIGION IN PUBLIC SCHOOLS

1. Sidney E. Mead, *The Lively Experiment: The Shaping of Christianity in America* (New York: Harper & Row, 1963), 68.

2. 333 U.S. 203 (1948); Miller and Flowers, 496.

3. 333 U.S. 203 at 209–10, 212; Miller and Flowers, 497.

4. 343 U.S. 306 (1952); Miller and Flowers, 507.

5. 343 U.S. 306 at 313–14; Miller and Flowers, 508.

6. 343 U.S. 306 at 323; Miller and Flowers, 510.

7. 343 U.S. 306 at 325; Miller and Flowers, 511.

8. 370 U.S. 421 (1962); Miller and Flowers, 511.

9. 370 U.S. 421 at 425; Miller and Flowers, 512.

10. 370 U.S. 421 at 431–32; Miller and Flowers, 513.

11. 370 U.S. 421 at 435; Miller and Flowers, 514.

12. *New York Times*, July 1, 1962, quoted in Leo Pfeffer, *Church, State, and Freedom*, rev. ed. (Boston: Beacon Press, 1967), 466. See Pfeffer, pp. 466–69 for a brief description of the variety of reactions to *Engel*.

13. 374 U.S. 203 (1963); Miller and Flowers, 516.

14. 374 U.S. 203 at 211; Miller and Flowers, 518.

15. For a short history of the Schempp family's involvement in initiating this case, and its aftermath, see Rob Boston, "Forever and Ever Amen: The 30 Years' War over Prayer and Bible Reading in the Public Schools," *Church and State* 46 (June 1993): 7–10.

16. 374 U.S. 203 at 225; Miller and Flowers, 522, quoting *Zorach* v. *Clauson* 343 U.S. 306 at 314; Miller and Flowers, 508.

17. The Court actually expanded on the language of *Schempp* in a *dictum* in *Stone* v. *Graham*, mentioned later in this chapter. "This is not a case in which the Ten Commandments are integrated into *the school curriculum, where the Bible may constitutionally be used in an appropriate study of history, civilization, ethics, comparative religion, or the like*." 449 U.S. 39 at 42 (emphasis added); Miller and Flowers, 547.

18. 333 U.S. 203 at 235–36 (emphasis added); Miller and Flowers, 503.

19. See Steven K. Green, "Evangelicals and the Becker Amendment: A Lesson in Church–State Moderation," *Journal of Church and State* 33 (summer 1991): 541–67.

20. 472 U.S. 38 (1985); Miller and Flowers, 548.

21. 112 S.Ct. 2649 (1992); Miller and Flowers, 597.

22. 112 S.Ct. 2649 at 2656–58; Miller and Flowers, 600–601.

23. *Scopes* v. *Tennessee* 289 S.W. 363 (1927). "S.W." represents the *Southwestern Reporter*, the reporting service in which Tennessee cases are reported.

24. 393 U.S. 97 (1968); Miller and Flowers, 542.

25. 393 U.S. 97 at 106; Miller and Flowers, 544.

26. It is interesting that fundamentalists gave so much energy to formulating a new strategy in the late 1960s and early 1970s. At the time *Epperson* came to the Court in 1968, only Arkansas and Mississippi had laws prohibiting the teaching of evolution in public schools, and there was no evidence that Arkansas had made any attempt to enforce its law since it had been passed in 1928. But the decision in *Epperson* corresponded with a dramatic rise of religious and political conservatism. Consequently, antievolutionists used the decision as a rallying cry for greater efforts to be expended to discredit evolution and to minimize its impact on public education.

27. See *McLean* v. *Arkansas Board of Education* 529 F.Supp. 1255 (1982). The opinion of Judge Overton is the best articulation of the fact that creation science is actually a religious concept and thus fails all three parts of the "*Lemon* test"—better than that in the Supreme Court case that came later.

28. 482 U.S. 578 (1987); Miller and Flowers, 566.

29. 482 U.S 578 at 593 (emphasis in original); Miller and Flowers, 569, quoting *Epperson* v. *Arkansas* 393 U.S. 97 at 106–7; Miller and Flowers, 544.

30. 367 U.S. 488 (1961); Miller and Flowers, 187. Remember that Article VI states that "no religious Test shall ever be required as a Qualification to any Office or public Trust under the United States." The Court decided the case on the Establishment Clause only, and did not have to decide whether Article VI applied to state as well as federal offices.

31. 330 U.S. 1 at 15; Miller and Flowers, 628.

32. 367 U.S. 488 at 495; Miller and Flowers, 188.

33. This point was forcefully made and litigated in *Smith* v. *Board of School Commissioners of Mobile County* 655 F.Supp. 939 (1986). For a commentary on that and a related case, see Ronald B. Flowers, "They Got Our Attention, Didn't They? The Tennessee and Alabama Schoolbook Cases," *Religion and Public Education* 15 (summer 1988): 262–85.

34. 347 U.S. 483 (1954).

35. 449 U.S. 39 (1980); Miller and Flowers, 546.

36. 449 U.S. 39 at 41; Miller and Flowers, 547.

37. 20 United States Code §§ 4071–74.

38. A phrase and concept derived from *Widmar* v. *Vincent* 454 U.S. 263 (1981); Miller and Flowers, 245, which will be discussed later in this chapter.

39. 496 U.S. 226 (1990); Miller and Flowers, 582.

40. An example is the chess club. The school had argued that it was curriculum-related because chess requires the same kind of logical thinking as mathematics. The Court held that that relationship was entirely too tenuous. The chess club was non-curriculum-related because the school did not teach chess or anything like it.

41. 496 U.S. 226 at 250 (emphasis in original); Miller and Flowers, 588.

42. 454 U.S. 263 (1981); Miller and Flowers, 245.

43. As noted earlier, the concepts of "limited open forum" and "equal access" which are so important in the Equal Access Act and *Board of Education* v. *Mergens* originated in this case.

44. 454 U.S. 263 at 273–74; Miller and Flowers, 246.

45. 113 S.Ct. 2141 (1993); Miller and Flowers 1993 Supplement, 63.

46. *City of Los Angeles* v. *Taxpayers for Vincent* 466 U.S. 789 at 804 (1984). Cf. also *Cornelius* v. *NAACP Legal Defense and Educational Fund* 473 U.S. 788 at 806 (1985).

8. BLUE LAWS, BARS, TAXES, AND PLASTIC REINDEER: THE COMPLEXITY OF ESTABLISHMENT CLAUSE ISSUES

1. Exodus 20:8–11 (RSV).

2. *Code of Justinian*, III.xii.3, quoted in *Documents of the Christian Church*, ed. Henry Bettenson, 2d ed. (New York: Oxford University Press, 1963), 26.

3. 366 U.S. 420 (1961); Miller and Flowers, 355.

4. 366 U.S. 420 at 445; Miller and Flowers, 360.

5. See also *Two Guys from Harrison-Allentown, Inc.* v. *McGinley* 366 U.S. 582 (1961), which reached essentially the same result.

6. 366 U.S. 599 (1961); Miller and Flowers, 380. See also *Gallagher* v. *Crown Kosher Super Market* 366 U.S. 617 (1961).

7. 366 U.S. 599 at 603; Miller and Flowers, 381.

8. 366 U.S. 599 at 616; Miller and Flowers, 384. Justice William O. Douglas wrote a long dissent, which applied to all the Sunday law cases. He ended it by quoting a letter from a pastor, saying that the pastor "has stated my views."

We forget that, though Sunday-worshiping Christians are in the majority in this country among religious people, we do not have the right to force our practice on the minority. Only a Church which deems itself without error and intolerant of error can justify its intolerance of the minority.

A Jewish friend of mine runs a small business establishment. Because my friend is a Jew his business is closed each Saturday. He respects my right to worship on Sunday and I respect his right to worship on Saturday. But there is a difference. As a Jew he closes his door voluntarily so that he will be able to worship his God in his fashion. Fine! But, as a Jew living under Christian inspired Sunday closing laws, he is required to close his store on Sunday so that I will be able to worship my God in my fashion.

Around the corner from my church there is a small Seventh Day Baptist Church. I disagree with the Seventh Day Baptists on many points of doctrine. Among the tenets of their faith with which I disagree is the "seventh day worship." But they are good neighbors and fellow Christians, and while we disagree we respect one another. The good people of my congregation set aside their jobs on the first day of the week and gather in God's house for worship. Of course, it is easy for them to set aside their jobs since Sunday closing laws—inspired by the Church—keep them from their work. At the Seventh Day Baptist Church the people set aside their jobs on Saturday to worship God. This takes real sacrifice because Saturday is a good day for business. But that is not all—they are required by law to set aside their jobs on Sunday while more orthodox Christians worship.

. . . I do not believe that because I have set aside Sunday as a holy day I have the right to force all men to set aside that day also. Why should my faith be favored by the State over any other man's faith?

At the end of that quotation, Justice Douglas ended his dissent by saying, "With all deference, none of the opinions filed today in support of the Sunday laws has answered that question." 366 U.S. 420 at 580–81; Miller and Flowers, 380.

9. 472 U.S. 703 (1985); Miller and Flowers, 384.

10. 472 U.S. 703 at 708; Miller and Flowers, 385.

11. 472 U.S. 703 at 709; Miller and Flowers, 385.

12. 463 U.S. 783 (1983); Miller and Flowers, 419.

13. 463 U.S. 783 at 792; Miller and Flowers, 421.

14. See *Katkoff* v. *Marsh* 755 F.2d 223 (1985), a federal court of appeals case, which upheld the constitutionality of military chaplains on the grounds contained in the preceding paragraph, and which clearly expresses that principle. (The "F.2d" in the citation refers to the *Federal Reporter*, second series, which is the official reporting document for cases in federal courts of appeals.)

15. 459 U.S. 116 (1982); Miller and Flowers, 401.

16. 459 U.S. 116 at 126–27; Miller and Flowers, 404, quoting *Abington Township School District* v. *Schempp* 374 U.S. 203 at 222; Miller and Flowers, 521.

17. 456 U.S. 228 (1982); Miller and Flowers, 407.

18. 397 U.S. 664 (1970); Miller and Flowers, 317.

19. 397 U.S. 664 at 678; Miller and Flowers, 320.

20. 397 U.S. 664 at 674–75; Miller and Flowers, 319.

21. 455 U.S. 252 (1982); Miller and Flowers, 255.

22. 26 United States Code § 1402(g).

23. 455 U.S. 252 at 257–58; Miller and Flowers, 255. No more concise statement of the "*Sherbert* test" could be found than this one. This was clearly before the Court's disastrous decision in *Employment Division of Oregon* v. *Smith*.

24. 455 U.S. 252 at 260; Miller and Flowers, 256. Notice that this language could be applied to conscientious objection to taxes beyond the narrow Amish objection to Social Security; for example, the nonpayment of income taxes because of objections to the government's expenditures for armaments and the waging of war.

25. 489 U.S. 1 (1989); Miller and Flowers, 328.

26. 319 U.S. 105 (1943); Miller and Flowers, 74. See chapter 3.

27. 493 U.S. 378 (1990); Miller and Flowers, 268.

28. 26 United States Code § 501(c)(3) (emphases added).

29. 470 F.2d 849 (1972).

30. 470 F.2d 849 at 852. Past-tense verbs replace present because Christian Echoes National Ministry no longer exists.

31. 470 F.2d 849 at 853–54 (emphasis in original).

32. 470 F.2d 849 at 854, 857.

33. Certiorari denied, 404 U.S. 561 (1972). Remember that denial of certiorari does not mean that the Court endorses or agrees with the opinion of the lower court, but it does mean that the opinion is the law.

34. 461 U.S. 574 (1983); Miller and Flowers, 257. Another case was decided with *Bob Jones, Goldsboro Christian Schools* v. *United States.* The facts in the two cases were essentially the same, except Goldsboro Schools were elementary and secondary, rather than at the collegiate level.

35. 461 U.S. 574 at 595–96; Miller and Flowers, 261, quoting *Walz* v. *Tax Commission* 397 U.S. 664 at 673; Miller and Flowers, 319.

36. 461 U.S. 574 at 603–04; Miller and Flowers, 263.

37. 490 U.S. 680 (1989); Miller and Flowers, 339.

38. 490 U.S. 680 at 691; Miller and Flowers, 341, quoting *United States* v. *American Bar Endowment* 477 U.S. 105 at 118 (1986) (emphasis added on final phrase).

39. 495 U.S. 472 (1990); Miller and Flowers, 348.

40. 465 U.S. 668 (1984); Miller and Flowers, 429.

41. 465 U.S. 668 at 680; Miller and Flowers, 432.

42. 492 U.S. 573 (1989); Miller and Flowers, 444.

43. 492 U.S. 573 at 600–01; Miller and Flowers, 449–50.

44. 492 U.S. 573 at 616, 620; Miller and Flowers, 453–54, quoting *Grand Rapids School District* v. *Ball* 473 U.S. 373 at 390; Miller and Flowers, 736.

9. FLASH POINTS AND THE FUTURE

1. Walter H. Capps, *The New Religious Right: Piety, Patriotism, and Politics* (Columbia, S.C.: University of South Carolina Press, 1990), 3.

2. President Reagan appointed 378 federal judges; President Bush appointed 185. Joan Biskupic, "Bush Boosts Bench Strength of Conservative Judges," *Congressional Quarterly Guide to Current American Government: Fall 1991* (Washington, D.C.: Congressional Quarterly, 1991), 104–7; Holly Idelson, "Clinton's Unexpected Bequest: Judgeships Bush Did Not Fill," *Congressional Quarterly Guide to Current American Government: Fall 1993* (Washington, D.C.: Congressional Quarterly, 1993), 86.

3. The paragraphs on *Smith* that follow here are similar to those in my article "The Reagan Court Is In," *Liberty: A Magazine of Religious Freedom* 87 (May-June 1992): 14, 28.

4. In *Smith* Justice Scalia gave examples of such "hybrid cases." Some are cases mentioned in this book: *Cantwell* v. *Connecticut* (which had a free-speech component), *Murdock* v. *Pennsylvania* (free speech), *West Virginia Board of Education* v. *Barnette* (which Scalia incorrectly said was decided "exclusively upon free speech grounds"), and *Pierce* v. *Society of Sisters* (right of parents to direct the education of their children—which is *not* a constitutionally enumerated right). See *Smith* 494 U.S. 872; Miller and Flowers, 173.

5. See *Jones* v. *Opelika* 315 U.S. 584 at 608 (1942), Robert T. Miller and Ronald B. Flowers, *Toward Benevolent Neutrality: Church, State, and the Supreme Court*, 4th ed. (Waco, Tex.: Baylor University Press, 1992), 69; *Murdock* v. *Pennsylvania* 319 U.S. 105 at 115 (1943); Miller and Flowers, 76; *United States* v. *Ballard* 332 U.S. 78 at 87 (1944); Miller and Flowers, 18. It must be acknowledged that in some of these quotes freedom of speech, press, and others are mentioned as preferred freedoms along with religion. But there is never even a hint that the others take precedence over religion

or that freedom of religion receives life only because of its affiliation with the others. Just the contrary is expressed in Justice Frank Murphy's dissent in *Jones* v. *Opelika* at 621, joined by three others: "Important as free speech and a free press are to a free government and a free citizenry, there is a right even more dear to many individuals—the right to worship their Maker according to their needs and the dictates of their souls and to carry their message or their gospel to every living creature."

6. 494 U.S. 872 at 888; Miller and Flowers, 174.

7. 494 U.S. 872 at 890; Miller and Flowers, 175.

8. *West Virginia Board of Education* v. *Barnette* 319 U.S. 624 at 638; Miller and Flowers, 89.

9. A wonderful statement on the purpose of the Bill of Rights, American liberty in general, and the cost of obtaining these was written by Chief Judge Ryder of the District Court of Appeal of Florida, Second Circuit, in *Collins* v. *Florida* 465 So.2d 1266 at 1268–69 (1985): "We fought a war to obtain these rights. This Nation pledged its wealth, its goods, its lives and many, many lives were, in fact, lost fighting that war against a then autocratic, dictatorial government to gain those rights. These rights were not easily won or wrestled away from that government across the sea whose agents here did their will at their whim in violating their own citizens' homes, papers, and persons by searches without cause, much less probable cause, but on mere suspicion or personal whim. The then continentals were often treated as merely chattels without rights. It was not merely because of a tea tax that this Nation fought the sovereign across the sea—it was not merely [because of] taxation without representation that this Nation undertook a cruel and lengthy war—it was more than that. It was to secure freedom for all peoples of this Nation, all citizens—not just a preferred few. And because of the abuses of power of the government across the sea, abuses directly against our pioneering predecessors, our founding fathers correctly believed that it was right, meet and proper that those abuses should not ever again be given a chance to be inflicted upon the citizenry under its new government; so much so, that inhibitions against the new government in the form of a Bill of Rights and other amendments to the Constitution were written down and passed into law, to be a permanent and basic, fundamental law of the land, forever protecting the citizens from despotism and the threat of its reappearance in this land." (The "So.2d" in the citation refers to the *Southern Reporter*, second series, which is the official reporting document for state courts in Florida and other states in that region.)

10. Peter Berger, "Religious Liberty and the Paradox of Relevance," *The Religion and Society Report* 5 (January 1988): 1 (emphasis in original); Berger spells this out in somewhat more detail in his essay "The Serendipity of Liberties," in *The Structure of Freedom: Correlations, Causes & Cautions*, ed. Richard John Neuhaus (Grand Rapids: Wm. B. Eerdmans Publishing Co., 1991), 14–16.

11. 494 U.S. 872 at 902–3; Miller and Flowers, 178.

12. I quote with appreciation the words of Judge Goldberg of the U.S. Court of Appeals for the Fifth Circuit: "[W]e do not labor within a majoritarian jurisprudence. Our responsibility is to apply not the majority ethos, but the Constitution. That great document enforces no religious orthodoxy; it permits no compelled religious expression. Its provisions protect not just the popular, but also the un-; not just the sensible, but also the (seemingly) silly. In return, the Constitution repays our investment of tolerance with a dividend of individual autonomy and social freedom— freedom, in great measure, from the religious hostilities and petty oppressions that

have rent nations throughout history and across the globe." (*Society of Separationists* v. *Herman* 939 F.2d 1207 at 1220 [1991].)

13. In describing the impact of *Smith*, professor of constitutional law Douglas Laycock says: "This is in fact a move to majoritarianism; the Court is getting out of the business of enforcing the religion clauses. Legislatures and enforcement agencies choose when to provide only formal neutrality and when to grant exceptions. Favored religions can be exempted from the rules that burden them, while disfavored religions are denied exemptions from the rules that burden them." "The Remnants of Free Exercise," *Supreme Court Review 1990* (Chicago: University of Chicago Press, 1991): 12.

Church–state authority Dean M. Kelley observes: "Some of [the Court's] members seem to feel that individuals should not have many rights that are judicially enforceable against the government. Apparently, individuals, minorities and courts should get out of the way and let the government—in its infinite wisdom—govern. That view, of course, would put the courts on the side of the strong against the weak and nullify the whole purpose of the Bill of Rights, which is to protect individual rights against government powers." "Statism, Not Separationism, Is the Problem," *Christian Century* 106 (January 18, 1989): 49.

14. One example, of many that could be cited, is the situation of a family of Hmongs whose son suffered a seizure while he was sleeping and was rushed to the hospital, where he died. Because the physicians did not know the cause of death, the medical examiner, pursuant to Rhode Island law, which requires an autopsy in those situations in which death occurs "in any suspicious or unusual manner," performed an autopsy on the young man without consulting his parents. Hmong religion prohibits any mutilation of a body, including autopsies and the removal of organs during autopsies. Such mutilation means that the spirit of the dead is not free, and thus would come back to take another person in the decedent's family. In a long and careful opinion in which it relied on the "compelling state interest test," the U.S. District Court for Rhode Island found that the Hmong family had a religion-based cause of damages against the medical examiner. However, it postponed the determination and awarding of damages until a later hearing. During the time the court was researching the case law in order to fix damages, the Supreme Court issued *Smith*. Subsequently the district court took the highly unusual step of issuing a second decision in the case—rescinding the earlier decision. Expressing "deep regret" because of his profound sympathy for the Hmong family, the judge noted that the *Smith* doctrine would not allow him to find for them, since the state law concerning autopsies is a law of general applicability. (*You Vang Yang* v. *Sturner* 750 F.Supp. 558 [1990]. At 559 the judge said: "While I feel constrained to apply the majority's opinion [in *Smith*] to the instant case, I cannot do this without expressing my profound regret and my own agreement with Justice Blackmun's forceful dissent.") So now, the state need not make any accommodation for religious objections to autopsies, so long as the law authorizing them is not aimed specifically at religious objections.

15. 42 United States Code § 2000bb.

16. Justice Byron White, who voted with Justice Scalia and the majority in *Smith*, retired in June 1993, when the Court's term ended. He was replaced by Justice Ruth Bader Ginsburg. At the time of her appointment, her views on church–state relationships were not clear. But her clear record in favor of guaranteeing the rights of

women and minorities suggest that she might be a strong supporter of religious freedom.

17. 465 U.S. 668 at 673; Miller and Flowers, 430, quoting first *Committee for Public Education and Religious Liberty* v. *Nyquist* 413 U.S. 756 at 760; Miller and Flowers, 669, and then *Zorach* v. *Clauson* 343 U.S. 306 at 314; Miller and Flowers, 508.

18. 472 U.S. 38 at 113; Miller and Flowers, 566.

19. 472 U.S. 38 at 107; Miller and Flowers, 564.

20. Laurence H. Tribe, *God Save This Honorable Court: How the Choice of Supreme Court Justices Shapes Our History* (New York: New American Library, Mentor Book, 1985), 55, 51 (emphasis in original). Professor of jurisprudence Harry Jones approaches the question of original intent this way: "To consider constitutional law as if it were a mere attempted reconstruction of the intention of the founding fathers is about as helpful as the old query: 'If I had had an uncle, would he have liked prunes?' Nowhere is this more true than in the constitutional law of church-state relations. *It is the task of the Supreme Court in this area to keep the historic purpose of the First Amendment a living influence in contemporary society.*" (Harry W. Jones, "Church-State Relations: Our Constitutional Heritage," in *Religion and Contemporary Society*, ed. Harold Stahmer [New York: Macmillan Co., 1963], 173 [emphasis added].)

21. That the Constitution is dynamic, as opposed to static, and should be interpreted as such, was expressed well by Chief Justice Charles Evans Hughes in *Home Building and Loan Association* v. *Blaisdell* 290 U.S. 398 at 442–43 (1934) in which he invoked two other greats of the Court, Chief Justice John Marshall and Justice Oliver Wendell Holmes, Jr.:

If by the statement that what the Constitution meant at the time of its adoption it means to-day [*sic*], it is intended to say that the great clauses of the Constitution must be confined to the interpretation which the framers, with the conditions and outlook of their time, would have placed upon them, the statement carries its own refutation. It was to guard against such a narrow conception that Chief Justice Marshall uttered the memorable warning—"We must never forget that it is a *constitution* we are expounding" (*McColloch* v. *Maryland*, 4 Wheat. 316, 407)—"a constitution intended to endure for ages to come, and consequently, to be adapted to the various *crises* of human affairs." *Id.*, p. 415. When we are dealing with the words of the Constitution, said this Court in *Missouri* v. *Holland*, 252 U.S. 416, 433, "we must realize that they have called into life a being the development of which could not have been foreseen completely by the most gifted of its begetters. . . . The case before us must be considered in the light of our whole experience and not merely in that of what was said a hundred years ago."

22. Another of those great principles is equality. But how do we achieve maximum equality before government for citizens of an increasingly diverse society? To do so, must we not insist that atheists or adherents to a wide variety of religions, most of them historically not related to Western culture, have equal rights? Does that not, in itself, preclude nonpreferentialism? That is, how does government treat all these religions the same, in an evenhanded way? And if government does manage to promote all these religions in a nondiscriminatory way, how does it manage, at the same time, to treat the nonreligious with equality?

23. The test is named after *Lemon* v. *Kurtzman*. See chapter 6.

24. See *Wallace* v. *Jaffree* 472 U.S. 38 at 110–12; Miller and Flowers, 565–66.

25. 465 U.S. 668 at 690, 688; Miller and Flowers, 435, 434.

26. 465 U.S. 668 at 687–88; Miller and Flowers, 434.

27. A shorter version of the next three paragraphs appears in my article "The Reagan Court Is In," *Liberty: A Magazine of Religious Freedom* 87 (May-June 1992): 13.

28. 492 U.S. 573 at 670 (1989); Miller and Flowers, 468.

29. Interestingly enough, in *Lee* v. *Weisman* 112 S.Ct. 2649 (1992); Miller and Flowers, 597, Justice Kennedy, who wrote the majority opinion, did not seem to push this position. But Justice Scalia, in a strongly worded, sarcastic dissent argued the view vociferously. The theme of his opinion is contained in the sentence: "Today's opinion shows more forcefully than volumes of argumentation why our Nation's protection, that fortress which is our Constitution, cannot possibly rest upon the changeable philosophical predilections of the Justices of this Court, but must have deep foundations in the historic practices of our people." 112 S.Ct. 2649 at 2679; Miller and Flowers, 612. Because he clearly believes that government accommodation of religion is embedded in that history, he argues that the Establishment Clause must be interpreted so that accommodationism can be accommodated.

30. Justice David Souter *may* be an exception to this generalization. See his concurring opinions in *Lee* v. *Weisman* 112 S.Ct. 2649 at 2667–78 (1992); Miller and Flowers, 605–12; and *Church of the Lukumi Babalu Aye* v. *City of Hialeah* 113 S.Ct. 2217 at 2240 (1993); Miller and Flowers 1993 Supplement, 15.

31. The use of the word "accommodate" is interesting. The proper sense of the word is consistent with strict separation. Government should accommodate religion by getting out of its way and letting it flourish. That is what the First Amendment seems to demand. But "accommodationists" interpret the word to mean affirmative government aid or assistance to religion. I am using the word in their sense—in order to examine it critically and disagree with it.

32. Russell H. Dilday, Jr., "Jesus and Politics," *Church and State* 37 (October 1984): 20.

33. "Church Colleges: The Price of Tax Aid," *Church and State* 28 (June 1975): 10–12.

34. 426 U.S. 736 at 775; Miller and Flowers, 701.

35. Joseph L. Conn, "Breach of Faith? In Order to Keep State Funds Flowing, Falwell and Company Drop Religion Requirements at Liberty University," *Church and State* 46 (July-August 1993): 12–13.

36. Defendant's Trial Brief, *McLean* v. *Arkansas Board of Education*, 14–15.

37. Thomas Jefferson, "A Bill for Establishing Religious Freedom"; see Appendix B.

38. It was pointed out in chapter 7 that voluntary *individual*, nondisruptive prayer has never been forbidden by the Court.

39. "A Memorial and Remonstrance against Religious Assessments"; see Appendix A.

40. *Zorach* v. *Clauson* 343 U.S. 306 at 324–25; Miller and Flowers, 511.

EPILOGUE

1. 370 U.S. 421 at 431–32; Miller and Flowers, 513.

Bibliography

Boles, Donald E. *The Bible, Religion, and the Public Schools*. 3d ed. Ames, Iowa: Iowa State University Press, 1965.

Carper, James C., and Thomas C. Hunt. *Religious Schooling in America*. Birmingham, Ala.: Religious Education Press, 1984.

Curry, Thomas J. *The First Freedoms: Church and State in America to the Passage of the First Amendment*. New York: Oxford University Press, 1986.

Davis, Derek. *Original Intent: Chief Justice Rehnquist and the Course of American Church/State Relations*. Buffalo: Prometheus Books, 1991.

Gaustad, Edwin S. "A Disestablished Society: Origins of the First Amendment," *Journal of Church and State* 11 (autumn 1969): 409–25.

———. *Faith of the Fathers: Religion and the New Nation*. San Francisco: Harper & Row, 1987.

Geisler, Norman L. *The Creator in the Courtroom; "Scopes II": The 1981 Arkansas Creation–Evolution Trial*. Milford, Mich: Mott Media, 1982.

Gilkey, Langdon. *Creationism on Trial: Evolution and God at Little Rock*. Minneapolis: Winston Press, 1983.

Hall, Kermit L., ed. *The Oxford Companion to the Supreme Court of the United States*. New York: Oxford University Press, 1992.

Harrell, Mary Ann, and Burnett Anderson. *Equal Justice under the Law: The Supreme Court in American Life*. Washington, D.C.: Supreme Court Historical Society, 1982.

Ivers, Gregg. *Lowering the Wall: Religion and the Supreme Court in the 1980s*. New York: Anti-Defamation League, 1991.

Karlen, Delmar. "Court, 2. Courts in Common Law Countries." *The Encyclopedia Americana: International Edition*. Vol. 8, pp. 103–9. Danbury, Conn., 1988.

Keim, Albert N., ed. *Compulsory Education and the Amish: The Right Not to Be Modern*. Boston: Beacon Press, 1975.

Levy, Leonard W. *The Establishment Clause: Religion and the First Amendment*. New York: Macmillan Publishing Co., 1986.

McCloskey, Robert G. "United States, 18, The Judicial System," *The Encyclopedia Americana: International Edition*. Vol. 27, pp. 631–36. Danbury, Conn., 1988.

Mead, Sidney E. *The Old Religion in the Brave New World: Reflections on the Relation between Christendom and the Republic*. Berkeley: University of California Press, 1977.

Michaelsen, Robert. *Piety in the Public School: Trends and Issues in the Relationship between Religion and the Public Schools in the United States*. New York: Macmillan Co., 1970.

Miller, Robert T., and Ronald B. Flowers. *Toward Benevolent Neutrality: Church, State, and the Supreme Court*. 4th ed. Waco, Tex.: Baylor University Press, 1992. Also annual supplement.

Noll, Mark A., Nathan O. Hatch, and George M. Marsden. *The Search for Christian America*. Exp. ed. Colorado Springs: Helmers & Howard, 1989.

O'Brien, David M. *Storm Center: The Supreme Court in American Politics*. New York: W. W. Norton & Co., 1986.

Pfeffer, Leo. *God, Caesar, and the Constitution: The Court as Referee of Church–State Confrontation*. Boston: Beacon Press, 1975.

———. *Religion, State and the Burger Court*. Buffalo: Prometheus Books, 1984.

Rehnquist, William H. *The Supreme Court: How It Was, How It Is*. New York: William Morrow & Co., 1987.

Vecsey, Christopher, ed. *Handbook of American Indian Religious Freedom*. New York: Crossroad, 1991.

Wilson, John F., and Donald L. Drakeman, eds. *Church and State in American History*. 2d ed. Boston: Beacon Press, 1987.

There are seven regularly published periodicals completely devoted to church–state concerns:

Church and State, published every month except August by Americans United for Separation of Church and State, 8120 Fenton Street, Silver Spring, MD 20910.

Journal of Church and State, published four times a year by the J.M. Dawson Institute of Church–State Studies, Baylor University, Box 97308, Waco, TX 76798-7308.

The Journal of Law and Religion, published twice a year at the Hamline University School of Law, 1536 Hewitt Avenue, St. Paul, MN 55104.

LIBERTY: A Magazine of Religious Freedom, published bimonthly by the Review and Herald Publishing Association, 12501 Old Columbia Pike, Silver Spring, MD 20904-1608.

Religion and Public Education, published quarterly by the National Council on Religion and Public Education, E262 Lagomarcino Hall, Iowa State University, Ames, IA 50011.

Religious Freedom Reporter, published monthly by the Church–State Resource Center of the Norman Adrian Wiggins School of Law, Campbell University, P.O. Box 505, Buies Creek, NC 27506, is a compilation of up-to-date information on current litigation and periodical articles in the field.

Report from the Capital, published biweekly by the Baptist Joint Committee on Public Affairs, 200 Maryland Avenue, N.E., Washington, DC 20002.

Index

the Presbyterian Outlook

BOOK REVIEWS

Thank you for your willingness to write a book review for The Presbyterian Outlook. Please limit your review to no more than two pages double-spaced (up to 400 words max). In addition, please select two brief quotations from the book (giving the editor a choice) for possible use on the cover of the magazine. The cover-quotes should be approximately 150 words in length, should cite the page number on which the quotation is found, and should be given an appropriate attention-getting headline.

Begin your book-review with full bibliographic information, in this format:

Book Title. By (author). Publisher. Year. Paperback? Pages. Price (if available).

Place your name at the end of the review.

If, after reading the book, you think it is not worthy of a review, don't bother to write one. Let me know your reaction, and keep the book anyway. I will send you another book.

Send your review to me at the address below. We need to have your review within four to six weeks.

If you have any question about the book, or about writing the review, please don't hesitate to contact me.

Many thanks.

LILLIAN M. TAYLOR, Outlook Book Editor
Post Office Box 1909
Elizabethtown, NC 28337
Phone: (910) 862-4722

PHONE (804) 359-8442 · 3711 SAUNDERS AVE. · RICHMOND, VA 23227